CHANGES IN THE FIELD OF TRANSPORT STUDIES

ESSAYS ON THE PROGRESS OF THEORY IN RELATION TO POLICY MAKING

in honour of

PROF. DR. J.P.B. TISSOT VAN PATOT

edited and introduced by

J.B. POLAK & J.B. VAN DER KAMP

1980

MARTINUS NIJHOFF PUBLISHERS
THE HAGUE/BOSTON/LONDON

in co-operation with
THE NETHERLANDS INSTITUTE OF TRANSPORT

The distribution of this book is handled by the following team:

for the United States and Canada

Kluwer Boston, Inc.
160 Old Derby Street
Hingham, MA 02043
USA

for all other countries

Kluwer Academic Publishers Group
Distribution Center
P.O. Box 322
3300 AH Dordrecht
The Netherlands

Library of Congress Cataloging in Publication Data   CIP

Main entry under title:

Changes in the field of transport studies.

    Contents: Blauwens, G.J. The spatial theory of the demand for freight transport. —
Gent, H.A. van and Kuyvenhoven, R.A. Prof. Dr. J.P.B. Tissot van Patot, his contribution
to the theories of transport policy and spatial economics. — Gwilliam, K.M. Realism and
the common transport policy of E.E.C. [etc.].
    1. Transportation and state — Addresses, essays, lectures.   2. Freight and freightage —
Addresses, essays, lectures.   3. Transportation — Addresses, essays, lectures.   4. Tissot
van Patot, Jan Pieter Bastiaan — Addresses, essays, lectures. I. Tissot van Patot, Jan
Pieter Bastiaan. II. Polak, J.B. III. Kamp, J.B. van der
HE193.C45   1079   380.5   79-11690

ISBN 90-247-2147-4 (this volume) ✓
ISBN 90-247-2330-2 (series)

PRINTED IN THE NETHERLANDS

PREFACE

This liber amicorum honours Professor Jan Tissot van Patot as a scholar, referring in particular to his concern with transport economics. The significance of his work grew out of his influence within Netherlands Railways as, with the passage of the years, he dedicated himself increasingly to the vastly wider field of transport economics. I would emphasize, however, that his theoretical knowledge and views in wider contexts have also been of great value to Netherlands Railways, and I greatly appreciate this opportunity of referring to this aspect in a few personal words.

It is characteristic both of his person and his attitude that his work was often the occasion for contacts of a more personal nature, contacts which were profoundly marked by his philosophy and convictions. Our relations date from more than thirty-seven years ago, when he asked me for a contribution for a magazine which he helped to edit at that time and which was concerned with the same field as I was. We became colleagues when he entered the service of NS, the Netherlands Railways. His sphere of work at that time was such that he was consulted more and more frequently by others. His particular value to NS has been the increased dimension of transport policy and decision making he added to the company's existing policy and decision making. His strongly developed objectivity, his desire always to lay theoretical foundations and his need to check them against precisely defined criteria meant that on many occasions he acted as the railways' conscience.

He also came to play an increasing role in international railway cooperation, and in his own country he helped build up institutes which aimed to give the theory of general transport economics the place which it more and more evidently deserved.

In his long career with the railways Jan Tissot started out as a practical man who nonetheless relied on theory; later on, when theory began to prevail over practice, this situation was reversed. His desire to pass on his methods and ideas in a wider sphere, at university level, was satisfied in 1964, when he was made a Professor at the Free University in Amsterdam.

Thus it was in his own career that he consistently gave shape to the synthesis of theory and practice, through interaction: the links between theory, policy and decision making always guided his thought and his work. His great merit has been that he has assisted many people, both inside and outside the railways, to develop their capacity for constructive analysis and theory formulation, and that he has shown them how to make sound judgements and to act consistently, while remaining open to the changes which constitute progress, in both theory and practice.

I reckon myself among the many people who feel grateful to him for this and who — I am sure — will value the fact that his flag covers a cargo which is worthy of being shipped from author to reader, in the form of this book.

M.G. DE BRUIN
President and Chief Executive
Netherlands Railways   *Summer 1979*

(

B

CHANGES IN THE FIELD OF TRANSPORT STUDIES

Developments in Transport Studies

VOLUME 1

CONTENTS

INTRODUCTION

J.B. VAN DER KAMP and J.B. POLAK

1. THE THEME OF THIS BOOK

Reflection on problems of policy has been part and parcel of economic science throughout its history. Additionally economists, besides dealing with problems of theory, have often personally taken part in the shaping of policy.

Transport economics and transport economists have been no exception to this general phenomenon. The person of Tissot van Patot is a striking example of someone who over a long period of time has been fascinated by the mutual relationship between transport economics as a theoretical subject and decision making in matters of transport.

Especially during the later, academic, part of his career, Tissot van Patot was confronted with the fact that transport economics entails more than the analysis of problems related to policy. In a collection of essays intended to honour the work of Tissot van Patot it seemed appropriate, for the reasons just mentioned, that ample place should be given to problems of transport policy, but only to the extent that a still considerable number of the contributions be devoted to other themes of transport economics.

The general aim — without trying to achieve it in a strictly systematic manner — has been that the essays taken as a whole should present the reader with an insight into the wide-ranging character of present-day transport economics.

In fact, as may appear from the title of the book, the scope has been rather more ambitious. It was considered a challenge to also trace and make visible certain developments that — at least in the opinion of the editors — have over the past few decades more or less changed the face of transport economics.

Given this aim, the question arises of whether there is a need for such work. Have not developments in transport economics already obtained sufficient attention elsewhere?

A great deal has indeed been written on the history of transport, both from a technical and from an operating point of view. It seems, however, that on the whole little attention has been given to the history of transport economics and certainly not to its more recent development. Some references to changes in the nature and the subject matter of transport economics can be found, of course. In the Netherlands, for example, Kuiler (1963) has considered the history of transport economics. Kuiler saw the development of transport economics as a reflection of the problems which have confronted transport enterprises in the course of time.

A decade later Thomson (1974) expressed the view that "two quite recent developments have entirely changed the appearance of the subject," viz. "a big shift towards quantitative analysis" and the fact that "transport is now treated as a branch of welfare economics in which market economics play a secondary role, rather than a branch of market economics with welfare implications."

Rakowski (1976) made the general statement that "the field had essentially been in a state of semi-dormancy since the 1920's," i.e. until about 1960. Listing new developments Rakowski refers to a "renewed interest in our [i.e. the U.S.] domestic transport system," to "the problems of physical distribution and the development of a new field which has come to be called business logistics," to an "expanded interest in all phases of urban transportation" and, finally, "to a great deal of research in the areas of transportation in the developing countries."

The present collection of essays attempts to identify some other changes regarding: (1) the nature of the subject matter of transport economics, (2) the methods with which issues in transport economics are being analyzed and explained and (3) the interaction of theory, policy and decision making.

As for (1), attention is drawn to two phenomena, viz. what could be called the *spatialization* of transport economics, and the evolution of transport-policy problems from ad hoc studies towards a *theory of transport policy*.

As regards category (2), noteworthy are developments towards a certain gradual *osmosis* between a purely economic approach to transport and approaches using methods and results derived from other disciplines.

In the area of (3), tendencies to change arise from the problems met by policy makers regarding the *societal implementation* of transport-policy objectives and decisions. This may be seen as equivalent to the need for improving preparatory activities in policy making in order to achieve better communication between the policy maker and the affected community — with all its conflicting desires, interests and opinions. It seems justified to qualify these changes as progress. The scope of transport economics being broadened and the scientific climate being influenced in particular by the two last-mentioned changes, it seemed appropriate to choose for the book the more encompassing title it now has.

2. THE "SPATIALIZATION" OF TRANSPORT ECONOMICS

Transport of course has been present for a very long time in the writings of economists. To mention but one famous example: the significance attributed to transport by Adam Smith in his exposition about the division of labour.

Though they did not always explicitly say so, it is clear that those who wrote about transport in the past must also have been aware of a close relationship existing between the concepts of "transport" and that of "space" (e.g. Knies, 1853).

Transport also figured in the context of location theory (see the contribution by Winkelmans). What is the picture, however, that one may form about the "reverse" question, i.e. whether the notion of a spatial structure has been present in transport economics? In the absence of any systematic study of the development of transport economics, there undoubtedly is a risk in answering this question.

It is a fact that in today's transport economics there is a still increasing stream of publications that introduce spatial characteristics in their explanation of transport flows. On the other hand, and not to be seen as a quite separate development, a great deal of attention is being paid to the question of how the transport system and other elements of spatial structure interact with each other. This trend in thinking is to be found both on the level of the explanation of behaviour and on that of its application, i.e. more particularly in the context of planning theory. Linking the study of transport with that of spatial structure seems to have become so much typical for the subject as it is treated today that one may well speak of the "spatialization" of transport economics. For a better understanding of this change in the nature of transport economics one would have to consider to what factors this change may be ascribed. Only a brief indication will be possible here.

A factor that immediately springs to mind is that space, or rather the relative shortage of it, has come to be an increasing concern in many societies. This factor may be seen as the reinforcement of another, lying in the field of theory. For a long time economists had been developing their ideas with utter neglect of an important aspect of reality, viz. space. This circumstance has been admirably expressed in Walter Isard's term of a "wonderland of no dimensions," to which Blauwens also refers in his contribution.

In a general sense the "spatialization" of transport economics may be seen, on the basis of the foregoing argument, as part of a wider phenomenon relating to economic theory in general. One would therefore be quite justified in asking whether the introduction into transport economics of a world where space, as one may also say, is heterogeneous, is able to add anything new to economic theory as a whole. Those who view transport economics and similar subjects merely as "applied economics" may tend to a negative answer. In a still fairly cautious attitude one may, however, follow the spirit of Schumpeter's words; discussing 19th century railroad economics, he wrote that it "ought to be able to repay the service by offering to general theory interesting special patterns and problems." (Schumpeter, 1954.) The fact is that developments in transport economics do not just follow general economics, but may equally well run ahead of it.

It is hoped that the reader will find some instances of Schumpetarian "repayments" but perhaps also proof of innovative activity of a more autonomous nature in the contributions in this book that deal with problems of transport in a spatial context. It will be clear that it is impossible to give more than a sample of those areas of transport economics that acquire a distinct nature through the introduction of spatial considerations.

In the first place, there is the purely micro-economic setting. This is represented by the article by *Blauwens*, who deals with demand for freight transport. Blauwens presents a survey, in very succinct terms, of the various kinds of models incorporating space that have been developed for this category of transport demand. The reader will easily note the difference between the spatial and the more conventional, a-spatial, approach to the subject that still often figures in textbooks. Will it ultimately be possible, one therefore wonders, to arrive at a *general* spatial theory of transport demand, i.e. one that applies to both freight and passenger transport? For one thing, developments in the theory of demand for passenger transport, like those discussed by Michon, may rather seem to drive both sectors further apart. Whether some kind of analogy, as far as the introduction of subjective factors is concerned, will be possible with respect to demand for freight transport remains as yet to be seen. At any rate this looks an attractive field for further study.

Klaassen's contribution in a sense is complementary to Blauwens' study, insofar as the former focusses on passenger transport. Klaassen's interest, however, is in infrastructural needs rather than in transport flows. At the core of his exposition is the view that transport infrastructure is an integral element of spatial structure. The immediate implication for the derivation of an "optimum use" of transport networks is that account will have to be taken of the mutual influence of transport and non-transport elements of spatial structure. The derivation of an optimum of course requires some standard with respect to which the optimum may be said to exist. To this end, a spatial welfare function for society is introduced. In the second part of his paper Klaassen moves on to the more practical question of the means at the disposal of governments for influencing traffic flows and, through these, infrastructure requirements. In all, the particular place of Klaassen's study among the other studies in this book that deal with spatial issues is determined by the fact that Klaassen looks at the relation between infrastructure and the spatial distribution of activities from the angle of welfare theory.

Hamerslag's contribution contains two distinct but closely related parts. In the first place a survey is given of the historical development of mathematical models that deal with the relationship between developments in the transport system and spatial development. The reader's interest will particularly center on the latest type of models, i.e. models with so-called elastic constraints. In these models the relationship between changes in the transport system and in the further elements of spatial structure—housing, employment — is taken to be of an interactive nature. In the second part of the article it is shown that with the model with elastic constraints it is possible to simulate in quite a realistic way what will happen to urban settlement under varying assumptions. It is worth stressing that the article ends on a cautious note as regards the possibilities for forecasting changes in spatial structure. Quite realistically, Hamerslag remarks that the transport system is only one of the factors to which spatial developments may be ascribed.

Santoro's interest is, one may say, in the same issue as the one dealt with by Hamerslag. The approach chosen, however, is very different. In the first place, Santoro discusses a particular case — that of the railways within the Italian national setting. More importantly, within the theme of the integration of the planning of transport with physical planning, he explicitly opts for a review of the main difficulties as they have been encountered in actual planning practice. So it appears that transport planning in the past has taken little or no account of effects on land use; that a problem exists of integrating a sectoral plan — i.e. for railways — within a plan for the transport sector as a whole; that there is much uncertainty about the role railways can play in less-developed regions. Questions like these will be found to transcend the purely Italian interest. The reader may want to speculate on the relative merits of a formalized approach as used by Hamerslag and the present one in which factual details and institutional matters take a prominent place. Should it not be concluded that each approach is able to make its own contribution and therefore possesses its own particular merit?

Winkelmans presents a critical appraisal of one of the oldest issues in spatially-orientated economics: the significance of transport in the locational behaviour of firms. A survey is first given of developments in theory. The article, however, is likely to evoke particular interest because of the evidence it contains about the weight given by firms to the presence of transport facilities in choosing their location. Contrary to what may be considered received opinion, it appears that the importance of transport as such is declining.

Certainly location theory cannot be seen as part of transport economics. In the more traditional definition of subjects location theory, i.e. in so far as it starts from a given endowment with transport facilities, may, instead of a part, rather be considered as the counterpart of transport economics. Apart from shedding light on still another aspect of transport—and therefore fully belonging to the domain referred to in the title of this book—the subject treated by Winkelmans is undoubtedly able to provoke further thinking about the future path of the relationship between spatial economics—to use the wider notion—and the economics of transport. It may prove to be one more element in the spatialization of transport economics.

3. FROM "TRANSPORT POLICY" TO A "THEORY OF TRANSPORT POLICY"

A tradition exists in transport economics of using the term "transport policy" in a double sense. "Transport policy" in the first place is used to denote a course of action taken or considered by some decision maker. On the other hand, the term can also be seen as indicating the theoretical study of transport policy. What may seem to be merely a terminological issue is very likely to possess deeper roots.

It is understandable that the earlier studies of problems of transport policy have been mostly conducted on an ad hoc basis. Gradually however, the need both for an explicit conceptional apparatus and for insights of a more general nature have manifested themselves. So one may say that there has been a transition from mere "transport policy," where the accent was mostly on the "doing," to a new and separate part of transport economics, the theory of transport policy.

It is not in the nature of the articles in this book to provide a rigid proof of the foregoing statement. The essays that deal with transport policy, taken as a whole, are meant to illustrate rather than to demonstrate the point that a change in the scope of transport economics has occurred. What is possible, however, is to formulate some general criteria that may guide judgement. So it should be asked, in the first place, whether explicit attention is presently being given to concepts for a theory of transport policy. A second question is whether the range of problems studied is sufficiently wide for explanations being able to transcend a mere ad hoc status. In the third place it should also be considered whether methods of general applicability have been, or are being, developed. Questions like these may be taken together by putting the general, though less operational question of whether writers show the awareness that the practice of policy making is one thing and a theoretical approach to problems of transport policy is something substantially different.

With the foregoing, the general framework has been sketched at the same time for the contributions to this book that deal with transport policy.

"Basic concepts" can be found with *Van Gent and Kuyvenhoven*'s survey of Tissot van Patot's contribution to the development of concepts for the theory of transport policy. First, it is indicated as characteristic for Tissot that his aim is to make maximum use of the concepts of the general theory of economic policy for the development of the theory of transport policy. A second main feature appears to be a certain reshaping of traditional economic concepts, notably through recourse to political science. As symptomatic for this may be seen the replacement of the concept of a "subject" of economic policy by that of an "actor" (see the article by Kuypers).

An impression of the variety of the problems the theory of transport policy takes into consideration can be obtained from the contribution by *Gwilliam*, dealing with the conditions for a common transport policy for a group of states. Gwilliam contributes to the development of concepts for the theory of transport policy. More in particular he provides a number of criteria which may serve to characterize different forms of transport policy. Among the criteria put forward it is the "style" of a transport policy which most attracts the attention, this notion enabling one to distinguish policies according to whether they are intended to be an integrated whole, or rather are "the ad hoc response to specific perceived problems." Gwilliam's main occupation, however, is not with concepts but with common transport policy. In the article the attention is focused on the fact that the development of a common EEC transport policy has almost come to a standstill. The task Gwilliam sets himself is that of making a suggestion for the solution of the deadlock. What he proposes is a lesser degree of centralization in the formulation of transport policy within the EEC. Valuable as the article is as an analysis of the problems of EEC transport policy, the interest it carries extends beyond that. Its statement of the conditions for creating a common transport policy within EEC may easily serve as a model that applies to any set of transport policies.

The role of models in the determination of a particular transport policy is the subject in the article by *Holtgrefe*. Taking the example of a government document on national transport policy in the Netherlands, he criticizes the non-quantitative nature of the way policy has been stated. Holtgrefe recognizes the possibility of, at least in principle, formulating a mathematical model for transport policy. His aim, however, is to show how, with a number of preliminary steps, i.e. devising flow schemes, a better understanding of the consequences of the policy maker's actions can already be obtained. Whether the road to building models for national transport policy should be followed to the end is a question that falls outside the scope of Holtgrefe's article. In the compact but highly illuminating assessment by Studnicki-Gizbert (1977) of the work on transport policy models during the last two decades, the question has been raised "whether we should admit that the task set by model builders is inherently impossible, and abandon it as the early scientists abandoned the search for a philosopher's stone." Reflecting on the merits of Holtgrefe's method may help to answer that question.

"The economic order in transport is of great importance because it is the framework within which the transport politician must take his decisions." (Tissot van Patot, as rendered by Van Gent and Kuyvenhoven, p. 29). The economic order occupies a central place in the contribution by *Kolarič*. More especially his article deals with the formation of transport policy in the context of the self-management system as existing in Yugoslavia. It appears that the self-management system offers an explicit structure for confronting and trying to integrate the ends of the various groups in society having interests in transport. Is it possible to draw any conclusion as to the results of this type of decision-making process, in comparison with the kind of society where action groups and pressure groups enter into decision making in a more random and ad hoc manner? In a wider sense, the merit of the article is that of stressing that the theory of transport policy can be enriched if it takes into account the existence of different kinds of economic order.

Aspects of the relationship between research and developing a particular transport policy are discussed by *De Waele*. Analysing developments within the framework of a large international body for co-operation in the field of transport policy, viz. the European Conference of Ministers of Transport (ECMT), he devotes his attention to the question of to what extent transport economics can lend assistance to policy makers in dealing with transport. The conclusions reached do not reflect a particularly optimistic view. That De Waele does not stand alone in this is made clear e.g. by the opinion professed by Hughes (1978): "Il existe encore un véritable fossé entre modèles théoriques et solutions pratiques," which is the more interesting as it derived from a synopsis of an ECMT symposium devoted to "The contribution of economic research to transport policy decisions."

De Waele's critical attitude points to a very serious problem, both for theory and for policy making. In view of this, it is worth while considering whether anything can be said about future developments in the relationship between theoretical transport studies and policy making for transport. It may be illuminating to approach this question both from a practical and from a theoretical point of view. The practical point of view may already be very sobering. Thus the former Prime Minister of Great Britain, James Callaghan, when asked how he looked upon his earlier post as Chancellor of the Exchequer, remarked: "You must have a knowledge of economics but you mustn't let it become your master. At the end of the day you must fly by the seat of your pants. You must trust your own instincts even when you have looked at all the statistics and the forecasts — which are frequently wrong anyway" (Harris, 1978).

On a less anecdotal level, one may ask whether it is in the nature of economics, and therefore also of transport economics, to come up with clear and immediately practicable solutions for the politicians' problems. For an answer one may look, as Hutchison (1977) points out, to the difference in "material" on which a science like physics on the one hand and the social sciences on the other are built. This difference must inevitably lead to the conviction that "failure to grasp limitations and a failure to try to bring them home to politicians and public, could certainly constitute a *very* serious fault, as would still more so, the fostering of excessive expectations."

4. SOCIETAL IMPLEMENTATION

It is true that the practice of policy making continues to provide an important stimulus for research into problems of transport policy. It is not true that all theory is expressly developed in order to help in solving practical problems, nor that it will always lend itself to practical application. Changes in the practice of policy making, however, will not fail to produce their effects on research and theory. Changes that are manifest in this respect should be analyzed and explained by revealing their various underlying causes. One of them certainly is the much more complicated character of the problems with which the policy and decision maker have been confronted in the last decade compared with those in former days, and — partly as a consequence of this — the broadened range of activities of the policy and decision maker in their role of assisting the community in clarifying its choices. According to Manheim (1973) this role "requires far-reaching changes in the way professionals and their organizations function." He further states: "The public no longer believes in the objectivity of the professional's analysis and is unwilling to accept his recommendation unquestioningly. The traditional model of the role of the professional in reaching a decision through "objective" analysis is no longer viable." This is what in Section 1 of this Introduction was called the phenomenon of "societal implementation," to be seen as a new cluster of problems in policy and decision making.

Tissot van Patot was on the right path indeed in introducing into his theory of transport policy the process approach implying that a policy (viz. a transport policy) is to be seen as a process of decision making by politicians (Van Gent and Kuyvenhoven, p. 28). Because the policy maker's tasks lie finally in consensus-maximization, there is a need of identification of the roles of the various actors in the decision-making process, actors such as planners, research workers, policy makers, politicians, community groups, individual citizens. Comprehensive transport planning (Wells, 1975) has become one of the techniques by which the objectives, the appropriate means for realizations and the impacts on the various community interests can be clarified, discussed and monitored in order to enable the community to make explicit choices among discrete, well-defined alternative programs, policies or projects.

It seems not yet possible to foresee in which way the relationship between theory and practice will be affected by the various aspects and requirements of "societal implementation." The articles in particular by *Holtgrefe*, *Santoro* and *De Waele* demonstrate how much is still in its infancy. A courageous and perhaps promising step in the field of comprehensive transport planning on a national scale seems to be the Swiss *Gesamtver-kehrskonzeption* (1977), not in the least from the point of view of striving for the highest possible degree of political consensus and — along the way of comprehensive planning — facilitating the solving of societal implementation problems in defining a long-term transport policy.

5. OSMOSIS, OR THE NEED OF INTERDISCIPLINARY APPROACHES

"Osmosis" between disciplines, as briefly indicated in Section 1 of this Introduction, is not yet a phenomenon that has been defined sharply, neither in its possibilities of enriching the theory of transport economics nor in the need that emanates from policy-making activities in transport, in particular when comprehensive plans have to be designed and implemented in society. When nevertheless in the eyes of the editors "osmosis" is to be labeled a change in the field of transport studies, it is just because of the growing consciousness that there is a gap to be bridged in this respect and that therefore it may be claimed that "osmosis" will become an object of special study and consideration, both for the sake of theory and policy making.

There is no reason whatsoever for criticizing the fact that the economic study of transport has become an important specialization and that it should be further developed in that sense. But for reasons of stimulating its possibilities in respect of theoretical explanation and formation of theory on the one hand and increasing its fruitful contributions to practical problems on the other, the trend for further progress should not merely be characterized by an extrapolation along straight lines of its notions, methodologies and outputs as they have been developed until recently. In introducing a book on urban transport economics, Hensher (1977) has pointed out that "in recent years there has been an extensive interdisciplinary effort in the search for an understanding of urban transport issues, and for this reason the economic emphasis has become part of a more diversified approach to issues having an economic theme. This has been mellowed by social, political and institutional constraints of sufficient magnitude to require their explicit consideration as major influencing forces in an economic exposition of transport requirements and policy prescription." Without other issues of that kind, urban transport economics' contribution in the field of transportation methods and practice would be, in the opinion of Hensher, insufficient. He lays an additional emphasis on the relationship between economics and other disciplinary implications of the urban transport problem. Also in more general contexts, certain needs of intersectoral and — often as a consequence — of interdisciplinary approaches have become manifest, just in behalf of realistic analyses and research, and for reasons lying in the real, "own" world of policy and decision makers, who have to design their "products" more and more as complete packages of projects and policies, conceived as a unified whole, taking account of the impact on society as a whole.

The editors' point is not to argue that the frontiers between transport economics and other disciplines should fade away or that we would be in need of some type of integrated theory far beyond the frontiers of transport economics as it exists. The fact that concrete reality only can be explained by considering it in its different aspects does not at all mean that this should or could be done by integrated theories embracing all aspects. Neither is there a place for one unified theory in the field of transport studies (Polak, 1968). The point, however, is that the professional who, as a transport economist, deals with a certain transport problem by using, of course, the knowledge and instruments from his own discipline, must nevertheless be fully conscious that the same problem has more aspects and also more ways of being approached. Generally speaking, the transport economist must be able to imagine what the problem looks like seen from the angle of another discipline and how it is or might be tackled through other disciplines. He must be inclined to take advantage of the notions, methodologies and results of others disciplines as much as possible. Partially this could be denoted as a new way of thinking, even as an attitude; partly it gives rise to rethinking organizational aspects of working. Not in the least could a growing degree of "osmosis" affect positively the relationship between theory and policy making in practice.

Could "osmosis" help in finding solutions for the practical problems indicated in De Waele's article? Is it the same phenomenon as touched on by Klaassen in the last section of his article? Whatever answer the reader may be inclined to give, the editors have also attempted to have reflected in this book this type of change.

In fact, *Kuypers'* article adds a non-economic dimension to the analysis of transport policy making. It is the contribution of a political scientist; not, as the author takes care to stress, to political science. The article is a patient unraveling of the political process of policy formation, applied to a transport setting. The key question of course is what can the more traditional, economic, analysis of transport policy gain from a confrontation with the (or "a") way of thinking in political science? It may be suggested that the gain could be a greater degree of realism in the analysis of transport decision making consisting of a better insight into the dynamics of the process of policy making. It may be interesting to note a basic similarity between the ends-means tree as it appears in Kuypers' analysis and the flow scheme which is Holtgrefe's main tool of analysis.

Heertje in his article emphasizes that in transport policy making one cannot ignore developments of a technological character, neither in their possible impacts in terms of influences of transport enterprises on the market positions, nor in terms of environmental effects which are still too much neglected by transport economists. Public authorities still have little grasp of the environmental effects of technological changes. Transport economists should devote more attention to technical changes and in general to macro-economic problems surpassing those of the market mechanism in terms of prices and money. Heertje stresses the "social scarcity" which seems to demand collective action to cope with societal impacts of technical change.

Travel demand has been a subject in transport economics which over the past decade or so has led to a profusion of writings. Though "demand" may once have seemed — or to some may still seem — the exclusive domain of economics, it is in particular this subject which, not very surprisingly, has attracted increasing attention in recent years from psychologists and sociologists.

The kind of contribution psychology is able to make to the analysis of an individual's travel behaviour is depicted, based on a number of concrete examples, by *Michon*. His main point is that psychology may not only, so to speak, play an external role (perform the function of an *aid*) in providing certain techniques for travel analysis, but may also be a *guide*, in being an active element in shaping or modifying the theory of travel behaviour. Should the trend as represented by Michon's article, one may ask, be interpreted as a reversion to the old position which held that the assumptions of the — economic —theory of consumer behaviour had to be derived from psychology? An economic theory of travel behaviour will remain characterized by the fact that individuals are confronted with scarcities. As to the question of which factors realistically are being experienced as "scarcities," economic theory indeed may expect guidance from psychology.

Kuiler shows some particular needs and possibilities of integrated sets of statistical information in the sense of complete spatial transport patterns with the relevant modal splits in some sectors of freight traffic in the Netherlands. A long way is still to be gone, but in the opinion of Kuiler the prospects are promising when one also makes the demand — as Kuiler does — that transport professionals, if needed, must be able to have an overall view, also statistically, on the whole of certain transport economic activities in their relevant interdependences. It must be clear that policy making by public authorities is a kind of management which requires adequate management information. Integralistic concepts in policy making ask for integralistic information systems. This too contributes to a broadening of view in the field of transport studies. It is not the least important condition for making real progress in the relationship of theory and policy making in the years ahead.

REFERENCES

Gesamtverkehrskonzeption Schweiz. Eidgenössisches Verkehrs- und Energiewirtschafts-Departement (1977):Bern.

Harris, K. (1978). "Callaghan: my way to the top", *The Observer*, 26 November.

Hensher, D.A., ed. (1977). *Urban transport economics.* Cambridge etc.: Cambridge University Press.

Hughes, M.P. (1978). "Contribution de la recherche économique aux prises de décisions en matière de politique de transport," *Transports* 23:326-336.

Hutchison, T.W. (1977). *Knowledge and ignorance in economics.* Oxford: Basil Blackwell.

Knies, K. (1853). *Die Eisenbahnen und ihre Wirkungen.* Braunschweig Schwetschke:37

Kuiler, H.C. (1963). *De ontwikkelingen van de vervoerseconomie en die van de Europese vervoersintegratie* ("The development of transport economics and that of European transport integration"). Assen etc.: Born.

Manheim, M.L. (1973). "Reaching decisions about technological projects with social consequences: a normative model," *Transportation* 2:1–24.

Polak, J.B. (1968). *Abstracties over Stapvoets en Supersoon* ("Abstractions about moving at foot-pace and at supersonic speed"). Leiden: Stenfert Kroese.

Rakowski, J.P. (1976). *Transportation Economics. A Guide to information sources.* Economics information guide series vol. 5. Detroit: Gale Research Company.

Schumpeter, J.A. (1954). *History of economic analysis.* London: George Allen and Unwin.

Studnicki-Gizbert, K.W. (1977). "Transport policy models and transport policy development — a major challenge or a search for a "philosopher's stone?" in E.J. Visser, ed., *Transport decisions in an age of uncertainty.* Proceedings of the third World Conference on Transport Research, Rotterdam, 26–28 April, 1977. The Hague–Boston: Martinus Nijhoff.

Thomson, J.M. (1974). *Modern transport economics.* Harmondsworth: Penguin.

Wells, G.R. (1975). *Comprehensive Transport Planning.* London: Charles Griffin.

THE SPATIAL THEORY OF THE DEMAND FOR FREIGHT TRANSPORT: A SURVEY

G.J. BLAUWENS

> The chief, geographic, element of a transport service, consists of the points between which the movement of passengers or commodities occurs. The connection between the two points, the so-called relation, is such an obvious feature, that it can properly be considered as the first element of a transport service.
>
> (translated from Tissot van Patot, 1952.)

Space is an essential element in any transport activity. When trying to explain transport demand, we should not proceed as if we lived in a "wonderland of no dimensions" (Isard, 1949). Space should be an explicit element in the analysis. Traditional economic theory, which does not consider the element of location, is inadequate for derivation and explanation of transport demand. It is unsuited even to understand the mere existence of such a demand.

Many spatial models of the demand for freight transport have been developed in economic literature. In the present paper we try to give a survey of that work. Section 1 contains a rough but useful classification of the various models. Section 2 concentrates on general spatial equilibrium. In Sections 3 and 4 some special cases are presented.

It is common practice to predict transport flows by means of a four-stage model comprising generation, spatial distribution, modal split and assignment. The latter two will be ignored in the present paper. Our exposition will focus on generation and, of course, on spatial distribution.

Both theoretical and applied models will be discussed. The emphasis however will be on operationality. There is little sense in developing endless variants of impractical constructions.

1. A CLASSIFICATION

A useful classification of spatial transport models can be based upon four criteria: the character of space, the number of commodities dealt with, the treatment of time and the assumed market behaviour.

1.1. Discrete space or continuous space

One class of models considers a finite number of locations between which freight flows occur. These models are said to operate in discrete space.

Another class of models considers space as a geometric plane, each point in the plane being a location that generates or attracts transport. The number of locations and consequently the number of freight flows is infinite. Models of this kind are said to operate in continuous space.

1.2. General or partial

A model which simultaneously defines the flows for all commodities in the whole economy is a general model. In applied versions of such a model it is always necessary to aggregate commodities. Otherwise the number of distinct goods would be astronomical and the cost of computation would prohibit any real use of the model. Conceptually however such a model remains general, as it defines the simultaneous equilibrium for all "commodities."

Quite an important set of spatial models give up the ambition of generality. They consider the flows of one single commodity. These models are partial.

1.3. Static or dynamic

All applied and nearly all theoretical models of spatial equilibrium are static. They explain transport flows by current variables only and they assume all adaptations to occur instantaneously. A few dynamic models have been developed however, specifying explicitly a time path with lagged reactions.

*   1.4. Competitive or non-competitive

In some models the economic agents are assumed to face pure competition: they are atomistic price takers, adapting their demand or supply to market prices. Their behaviour is competitive.

Other models are based on non-competitive behaviour. For instance, they assume collusive oligopoly, where suppliers set prices or quantities at such levels that profits are maximized for the industry. The spatial equilibrium under such an assumption will of course be different from the competitive equilibrium.

2. GENERAL SPATIAL EQUILIBRIUM

Let us start our survey with those models that are, in terms of our classification, "*general*," i.e. models which treat all commodities simultaneously.

A convenient starting point is the general model in *discrete space*, with *static* equilibrium and *competitive* market behaviour:

$$S_k^i(P_1^i, P_2^i, \ldots P_K^i) = \sum_{j=1}^{I} x_k^{ij} - \sum_{j=1}^{I} x_k^{ji} \ (i = 1 \ldots I, k = 1 \ldots K) \tag{2.1}$$

$$P_k^j - P_k^i \le c_k^{ij} \ (i,j = 1 \ldots I, k = 1 \ldots K) \tag{2.2}$$

$$(P_k^j - P_k^i - c_k^{ij}) x_k^{ij} = 0 \ (i,j = 1 \ldots I, k = 1 \ldots K) \tag{2.3}$$

$$x_k^{ij} \ge 0 \ (i,j = 1 \ldots I, k = 1 \ldots K) \tag{2.4}$$

In the notation of this equilibrium system superscripts indicate locations, while subscripts indicate commodities. The number of locations is I, the number of commodities K. The symbols have the following meaning:

S_k^i = excess supply of commodity k at location i, in other words supply minus demand of commodity k at location i. When $S_k^i > 0$, location i is a net supplier of k. When $S_k^i < 0$, there is a net demand for k at place i.

P_k^i = price of commodity k at location i.

$S_k^i(P_1^i, \ldots P_k^i)$ = excess supply function, giving the excess supply of k at location i, as a function of all prices at that location.

x_k^{ij} = transport flow of commodity k from location i to location j.

c_k^{ij} = transfer cost of commodity k from location i to location j (that means the total cost per unit of k, including transportation, insurance, package, risk, interest and any other cost due to the transfer from i to j) (Ohlin, 1933). In our model transfer costs are treated as autonomous variables, because we want to focus the analysis on demand. The supply side of transportation of course could be introduced by cost functions, giving c_k^{ij} as dependent on the flows x_k^{ij} and on factor prices $P_1^i \ldots P_K^i$.

The equilibrium system (2.1) to (2.4) is easily understood:

The I.K. equations (2.1), are balance equations. They require that a net supply ($S_k^i > 0$) of commodity k at location i is carried off to other locations, or that a net demand ($S_k^i < 0$) is carried in.

The I^2. K. equations (2.2) could be called limits of price difference. Their meaning is clear: the price difference between two locations can never exceed the transfer cost. If it would, anybody could immediately realize a profit by starting transportation.

The equations (2.3), also numbering I. K., are transport prohibitions. They prohibit transportation on relations where the price difference is less than the transfer cost, i.e. where the value of transportation does not pay off its cost. In conjunction with the limits of price difference (2.2), the transport prohibitions state that

— either the price difference equals the transfer cost $(P_k^j - P_k^i = c_k^{ij})$ and the flow x_k^{ij} can differ from zero;
— or the price difference is less than the transfer cost $(P_k^j - P_k^i < c_k^{ij})$ and the flow x_k^{ij} is necessarily zero.

Finally, the equations (2.4) are very obvious. They restrict the transport flows to non-negative quantities.

Our system (2.1) to (2.4) thus specifies spatial equilibrium as a situation where each net demand and each net supply is balanced by transport flows, which are non-negative and which have to force down every price difference to at most the transfer costs, without on the other hand occuring between locations where the price difference is less than the transfer cost.

The model operates in *discrete space*, with a finite number of locations I. It is *general*, as it treats all commodities simultaneously.

It is *static*, as it contains current variables only. And it is *competitive*, with price takers adjusting their net supply to market prices and their transport demand to price differences and transfer costs.[1]

The extension of the model to continuous space, dynamic equilibrium and non-competitive behaviour is discussed in the remainder of this paragraph.

The introduction of *dynamic* considerations, as a first exercise, is straight-forward: one can introduce lagged prices into the excess supply functions. One can express that a transport flow x_k^{ij} leaves origin i during period t and reaches destination j one or more periods later, etc. ...

Less obvious is the extension of the theory to *non-competitive* behaviour. Collusive oligopoly with joint profit maximization for the K industries, as an example, would require a formulation like the following one:

$$\text{Max} \sum_{i=1}^{I} \sum_{k=1}^{k} (P_k^i D_k^i - c_k^i x_k^i) - \sum_{i=1}^{} \sum_{j=1}^{} \sum_{k=1}^{} c_k^{ij} \cdot x_k^{ij} \qquad (2.5)$$

$$D_k^i (P_1^i, P_2^i, \ldots P_K^i) = \sum_{j=1}^{I} x_k^{ji} \quad (i = 1 \ldots I, k = 1 \ldots K) \qquad (2.6)$$

[1] Equivalent optimization models can be developed, using social utility as an objective function and transformation functions as restrictions (Lefeber, 1958; Von Böventer, 1962).

$$x_k^i = \sum_{j=1}^{I} x_k^{ij} \quad (i = 1 \ldots I, k = 1 \ldots K) \tag{2.7}$$

$$P_k^i - P_k^i \leq c_k^{ij} \quad (i,j = 1 \ldots I, k = 1 \ldots K) \tag{2.8}$$

$$x_k^{ij} \geq 0 \quad (i,j = 1 \ldots I, k = 1 \ldots K) \tag{2.9}$$

where D_k^i is demand for commodity k at location i (function of all prices);
x_k^i is production of commodity k at location i;
c_k^i constant average and marginal cost of commodity k at location i.

This new model maximizes the excess of total revenue over production and transfer costs.

In this maximum problem the delivered prices P_k^i, the production quantities x_k^i and the consignments x_k^{ij} are instrument variables. The transfer costs c_k^{ij} and the production costs c_k^i are given and in the present case assumed to be constant. As in the system (2.1) to (2.4) demand is a function D_k^i of all prices. Unlike that system, however, it is impossible to represent supply by a simple supply function. An adequate representation of supply needs a maximum formulation.[2]

The conversion of our model (2.1) to (2.4) in order to suit a continuous space requires a different indexation of the variables. Instead of a discrete locational superscript i or j we have to use couples of real-valued coordinates such as uv or st. Throughout the system (2.1) to (2.4) we introduce the following modifications:

— We replace a price P_k^i at location i by a price $P_k(u,v)$ as a continuous function of coordinates u and v.
— We replace a supply S_k^i at location i by a supply $S_k(u,v)$ again as a continuous function of coordinates.
— We replace a transport flow x_k^{ij} by a flow density $x_k(u,v,s,t)$ which is a continuous function of origin coordinates uv and destination coordinates st.
— We replace a summation of outflows $\sum_{j=1}^{I} x_k^{ij}$ by the double integral

$$\int_{s=0}^{S} \int_{t=0}^{T} x_k(u,v,s,t) \, dt \, ds$$

which gives the total flow leaving point uv to point st between the boundaries S and T of the plane.
— We replace a summation of inflows $\sum_{i=1}^{I} x_k^{ji}$ by the double integral

$$\int_{s=0}^{S} \int_{t=0}^{T} x_k(s,t,u,v) \, dt \, ds$$

---

[2]A partial variant of (2.5) to (2.9), restricted to one commodity, is given by Kuenne (1977).

— We replace a transfer cost c_k^{ij} by a continuous function $c_k(u,v,s,t)$ (for instance when the transfer cost is proportional to Euclidean distance, this function is simply $c_k = c \cdot \sqrt{(u - s)^2 + (v - t)^2}$, with c as proportionality constant).

— Finally, instead of imposing the equations (2.1) to (2.4) for each location i (i = 1 ... I) we require these equations to hold identically for all values of u, v, s and t in the plane (this identity is the continuous counterpart of the discrete proposition "for each i").

All these modifications are self-evident. The mathematical complexity of the resulting model however should not be underestimated.

3. SPECIAL CASES IN CONTINUOUS SPACE

A *competitive*, *static* and *general* equilibrium model in *continuous space* has been presented by Schweizer and Varaiya (1976, 1977) and by Scott (1976), who makes nearly the same assumptions but focusses his attention on land rent.

Supply is defined simultaneously for the K commodities by means of Leontief production functions. A drastical assumption however is made to simplify the spatial patterns of transport. Final demand is concentrated in one single point, called the Central Business District. Land outside this point is devoted exclusively to production and no production occurs in the Central Business District.

Partial models for one commodity in a continuous space have been developed by Hurter and Lowe (1976), Isard and Liossatos (1975), Beckmann (1972), and others.

Hurter and Lowe assume production to be concentrated in two plants and demand to be uniformly distributed over the plane. Transfer costs are directly proportional to Euclidean distance, but the constant of proportionality may differ between plants. The quantity produced in each plant and the two marketing regions are defined, assuming *monopolistic* and *static* profit maximization.

Isard and Liossatos even introduce *dynamic* considerations, but at the cost of dubious analogies with the physical features of waves. Transport is considered as the counterpart of wave propagation while transfer cost is the equivalent of friction.

Beckmann treats a *static* and *non-competitive* case, again at the cost of heroic simplification. Two competitors face a spatially homogeneous market, with the same simple demand function in all points: quantity is 0 if price exceeds a critical level; quantity is 1 if price does not exceed this level.

The most notable feature of all these continuous models is their complete lack of practical application. This may be explained partly by the fact that economic statistics do not treat space as a continuous variable. If in any way these statistics have a spatial dimension, they consider at most discrete space: they give production and consumption in a finite number of regions, transport flows between a finite number of origins and destinations, prices in a finite number of locations. Statistics with continuous spatial dimensions, such as decline in production density per km distance from the Central Business District or probability to observe an industrial activity, as a function of coordinates, can be conceived in theory. In practice however such data have not been collected so far. This of course hampers empirical work with continuous models.

A second explanation for the lack of practical applications is the highly unrealistic character of present model building in continuous space: transport costs proportional to straight-line distance, concentration of demand or supply in one single point, uniform distribution of supply or demand with identical properties in all points of space, etc ... One cannot reasonably expect to base an accurate explanation of real transport flows on academic assumptions of this kind.

4. SPECIAL CASES IN DISCRETE SPACE

For a simple application of the model (2.1) to (2.4), we can partialize the system to one single commodity: we simply suppress the subscript k and apply the model as if only one commodity exists. The resulting *partial, static* and *competitive* equilibrium problem in *discrete space* has been discussed originally by Enke (1951), Samuelson (1952) and Smith (1963). One of the first empirical applications was made by Morill and Garrison (1960).

A useful variant of the model (2.1) to (2.4), again static and competitive, is obtained by assuming the excess supply S_k^i to be completely inelastic. For each commodity k (k = 1 ... K), such an assumption of inelasticity produces the following linear programming model

$$\text{Min} \sum_{i=1}^{I} \sum_{j=1}^{I} c_k^{ij} \cdot x_k^{ij} \tag{4.1}$$

$$\sum_{j=1}^{I} x_k^{ij} - \sum_{j=1}^{I} x^{ji} = S_k^i \quad (i = 1 \ldots I) \tag{4.2}$$

$$x_k^{ij} \geqq 0 \quad (i,j = 1 \ldots I) \tag{4.3}$$

The relation between this optimization model and the original system (2.1) to (2.4) is not obvious at first sight: one immediately recognizes in

(4.2) the original balance equations (2.1), but the limits of price difference (2.2) and the transport prohibitions (2.3) seem to have vanished. Yet these limits and prohibitions are represented in the objective function (4.1). It has been shown that under this objective function, the dual variables of S_k^i can be interpreted as prices P_k^i, satisfying both the limits of price difference and the transportation prohibitions (Hadley, 1965).

The linear programming model (4.1) to (4.3) has been used in several applied studies of transport demand (Nijkamp, 1975; O'Sullivan 1972; Mera, 1971; Howes, 1967). Other linear programming formulations can be obtained by relaxing the inelasticity assumption and defining S_k^i $(i = 1 \ldots I, k = 1 \ldots K)$ from a set of linear constraints and objectives. This is the basic approach of the famous model that was proposed by Leon Moses in 1960 (cf. Stevens, 1968). Moses assumes that the net supply quantities S_k^i are not entirely inelastic. Only final demand y_k^i $(i = 1 \ldots I,$ $k = 1 \ldots K)$ and production capacity c_k^i $(i = 1 \ldots I, k = 1 \ldots K)$ of commodities k at locations i are inelastic and predetermined. Total outputs x_k^i $(i = 1 \ldots I, k = 1 \ldots K)$ have to satisfy these demand and capacity restrictions under a Leontief technology with fixed technical coefficients a_{kh}^i $(i = 1 \ldots I, k, h = 1 \ldots K)$ and under the objective of minimizing primary production costs (w_k^i per unit of k produced at location i) plus transport costs. The model can be written

$$\text{Min} \sum_{k=1}^{K} \sum_{i=1}^{I} w_k^i \cdot x_k^i - \sum_{k=1}^{K} \sum_{i=1}^{I} \sum_{j=1}^{I} c_k^{ij} \cdot x_k^{ij} \qquad (4.4)$$

$$\sum_{j=1}^{I} x_k^{ij} - \sum_{j=1}^{I} x_k^{ji} = x_k^i - \sum_{h=1}^{K} a_{kh}^i \cdot x_h^i - y_k^i \ (i = 1 \ldots I,$$

$$k = 1 \ldots K) \qquad (4.5)$$

$$x_k^i \leqq c_k^i \quad (i = 1 \ldots I, k = 1 \ldots K) \qquad (4.6)$$

$$x_k^i, x_k^{ij} \geqq 0 \quad (i, j = 1 \ldots I, k = 1 \ldots K) \qquad (4.7)$$

Unlike the simple LP model (4.1) to (4.3) where every commodity k is programmed independently from other commodities, the Moses model (4.4) to (4.7) is a true general K commodity model with interdependencies between goods. Again it is possible to demonstrate that the shadow prices satisfy limits of price difference and transport prohibitions.

A lot of variants on the Moses model have been developed, either by modifying the capacity restrictions and the objective function, or by introducing *dynamic* input-output concepts (Takayama and Judge, 1971; Fujita, 1975; Heady and Egbert, 1962; Greenhut, 1967; Ghosh, 1965; Ghosh and Chakravarti, 1970; Hurter and Moses, 1964). Some of these extensions are of great mathematical beauty but of little operational value.

Linear programming models of the kind (4.1) to (4.3) or (4.4) to (4.7) are considered by many authors as useful instruments in predicting the demand for freight transport.

The alternative to linear programming models are gravity models. Properly speaking these models seem to be the only alternative to linear programming. Nearly all applied spatial models of freight transport are based either on linear programming, or on a gravity model. The choice between these two approaches is for that matter an important issue in the debate on spatial transportation modelling (Nijkamp, 1975; Hartwick, 1972; Gordon, 1974; Hartwick, 1974; O'Sullivan, 1972; Blauwens, 1974).

The general consensus seems to be that high levels of commodity aggregation exclude the use of linear programming and require gravity modelling, while disaggregation of commodities improves the performance of linear programming without equally improving the results of gravity models. Nevertheless it remains difficult to beat gravity models. They continue to explain very well even when commodities are highly disaggregated (Black, 1972).

In its most primitive version a gravity model can be specified as follows:

$$x^{ij} = \alpha \frac{O^i \cdot D^j}{P} \cdot (c^{ij})^\beta \cdot e^{\epsilon^{ij}} \tag{4.8}$$

with x^{ij} = flow from region i to region j;
   c^{ij} = transfer cost from i to j (or a proxy for this);
   O^i = origin potential of region i (a parameter expressing the importance of region i as a transport origin; for instance industrial production, total exports);
   D^j = destination potential of region j (a parameter expressing the importance of region j as a transport destination, for instance regional inputs of the good);
   $P = \left[\sum_i O_i\right]^{1/2} \left[\sum_j D_j\right]^{1/2}$ = average potential;
   α, β = coefficients to be estimated;
   ϵ^{ij} = disturbance;
   e = base of natural logarithm.

Although this model, in all its simplicity, can perform remarkably well (Meyer and Straszheim, 1971; Linnemann, 1966), it is desirable to introduce cross price effects of transfer costs c^{uv} upon x^{ij} (ij $\neq$ uv). Quite obviously, when we consider a gravity model as a commodity-aggregated approximation of general system like (2.1) to (2.4) or (2.5) to (2.9), we have to recognize that a transport demand x_k^{ij} (or its aggregate x^{ij} over some commodities k) depends not only on its own transfer cost c_k^{ij} but on all transfer costs in the whole economy.

Such a dependence on more than one transfer cost is often expressed in specifications like (4.9) or a variant of this:

$$x^{ij} = \alpha \cdot \frac{O^i \cdot D^j}{P} (c^{ij})^\beta \cdot \Big[\frac{1}{P_d} \sum_{\substack{v \\ v \neq j}} D_v c^{iv}\Big]^\gamma \Big[\frac{1}{P_0} \sum_{\substack{u \\ u \neq i}} O_u c^{uj}\Big]^\lambda \cdot e^{\epsilon ij} \qquad (4.9)$$

with $P_d = \sum_v D_v$

$\quad\quad P_0 = \sum_u O_u$

and where we expect the coefficient β to be negative while γ and λ ought to be positive.

Gravity models are not limited to a specific market form. In that sense they are less specific than linear programming which necessarily assumes either a competitive equilibrium or a non-competitive but collusive or monopolistic maximization of a very specific kind.

Both gravity models and linear programming can be adapted to handle *dynamic* effects. One only has to introduce lagged transfer costs as explanatory variables in the gravity model or as coefficients in the objective function. In applied forecasts however this has not been attempted yet.

5. CONCLUDING REMARKS

An impressive body of literature exists on the subject of spatial demand theory for freight transport. To a high extent this work is purely theoretical: a range of models have been developed, including sophisticated dynamic variants, in continuous space, with non-competitive behaviour etc... From this range of models, just two are being applied to real forecasting problems: linear programming and gravity models, both in their static form.

An essential limitation of these two models is their *discrete spatial structure*, but this is not a serious handicap, given the character of available economic statistics. One certainly should not expect the predominant role of gravity models and linear programming to be taken over by continuous models in a near future.

On the theoretical level it may be interesting to concentrate efforts on the establishment of a common theory for passenger transport as well as freight transport. The whole body of theory treated in our survey is limited to commodity transport. As such our equilibrium systems are meaningless when applied to passengers. At least such an application would be extremely artificial.

Gravity models, admittedly, do apply both to commodities and passengers, but this generality is due more to a lack of explicit economic theory than to superior conception.

REFERENCES

Beckmann, M.J. (1972). "Spatial Cournot Oligopoly," *Papers of the Regional Science Association* 28:37–47.

Black, W.R. (1972). "Interregional Commodity Flows: some experiments with the gravity model," *Journal of Regional Science* 12:107–118.

Blauwens, G. (1974). "De vraag naar goederenvervoer en potentiaalmodellen," *Economisch en Sociaal Tijdschrift* 28:227–248.

Böventer, E. von, (1962). *Theorie des räumlichen Gleichgewichts*. Tübingen: J.B. Mohr (Paul Siebeck).

Enke, S. (1951). "Equilibrium among spatially separated markets: solution by electric analogue," *Econometrica* 18:40–47.

Fujita, M. (1975). "On optimal development in a multi-commodity space system," *Regional Science and Urban Economics* 5:59–89.

Ghosh, A. (1965), *Efficiency in Location and Interregional Flows*. Amsterdam–London: North Holland.

Ghosh, A. and Chakravarti, A. (1970). "The problem of location of an industrial complex," in A.P. Carter and A. Brody, eds., *Contributions to input-output analysis*. Amsterdam–London: North Holland.

Gordon, I.R. (1974). "The gravity hypothesis and transportation cost minimization. A comment," *Regional Science and Urban Economics* 4:1–9.

Greenhut, M.L. (1967). "Interregional Programming and the demand factor of location," *Journal of Regional Science* 7:151–161.

Hadley, G. (1962). *Linear Programming*. Reading, Mass. etc.: Addison-Wesley.

Hartwick, J.M. (1972). "The gravity hypothesis and transportation cost minimization," *Regional Science and Urban Economics* 2:297–308.

Hartwick, J.M. (1974). "The gravity hypothesis and transportation cost minimization. A reply," *Regional Science and Urban Economics* 4:1–9.

Heady, E.O. and Egbert, A.C. (1962). "Programming models of interdependence among agricultural sectors and spatial allocation of crop production," *Journal of Regional Science* 2:1–20.

Howes, R. (1976). "A test of a Linear Programming Model of Agriculture," *Papers of the Regional Science Association* 28:123–140.

Hurter, A.P. and Moses, L.N. (1964). "Regional Investment and Interregional Programming," *Papers of the Regional Science Association* 17:105–119.

Hurter, A.P. and Lowe, T. (1976). "The market area problem with two plants," *Regional Science and Urban Economics* 6:173–191.

Isard, W. (1949). "The General Theory of Location and Space Economy," *The Quarterly Journal of Economics* 63:476–506.

Isard, W. and Liossatos, P. (1975). "Parallels from physics for space-time development models," *Regional Science and Urban Economics* 5:5–40.

Kuenne, R.E. (1977). "Spatial oligopoly: price location interdependence and social cost in a discrete market space," *Regional Science and Urban Economics* 7:339–358.

Lefeber, L. (1958). *Allocation in Space*. Amsterdam: North-Holland.

Linnemann, H. (1966). *An econometric study of international trade flows*. Amsterdam: North Holland.

Mera, K. (1971). "An evaluation of Gravity and Linear Programming Models for Predicting Interregional Commodity Flows," in J. Meyer and M.R. Straszheim, eds., *Techniques of Transport Planning*, vol. 1. Washington D.C.: The Brookings Institute.

Meyer, J. and Straszheim, M.R. (1971). *Techniques of Transport Planning*, vol. 1. Washington D.C.: The Brookings Institute.

Morill, R.L. and Garrison, W.L. (1960). "Projections of Interregional patterns of trade in wheat and flour," *Economic Geography* 36:116–126.

Moses, L.N. (1960). "A general equilibrium model of production, interregional trade and location of industry," *Review of Economics and Statistics* 42:373–399.

Nijkamp, P. (1975). "Reflections on Gravity and Entropy Models," *Regional Science and Urban Economics* 5:203–225.

Ohlin, B. (1933). *Interregional and International Trade*. Cambridge: Harvard University Press.

O'Sullivan, P. (1972). "Linear Programming as a forecasting device for Interregional freight flows in Great Britain," *Regional Science and Urban Economics* 2:383–396.

Samuelson, P.A. (1952). "Spatial price equilibrium and linear programming," *American Economic Review* 42:283–303.

Schweizer, V. and Varaiya, P. (1976). "The spatial structure of production with a Leontief technology," *Regional Science and Urban Economics* 6:231–251.

Schweizer, V. and Varaiya, P. (1977). "The spatial structure of production with a Leontief technology — II: substitute techniques," *Regional Science and Urban Economics* 7:293–320.

Scott, A.J. (1976). "Land use and commodity production," *Regional Science and Urban Economics* 6:147–160.

Smith, V.L. (1952). "Minimization of Economic Rent in Spatial Price Equilibrium," *Review of Economic Studies* 30:24–31.

Stevens, B.H. (1958). "An interregional linear programming model," *Journal of Regional Science* 8:60–68.

Takayama, T. and Judge, G.C. (1971). *Spatial and Temporal Price and Allocation Models*. Amsterdam–London: North Holland.

Tissot van Patot, J.P.B. (1952). *Het concentratieverschijnsel in het binnenlandse vervoerswezen* ("The phenomenon of concentration in interior transport"). Ph.D. dissertation, Rotterdam.

PROFESSOR J.P.B. TISSOT VAN PATOT: HIS APPROACH TO THE THEORIES OF TRANSPORT POLICY AND SPATIAL TRANSPORT ECONOMICS

H.A. van Gent and R.A. Kuyvenhoven

1. INTRODUCTION

Tissot van Patot, appointed at the Free University in Amsterdam in 1964, was the first to occupy the University's Chair of Transport Economics. Quite naturally, therefore, his primary task was to create a structure for teaching the subject, which furthermore might serve for purposes of research.

Tissot van Patot during his academic career mostly devoted himself to his teaching duties. Extensive summaries of his lectures were made available to his students, copies of which usually were also presented to his closest colleagues.

The editors of the present collection of essays felt that Tissot van Patot's style in analyzing the problems of transport economics in his lectures had something distinct, which would merit bringing it before a wider public.

To this end we have chosen two subjects out of the large number, approximately 40, which were taught by him in the course of years and which may be said to characterize most his methods and style of thinking and teaching, namely his analysis of the theory of transport policy and his treatment of the function of the transport system in urban development. We thus, in accordance with the intentions of the editors of this book, on the one hand deal with a theme which, so to speak, is "classic" in Tissot's work, and on the other, shows his open-mindedness towards new developments within the field of transport economics.

In setting out Tissot's approach of these two subjects we will follow the main lines of the summaries of his lectures.

2. TRANSPORT POLICY

2.1. Towards an analysis of transport policy

Introducing the subject, Tissot (1973–74) begins by saying that the term "(transport) policy" not only has to be considered as denoting activities of persons and/or organizations, but also as the field of scientific studies which takes these activities as its empirical object. The usefulness of this field of studies is twofold. First there is a theoretical usefulness, since one learns to analyze the activities, irrespective of the values and the goals of the policy maker, in all their different elements; this leads to an insight into a phenomenon which is very complicated and therefore not easy to investigate. Secondly there is a usefulness of a practical character as the result of the greater insight into the structure and functioning of the transport system.

Tissot has attempted to obtain insight into this subject matter by taking as a point of departure two characteristics of transport policy: (1) on the one hand transport policy is a specific instance of economic policy, the same as the latter is a specific instance of policy in the most general sense; from general policy it derives certain characteristics as regards basis, principles, targets and means; (2) on the other hand transport policy deals with the peculiarities of the transport sector itself.

In literature the typical characteristics of transport are often designated as "special aspects." According to Tissot however the characteristics of transport are not to be considered as a particular feature of this branch of services; they also arise in other branches of services. Therefore the exclusive term "special aspects" should not be used; one should rather use the general term "characteristics." However, the characteristics of transport, such as the derived nature of demand, the lack of balance of demand in time and in space, the long technical length of life of equipment as well as the many-sided applicability of the equipment, are important in that they result in the need for a transport policy whose main objectives are the preservation, respectively the re-establishment, of balanced demands and supplies as well as an equilibrium between costs and revenues at least over a certain period of time.

Scheme 1. The connectedness of transport policy with general policy and with economic policy.

Elements of transport policy	Typifying characteristics	Source
basis	● law and public safety	general policy
principles	● public justice	general policy
	● optimal welfare	
	● efficient use of means of production	economic policy
targets	● promotion of general interest	general policy
	● optimum contribution to welfare	economic policy
lower-level targets	● equilibrium among demand and supply, costs and prices.	characteristics of mode of transport
means	● regulation of capacity	lower-level
	● regulation of rates	targets of transport policy

The first characteristic of transport policy, its connectedness with general policy and with economic policy, may appear from Scheme 1.

2.2. A process approach

A consequence of the view that transport policy is a specific instance of general policy and of economic policy is, according to Tissot van Patot, that the transport economist has to be apprenticed to political science in order to be able to make a structured analysis of transport policy. Political science will have to provide him with the instruments for bringing structure into the diversity of the measures that occur in transport policy.

It is for this reason that in his analysis Tissot has followed the method that sees politics as a process of decision making, consisting of various stages, and also corresponding to the kinds of decision as taken in a private firm (Kuypers, 1973).

The various stages are:

— defining the existing situation;
— indicating the situation to be expected in the future;
— acceptance of principles by which the future situation must be tested;
— determining the desired situation (=target);
— choosing the means to achieve the target.

This process is depicted in Scheme 2.
On the basis of these stages a transport policy can be analyzed as well as be built up.

Scheme 2.   Scheme of the political process.

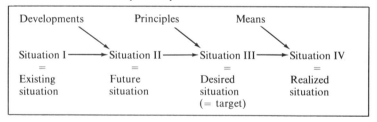

2.3. Existing and future situation

The *existing* situation and the changes in this situation form the basis for the actions of the political actor. Political actors are all the individuals and groups participating in a political process: transport firms, government, political parties, etc. Each actor judges the existing and future situation on the basis of his principles about a desired or undesired future situation. A correct insight in both the existing and the future situation is therefore of paramount importance for the political actor. If his insight is incorrect, the next stages of his acting will be incorrect also, so that he will not reach the situation which appears to him the most desirable one.

The descriptions of the existing situation should take place by means of an analysis of the economic order existing in the transport sector, the economic structure of transport and the economic process in transport.

The economic *order* in transport is of great importance because it is the framework within which the transport politician must take his decisions. However, that order is not an unchangeable feature. It can be altered and be moved to one of its two poles, viz. a completely unregulated market economy versus a completely centrally-planned economy. Changes in the economic order generally take a long time.

Knowledge of the economic *structure* of transport (i.e. structure of demand and supply; nature of markets) is a necessity because measures taken by the political authorities aim at or often result in changes in the structure.

Knowledge of the economic *process* in transport (i.e. the process by which transport demands are being satisfied) is necessary if the transport politician wants to take measures to regulate the process. He will especially need this kind of knowledge in taking decisions relating to unbalances in the field of supply and demand (overcapacity and transport prices).

Describing the economic order, the structure and the process for the transport sector, however, is insufficient. Such descriptions yield an incomplete picture of reality. A good insight requires describing the relations between the different phenomena, e.g. by means of demand and supply models.

The *future* situation will develop from the existing one by changes in the elements which characterize the existing situation. Not all the elements are variables lying within the power and competence of the transport economist or the transport politician for changing them. Keeping the variables that can be changed constant, thus continuing the existing transport policy, yields a future situation in terms of a forecast. Manipulating the variables enables us to design a number of possible future situations in terms of scenarios.

2.4. Principles

The transport politician cannot formulate the targets of his acting without having judged whether the situation as to be expected without his taking any action is desirable or not. This will depend on the principles accepted by him. It follows that principles are an indispensable element for the formulation of targets. Principles and targets are not synonymous and it is therefore going too far to identify principles with targets, as does Oettle (1967).

Considering transport policy as a specialization of economic policy in general and this again as a specialization of public policy in its broadest sense, it is possible to point to a hierarchy of principles, adhered to by the government:

— the highest ranked principle, belonging to the general policy (general interest of society);
— the middle principles, belonging to economic policy (optimal welfare);
— the lower principles, i.e. those of transport policy ("the general transport interest").

This hierarchy is determined by the relationship "aim:means". The lower principle is derived from the higher one and is in fact an elaboration of it. Consequently the principles of any particular transport policy cannot duly be discussed without looking at the higher and the middle principles. Both these sets of principles are data for a transport policy. In addition to these, the transport politician of course also has to do with principles of other, non-economic, fields, such as social principles.

It is clear that the general scheme described above can only prove its usefulness when it fits an actual situation. Thus the scheme is being put to a test by applying it to the situation in the Netherlands. Tissot van Patot draws the conclusion that the principles of transport policy in the Netherlands correspond with the accepted economic order: the free market economy and a free choice for the shipper. This means that in normal times Dutch transport policy is characterized by a limited measure of governmental intervention. The transport sector is neither centrally directed nor totally free; it is a mixed sector in which government grosso modo only intervenes where and when there is a danger or a situation of unbalance.

2.5. Targets of a transport policy

Tissot follows Predöhl (1964) in distinguishing two main categories of goals of transport policy, viz. internal goals, i.e. desired situations within the transport sector itself, and external goals, i.e. desired situations outside the sector. Of course it is interesting to see what specific content Tissot gives to these very broad notions. As the main internal goals he mentions (Figure 1) the situations of optimum (Q1), of maximum (Q2) and of subsidized (Q3) satisfaction of needs, as well as the situations of cost covering (Q4) and of maximum profits (Q5).

Again it is worth while to see in what relation this classification stands to reality. It can easily be seen that many of these internal goals are to be found in practice. For the Dutch situation, for example, the goal of cost

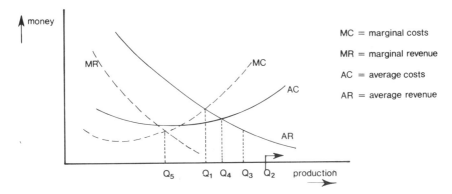

Figure 1. Internal goals.

covering till the end of the sixties applied to public passenger transport. Since then, however, the subsidized satisfaction of needs is the goal of policy. For the other sectors of transport the goal is a satisfaction of needs at a cost-covering basis, resulting from the competition between the various enterprises, each of them trying to gain a maximum result within the framework of government measures aiming at a balance between supply and demand of transport services.

The goals lying outside the transport sector which nevertheless can benefit from transport policy, are manifold. A well-known external goal is the contribution of the transport sector to a regional growth policy or, more in general, its contribution to spatial development.

2.6. Means

The actor in transport policy will have to choose the most adequate and effective means in order to arrive at the desired situation. He will make that choice on the basis of the principles he adheres to, the political chances for realization, the efficiency of the means, the strategy to be followed and the tactics to be employed. During the whole of the decision-making process the transport economist will be able to assist the politician with his knowledge.

Scheme 3 illustrates the relation of the economics of transport as a theoretical subject to the practice of policy making. The means needed in behalf of a rational and efficient policy-preparation process are called "auxiliary means." It appears that in all stages of the process of decision making with respect to transport policy, transport economics can lend assistance in rationalizing the process.

Scheme 3.   Auxiliary means.

Stage of decision making	Auxiliary means	
(1) Definition of existing situation	Observations Statistics Literature	demand/supply models
(2) Prediction of future situation	Forecast	
(3) Choice of principles	Doctrine	
(4) Determination of target (5) Choice of means	Target function Investment criteria (cost-benefit analysis) Traffic plans	

2.7. Evaluation

Taking a general look at the ideas of Tissot van Patot about the theoretical approach to transport policy, it is striking to see his consistent application of the various stages of the political decision-making process, with emphasis on transport policy to be seen as a specialization of economic policy in general. Tissot has made clear how the complicated process of the formation of a transport policy can be explained by systematically analyzing the various stages, without losing sight of the dynamics of the whole. Joining results from the field of political science with economic analysis, more in particular with the consideration of the economic aspect of transport policy, proves to be of great value.

The application to practical policy making of such a conscientious systematic approach, however, is not so easy and not yet common. The formulation of principles on the whole has remained very limited and vague. From Tissot's analysis, as presented in brief above, it will be clear that this must hamper the testing of the future situation in the case of unchanged policy, whether that situation is desired or not. In addition, the prediction of the future situation itself is something very difficult. The complexity of the transport system can lead to predictions only on the basis of a number of assumptions and of complicated methods for estimation. This will not benefit the reliability of the predictions and therefore the efficiency of the means used cannot always be stated clearly.

We can only agree with Tissot van Patot's own conclusion in this respect that this unsatisfactory situation, viz. the insufficient knowledge of the transport process, has to be considerably improved in the interest of sound decision making in the context of transport policy. The theory of transport economics can and still has to make a large contribution towards this end.

3. THE FUNCTION OF THE TRANSPORT SYSTEM IN URBAN DEVELOPMENT

3.1. Introduction

In 1970 Tissot van Patot first introduced into his lectures the subject of transport in spatial development. His main theme was the interrelationship between transport and physical planning on the three levels of the national, the regional and the urban territory. In rendering his views we will limit ourselves to the interrelationship between urban structure and the transport system (Tissot, 1972/73).

The difficulty of solving the problem of the interrelationship between urban structure and transport system is that the problem is the object of two different disciplines, physical planning and transport economics, using different languages. Tissot van Patot has tried to bridge the gap between the two disciplines by translating the physical planners' ideas into the terms of transport economics.

Transport economics is suited for this, as it sees demand as a derived phenomenon and supply as an economic reflex of demand. The problem of the interrelation can then be put as follows: what influence do physical planning structures have on demand for movement and on supply within the transport system and, conversely, what is the influence that supply and the forms of the transport system have on urban structure?

For gaining an understanding of this interdependence Tissot van Patot has adopted the method of bringing to the fore some typical characteristics of both elements that to an important degree determine the picture. This method of stylizing he deemed necessary in order to be able to throw a clear light upon the basic relationships.

For his exposition Tissot defined the town as a concentrated bundle of interrelated human activities that generates demand for movements of people and goods in a restricted spatial territory. Defined in this way each town has some elements that are very important from the point of view of movements, viz. its *functional structure* (with emphasis on economic aspects), its *spatial structure* (the location of economic and other activities) and its *shape* (the outward form of the town as it is situated in geographical space).

The transport system is defined by Tissot as the infrastructure available for traffic together with the transport services making use of it. Transport services have a number of quality aspects, several of which are interconnected. In explaining how the transport system influences urban structure attention can be restricted to the *density* of the networks and of the transport services, the *speed* of traffic and conveyance, the *capacity* of infrastructure and vehicles, and the *cost of transportation*.

3.2. The influence of the transport system on the structure and the shape of the town

The *density of the networks* is of course the most determining element as regards the accessibility of the different parts of the town, especially its centre. It influences the evenness of the distribution of economic activities over the urban area, both as far as locations (horizontal structure) and the density of building (vertical structure) are concerned. A lesser density of networks as a rule means the presence of relatively high buildings near the transport facilities. A higher density results in a more even distribution of higher and lower buildings over the whole of the urban territory. If the density of the transport networks and of transport services in all directions is high, the shape of the town will be in principle that of the round town; every place in the urban area may then be linked up in an equal way with the city centre. In the opposite case, the town will have an oblong shape, an example of which are the so-called dyke villages in the Netherlands.

Travel *speed* has its influence in the sphere of interaction between the different kinds of settlement located in the town. It immediately influences the distance one is inclined to travel for certain activities within a certain period of time. Through this it determines the question of what the distance between places of residence, working and recreation within the town can be. The lower the speed, the less residential low building will be effected in places relatively far away from the centre. As for the shape of the town, an uneven distribution of travel speeds will stimulate the expansion of the town alongside the most rapid routes; in that case towns will be either of an oblong or of a star-like shape.

The *capacity* of the transport system is one of the determining factors as regards the kind of activities that can be performed at a certain location, e.g. stores near motorways, light industries near roads of low capacity. The capacity also determines in what degree high versus low building can or has to be realized; this because the number of workers that can be brought together at a certain location depends on the capacity of the transport system.

If all roads have a capacity adequately adapted to transport demand, the town will in principle be of a round shape: all places outside the centre are connected with it at the same time costs. If capacities no longer correspond with transport demand, the shape of the town will be determined by the parts of the transport system where surplus capacity exists: those parts entailing the lowest costs.

Transport costs, finally, determine the location of those activities whose functioning depends primarily on accessibility. A city centre, e.g., which is accessible only at high costs (including cost of congestion) will in principle drive out industries which to a high degree are dependent on physical accessibility.

For the same reasons as speed and capacity, transport costs have their impact also on the "third dimension" of a town. Low costs in money and in time will make a greater number of people willing to travel to one single point of concentration; high building will be stimulated. If all modes of transport involve equal costs per unit of distance for the whole of the urban area, the town will acquire a round shape. Otherwise the town will show bulges along the routes involving lower travel costs.

As for the impact of these four dominant and interrelated elements on the shape of a town, Tissot van Patot referred to Von Stackelberg's Law of Refraction. Though this law deals with the relation between transport costs and the routes along which transport will take place in general, it can be applied to the shape of a town and its development (Von Stackelberg, 1938).

In conclusion Tissot van Patot points out that from an analysis as summarized above one can derive instruments for purposes of town planning, e.g. for the reinforcement of the economic functions of towns, the preservation of the functions of business centres, and the control of developments relating to the spatial structure and the shape of the town. Actually the analysis as such is an elaboration of the well-known fact that towns are the product of traffic.

3.3. The influence of the town on the transport system

In analyzing the influence of the functional structure, the spatial structure and the shape of the town on the nature and volume of transport demand and on the cost of transport, Tissot van Patot — just as he did in the opposite relation (Section 3.2.) — limits himself to the treatment of some dominant elements. In analyzing this relationship he proceeds in a similar way as described in our previous section.

On the basis of his analysis he put the question of what qualities of the structure and the shape of a town correspond — especially regarding commuter traffic flows — with a transport system functioning at the lowest level of money costs. It should be added that for the sake of simplicity it is assumed that both the benefits arising from the transport system and the costs of it — which are not in the first instance of a monetary character — are constant.

As the economic functions of a town appear to be the main determining factor in this context, Tissot concentrated his considerations concerning the influence of the *functional structure* mainly on that element.

With regard to *spatial structure* the answer is that a type of town obviously is to be preferred in which residences and working places are situated close to each other; the city centre should not only be a business centre, but should also have a residential function; business establishments in the city centre must preferably be of a type that asks for relatively few workers and for relatively many visitors (off-peak movements), while establishments that attract a relatively large number of workers and few visitors preferably have to be situated outside the city centre. Furthermore the density of building has to be high. This will lead to large but brief traffic flows, favourable to space-saving means of transport: public transport, pedestrian and bicycle traffic.

With regard to the *shape* of towns Tissot van Patot took into consideration the star-shaped, the oblong, the elliptical and the round town. The last one is the type with the shortest travel distances and with the best opportunities for bundling traffic flows on radial roads. The former types of towns will entail higher costs from the point of view of the transport system required for their functioning.

3.4. Evaluation

Urban transport all over the world presents great problems. The authorities that bear the responsibility mostly try to solve these problems by taking physical measures, such as restrictions on parking, free lanes for public transport, etc. Generally speaking the result so far has been a transfer of the problems from one part of the town to another part. It is seldom that these problems are taken in hand in a fundamental way. In our opinion it is the merit of Tissot van Patot that he has tried to examine the problems of urban transport in a more structural way by showing, along theoretical lines, the interconnections and the interdependence of the dominant elements of the town on the one hand and of the transport system on the other.

Tissot van Patot has put these problems in general terms and he gave some indications for possible solutions. He draws attention to the contradictory desiderata of transport economists and town planners. Together they will have to find an optimum which renders the greatest contribution to national welfare. The results of this analytical and deductive way of thinking seem to point in the direction of packages of rules and measures for town planning that in the long run might alleviate the problems of urban transport.

Tissot van Patot's way of tackling the problems may be of a somewhat schematical and mainly qualitative nature; his analysis and conclusions can undoubtedly be helpful in trying to find our way in the complicated interwovenness of traffic and transport, town planning and urban design.

REFERENCES

Kuypers, G. (1973). *Grondbegrippen van politiek* ("Basis concepts in politics"). Utrecht/ Antwerpen: Het Spectrum.

Oettle, K. (1967). *Verkehrspolitik.* Stuttgart: C.E. Poeschel.

Predöhl, A. (1964). *Verkehrspolitik.* Göttingen: Vandenhoeck & Ruprecht.

Stackelberg, H. von (1938). "Das Brechungsgesetz des Verkehrs," *Jahrbücher für National-ökonomie und Statistik* 50:680-696.

Tissot van Patot, J.P.B. (1972/73). *De functie van het verkeers/vervoersstelsel in de stedelijke/ stadsgewestelijke ontwikkeling* ("The function of the traffic/transport system in urban/agglomerational development"). Amsterdam: Vrije Universiteit.

Tissot van Patot, J.P.B. (1973/74). *Inleiding tot de vervoerpolitiek* ("Introduction to transport policy"). Amsterdam: Vrije Universiteit.

REALISM AND THE COMMON TRANSPORT POLICY OF THE EEC

K.M. GWILLIAM

INTRODUCTION

There appears to be a wide measure of agreement that the development of a common transport policy for the European Economic Community (EEC) has been very slow; some would go so far as to regard the present position as one of complete stagnation. It is also clear that this has occurred largely as a result of incompatibilities between existing national transport policies and the new policies which the EEC Commission has been attempting to develop. What is less clear is how the present deadlock can be resolved. It is to consideration of that issue that the present paper is devoted.

Our approach is as follows. In Section 1 we attempt to identify the dimensions within which transport policy can be described and formulated. In Section 2 we examine the current transport policy of the U.K. as an example, hopefully not untypical, of the kind of stance that a national government may adopt towards transport policy. In Section 3 we examine the essential elements of EEC transport policy. In Section 4 the inconsistencies in stance and content between the national and the EEC policy levels are identified as the basis for the suggestion, contained in Section 5, of a means of reconciling the national and supranational dimensions in transport policy.

1. THE NATURE AND SCOPE OF TRANSPORT POLICY

We would suggest four dimensions within which transport policy can be described and appraised. These are the style of the policy approach, the objectives of policy, the instruments used to achieve policy objectives and the organizational arrangements within which transport policy is administered. We shall discuss each in turn.

1.1. Style

Commentators frequently refer to "transport policy" as though there exists a coherent, well-integrated philosophical framework into which all items of transport legislation or administration can be fitted and from which all laws and regulations can be uniquely deduced.

In many countries, however, the reality is quite different. Transport legislation is diffuse and diverse. It has been developed incrementally over a long period by the addition of new laws or institutions to an established situation. Moreover, whilst the addition of these increments has often been given the appearance of stemming from a comprehensive policy review, it has not generally been associated with a thoroughgoing reassessment of transport legislation as a whole. For example, while it is possible to characterize British transport policy from 1948–53 as being one of "administrative coordination" or from 1962 onwards as being "coordination through a managed competitive market" it is not difficult to find elements of policy in each period which are very ill-described in those simple general terms.

This is not to argue that governments do not occasionally attempt to introduce comprehensive, rationally-founded and radical changes in "transport policy." Certainly the U.K. measures of 1947 and 1962 and the German "Leber plan" of 1968 had such intent. Simply one is arguing that the potential scope of transport legislation is so great, and the potential content so complex, that it is unrealistic always to presume a monolithic structure within that body of legislation, with all measures conforming to some simple unifying philosophy which can from time to time be radically and comprehensively overhauled. These observations suggest an important distinction in the styles of transport policy which may be adopted. At the one extreme "active" policy making involves a continuous attempt to establish and maintain rational comprehensive and well-integrated policies and institutions conforming to a clear logical structure. In contrast "reactive" policy making may be characterized as the ad hoc response to specific perceived problems as they acquire some critical gravity (Mayntz and Scharpf, 1975). In alternative terminology the distinction may be seen as that between "rational comprehensivism" and "disjointed incrementalism" (Lindblom, 1968).

1.2. Objectives

The second dimension of transport policy is that of objectives, where there appear to be two interacting distinctions to be made.

Firstly, there is the distinction between the pursuit of objectives which are internal to the transport sector as compared with the external relationship of the transport sector to the rest of the economy. For example, the kind of transport pricing policy which is pursued does seem to depend on the extent to which the responsible authority considers that transport should be used as an instrument of higher level policy (e.g. on income distribution or regional balance), possibly to the detriment of the internal performance of the sector.

Second, there is the distinction between social and economic objectives. Again, pricing policies will depend crucially on the extent to which governments consider that, whether within the transport sector or in the economy at large, equity and efficiency should be pursued by the use of different instruments. For example, statutory control of railway rates and conditions of carriage, initially developed as a protection against exploitation of railway monopoly powers in the latter part of the 19th century, have subsequently been developed as instruments of urban planning as in France and Germany, as means of stimulating selected regional developments as in Italy and Germany, as barriers to foreign competition in industry as in Germany, and as instruments of distribution of income.

Within each of these dimensions there is also the issue of the level of detail to which objectives are specified. For instance, the social objective may be set at the general level of achieving an acceptable level of public and private transport facilities. Or it can be formulated in more detail to require some minimum level of accessibility and mobility for all locations, social groups, or even individuals. The choice of detail in which the social objectives in transport are to be formulated almost certainly carries significant implications for the choice of instruments of transport policy.

Similarly there are at least four levels at which the objective of economic efficiency in transport needs to be pursued.

(i) At the sectoral level, the total amount of transport provided should be adequate but not excessive. (In theoretical terms the marginal productivity of factor inputs in the transport sector should be equal to those in other sectors).

(ii) Within the transport sector we need an efficient allocation of resources and traffics between modes. This we shall call the intermodal resource allocation dimension.

(iii) The structure of each mode of transport should be that which allows the demand for that mode to be met at least cost. (In theoretical terms this would be achieved if, for every output, the short run and long run marginal cost had been equated through the adaptation of plant or system size).

(iv) Each individual operator must also be operating in such a way as to make efficient use of the assets at his disposal in the short run. This we shall call the X-efficiency dimension.

In transport, as in other sectors, the existence of indivisibilities, of uncertainty, of finite gestation periods for investment, of externalities, and of varying incidence of economies of scale makes the simultaneous achievement of all these levels of efficiency extremely difficult to attain.

1.3. Instruments

There would appear to be four main sets of instruments available to governments, namely those of direct execution, of organization, of regulation and of taxation. In many countries, but not all, the government is the direct executive agency for provision and maintenance of the trunk-road system; in some (e.g. Italy) the railways are also operated as a direct instrument of governments. Slightly less directly governments can determine the scope, administrative structures and operational objectives of the nationalized industries. The powers of regulation include the regulation of entry to the sector or to parts of the sector; control of the physical and commercial conditions of operation in the sector; and general and specific price controls. The financial powers consist mainly of control over the level and structure of taxation of road users on the one hand, and the level and structure of subsidies to public transport agencies, whether nationally, locally or privately owned, on the other.

It is of particular interest for our present purpose to note that the pursuit of any one of the policy objectives usually involves several of these policy instruments. Moreover, any one instrument may simultaneously be serving a number of purposes and be justified by reference to more than one objective. We shall develop this point by showing, with respect to different objectives and different transport markets, how various packages of policy instruments have developed in U.K. transport policy. It is our belief that other countries, with similar objectives and similar ranges of instruments at their disposal, may quite sensibly and legitimately pursue their objectives with rather differently comprised packages.

1.4. Administration

Whatever the objectives pursued or the instruments chosen the effectiveness of a transport policy will depend on the way in which it is administered. The nature of the institutions adopted, and the relationships between them will not, of course, be totally independent of the style of policy, the objectives and the instruments. Direct executive responsibility for road infrastructure, for instance, requires a department of government with appropriate budgets and executive powers. But neither are the institutions entirely determined. Important variety in administrative arrangements may appear in three dimensions.

Firstly, and of particular importance in the context of EEC transport policy, is the relationship between legislative, executive and administrative powers. Typically for democratic nation-states the legislature sets the framework of law; the executive determines current policy within the rule of law; and the administration implements the policies so determined. But within this paradigm there are important variations in detail. The government has a much stronger and more secure control of the legislature in the U.K. than in the U.S.A. Administrative discretion in the implementation of policy is also greater in some countries than others. Most curiously of all, in the EEC the initiation of policy falls to the administrative institution, the Commission; the legislative function falls to the Council of Ministers (i.e. the national executive bodies); whilst the Parliament is bereft of the typical range of legislature powers.

Second, the degree of decentralization and delegation of powers is very variable. In the unitary nation-state this is essentially determined by the executive and may typically vary according to the needs of the policy objectives and instruments adopted. In federal states the division of powers is more typically contained in a constitution and is hence less immediately flexible. It then becomes extremely important that government does not attempt to adopt policies and instruments inconsistent with its constitutional ability to implement.

Thirdly, there appear to be significant variations in the attitude to functional specialism. At the one extreme the U.S.A. exhibits a great commitment to countervailing rather than coordinated institutions. In that case the institutions tend to be endowed with legal autonomy within the constitution, and to operate through the subtle process of the balance of political power between institutions. At the other extreme the functions may be coordinated "logically" through a hierarchical structure with central government at the focal point.

2. NATIONAL TRANSPORT POLICIES

The purpose of this section is to examine the typical structure of a national transport policy in Western Europe. British transport policy, which has been subject to a comprehensive review in 1976–77, is taken as an example to show how objectives may be formulated and a range of instruments fitted together into a policy. Reference is made to other countries where it appears that British experience is not typical.*

The British Transport Policy Review (Cmnd 6836, 1977) identified three principal policy objectives. Firstly, to contribute to economic growth and to higher national prosperity, particularly through providing an efficient service to industry, commerce and agriculture. Second, to meet social needs by securing a reasonable level of personal mobility, in particular by maintaining public transport for the many people who do not have the

---

*This section does not refer to any changes in policy which have emerged since the election of a Conservative Government in May 1979.

effective choice of travelling by car. Third, to minimize the harmful effects of transport, in loss of life and damage to the environment.

The pursuit of these principal objectives is recognized as being subject to a number of constraints. The need to restrain public expenditure, to ensure that changes are accomplished in the context of full trade union involvement, to leave as much freedom of choice as possible both to users and to local democratic decision, and to fit transport into the context of other sectoral plans, are all identified as limitations in the construction of transport policy.

At this level of generality there is likely to be relatively little dispute about objectives. But conflict is likely to arise when one considers the instruments for achieving these objectives and the institutional arrangements within which they are to be pursued. In Britain the government has declared that a wholly free market is unacceptable because it would result in an inefficient use of resources as well as an inequitable distribution of benefits. The contrary extreme view, that the transport problem should be approached through centralized national demand forecasting and planning, is also rejected. It is argued that such an approach is insufficiently sensitive or flexible to meet the constantly changing patterns both of industrial demand and personal preferences. What the government claims to be seeking is a balanced transport policy which draws on the best elements of planning while rejecting impracticable and unacceptable features.

2.1. Efficiency objectives

The current package of measures to try to achieve efficiency in British transport may now be briefly summarized for each of the major market sectors — urban passenger, non-urban passenger and freight.

In *urban transport* the main concern has been with the intersectoral and intermodal resource allocation dimensions.

The current view is that we need better and more coherent planning at the local level, which should be part of the wider planning for the areas concerned and should be under local democratic control. This implies that local authorities should have comprehensive transport planning responsibilities and powers and should have the widest range of possible instruments of planning at their disposal. Much of recent institutional change in the U.K. is devoted to this end. (Gwilliam, 1976).

This does not leave the local authorities completely free from central-government control. Firstly, insofar as part of the funding for local transport policy comes from central sources, it is inevitable that central government will wish to set some limits to the purposes for which, and ways in which, such funds can be used. Secondly, and more important, central government will wish to retain control over the amount of money which it gives to local authorities. Hence it will not be willing to give open-ended support to any specific policy instrument or to any particular authority. Already there have been severe conflicts between central government and local authorities wishing to use increased levels of public-transport subsidy as a policy instrument. Many local authorities believe that their discretion in local transport policy is, for this reason, more apparent than real. But it is clear that, in the long run at least, there could well emerge widely differing local transport strategies (Gwilliam, 1977). For instance, restraint of private car traffic would be variously achieved by stringent parking policy, by congestion pricing or by large public-transport subsidy. Any national, or supranational, policies superimposed on this basis would need to be compatible with a wide variety of local policies. One of the crucial questions which we shall be asking later is whether the higher level policies which are presently being developed are sufficiently versatile to permit this. Concerning the organization of public transport, there is wide agreement that a very high degree of administrative coordination is desirable, requiring either monopoly or a monopolistic franchise system.* The only real controversy arises on the question of whether control should be vested entirely in the local political authority or should be shared with the traditional institution of the traffic commissioners who have, since 1930, possessed extensive powers to control route structures, schedules and fares for buses.

The issue of X-efficiency has until recently received little attention. But increasingly, as local authorities grant public-transport subsidies both for welfare and intermodal allocation reasons, there is concern to provide management objectives which are better related to the fundamental local authority objectives than traditional commercial objectives seemed to be (Nash, 1978). London Transport, for example, has been given the objective of maximizing passenger miles subject to an overall budgetary constraint.

For *inter-urban transport* both intersectoral and intermodal efficiency is sought by attempting to ensure that each mode meets the costs properly attributable to it. This means that the costs of providing road infrastructure should be covered by the taxation levied on the users and that public road and rail operators be set broadly commercial objectives. Structurally, the railways operate as a unified national system whilst in the bus industry control of entry and route-service licensing operates in such a way as to combine monopoly route franchises with a limited freedom to seek entry by development of new markets. National ownership of a large proportion of the bus industry is accompanied by much decentralization in management. For X-efficiency the separate modes have commercial objectives and

---

* Note that the Conservative administration, elected in 1979, takes a more liberal view of the bus licensing arrangements, though not committed to its abolition.

inducements with substantial freedom to use discriminatory pricing structures to secure traffic in competition with each other. Similarly, in controlling domestic air transport, the Civil Aviation Authority is required to ensure that revenues cover full costs in the long run, whilst structurally the control of entry protects the achievement of economies of scale in operation on the major routes. Although C.A.A. also regulates fares, in doing so it has allowed the major operators freedom to introduce promotional fares so long as they meet the general obligation to cover costs.

There are a number of weaknesses and areas of judgement in operating this regime. The theoretical basis for the allocation of road-track costs is widely thought to be weak; the definition of the "proper contribution" which intercity rail services should make to the joint costs of system operation is essentially arbitrary; and the possibility of competitive overinvestment in capacity between the modes is a source of concern for the government. But, subject to these limitations, a structure does exist within which the modes are expected, through the pursuit of traditional commercial objectives, to secure an efficient service. The real problems arise in the non-urban transport demands which do not fall on the major intercity corridors. Here the problem is that demand is often so sparse that rail transport services cannot be viably maintained, and in some circumstances no public transport services at all would be provided if the market mechanism was relied upon. The mechanism for deciding whether such unremunarative services should be provided, and on what terms, is discussed later in the context of the social objectives.

Efficiency in the *freight* market is also intended to be achieved primarily through market forces. The main aim of the government here is to secure fair competition between road and rail by the removal of direct or indirect subsidies to freight, whether by road or rail. As with intercity passenger service this is based upon the structure of road taxes covering track costs for all categories of road freight vehicle and the railways being required to cover all the avoidable costs of rail freight from revenue. The difference between the passenger and freight requirements is that where track is shared between types of service, rail freight is only required as a minimum to cover avoidable costs, whereas intercity passenger services are expected to make a contribution to system costs. Much more serious problems also arise in freight in respect to the analysis and interpretation of the structure of road-track costs. It has recently been suggested that, whilst for freight as a whole track costs are being covered, the same is not so true of the heaviest and highest mileage categories of road vehicles. As these are likely to be the vehicles performing the services most closely substitutable for rail transport, this is a matter of great concern and controversy.

The structure of the road-haulage industry is uncontrolled, in the implicit belief that there are no significant economies of scale in road haulage and that the freedom to enter and expand will produce optimum adaptations in scale. Nor, since the abandonment of the quantity licensing system in the U.K. in 1968, is there any overall control on the level of capacity provided in the industry.

It is in this aspect of policy that British policy is least typical. Entry to the road-haulage industry is controlled by a licensing system in all of the other Western European countries; in all cases with the exception of the Netherlands this regime is operated restrictively to protect rail transport. This closer regulation of competitive provision has, however, often been accompanied by tighter control over rail pricing with the effect that the financial situation of railways is not necessarily improved in consequence. In Germany, for instance, rail rates are kept down by the combined pressures of trade unions, industrial transport users and regional authorities (*Länder*). Thus despite the most rigorous constraints on competition the deficit per traffic unit exceeds that of all other EEC countries except Italy.

2.2. Social objectives

In Britain the social objective is defined as that of securing a reasonable level of personal mobility, in particular by maintaining public transport for the many people who do not have the effective choice of travelling by car. This objective is qualified by recognizing that the need to constrain public expenditure means that subsidies must be controlled to ensure that they go where they are most needed. This is interpreted as being to support public-transport services that would not otherwise exist or to help people who could not otherwise afford to use services that are running anyway. For the most part the responsibility for applying these principles is passed on to local authorities who are now specifically required to produce an annual public-transport policy statement. Only in the case of certain rail services which the government may require British Rail to maintain as part of the general public service obligations does the administration of the subsidy rest in central-government hands. In all other cases, however, the government operates at one remove, using the leverage it has as the provider of part of the funds from which local authorities finance their transport expenditures.

Some guidance is offered. It is argued that there is rarely a case where public-transport subsidies are likely to be justified as optimal instruments to secure efficient use of infrastructure. Thus the justification must be that of the distributional effects. Here it is asserted that simply to use subsidies to disguise what are the real costs of transport is a blind policy, which may even have the perverse effect of causing the poor to subsidize the rich. This danger is particularly alluded to in the case of subsidies to intercity rail transport, which is predominantly consumed by higher income and business travellers.

Recent U.K. experience does not fit comfortably within those prescriptions. Bus subsidies have gone predominantly to finance global restrictions on fare levels in the largest conurbations. Moreover, there is little evidence that any operable regime of subsidy management has been devised whereby the principles can be efficiently implemented.

The outcome can be characterized as follows. The principle of public-transport subsidy to meet social needs is now widely accepted. Rather more than half of total subsidy expenditure, however, will be devoted to the maintenance of the public service obligation rail network, much of that going to passenger services in London and the South East. Of the bus subsidies the bulk will continue to go to non-specific fare subsidies in the conurbations. Although the trend is to an increasing proportion of specific service-maintaining subsidies in more rural areas, only about 5 percent at most will go to these types of support in the foreseeable future (Beesley and Gwilliam, 1977).

There are some significant differences between European countries in this respect. Specific social concessionary fares are much more common in France, whilst general fare control for macro-economic reasons, which was experienced in the U.K. between 1973–75, has been adopted as normal policy in Italy and the Netherlands as well. Hence, both the balance between economic and social objectives and the specific way in which the chosen balance is obtained differs between nations.

2.3. Safety and environment

In the U.K. considerations of safety and environment are handled almost exclusively by the prescription of standards of construction and operation. Whilst there are arguments for charging heavy lorries more than their direct user costs in recognition of the noise, vibration and pollution that they cause, it is argued that such costs cannot be measured in any objective way. Moreover, even if they could, it would be difficult to arrange for the transfer of the appropriate revenues to sufferers in a welfare-maximizing way. So, whilst the government reserves the right to charge road users more than the costs of provision and maintenance of the roads, it also proposes to use various kinds of direct intervention to pursue environmental objectives. Amongst these are the capital grants for the construction of private rail sidings where there appears to be substantial environmental benefit to be obtained from the transfer of traffic from road to rail; the use of local (though not national) traffic regulation powers to control the routing of heavy traffic; special attention to safety and environmental issues in determining road investment programmes; and the maintenance of stringent regulations on construction and use of lorries and the conditions under which they are operated. A similar range of objectives and instruments can be found in most European countries, with perhaps more emphasis on global protection of rail than is found in the U.K. being typical. In all cases, however, part of the responsibility will be exercised nationally and part locally. Thus, the way in which public authorities' actions affect the individual business will vary according to the nature of that business and the locations in which it is carried out.

3. THE ESSENCE OF THE EEC TRANSPORT POLICY

The common transport policy of the EEC originates in the Treaty of Rome, which declares that a common transport policy is necessary to support the general aim of the treaty to create a free, competitive market in goods and services. To this end the treaty contains, in Articles 76–82, a series of specific injunctions on the kinds of discrimination in the transport sector which might jeopardize the undistorted operation of the free market. In this respect the common transport policy would appear to have very narrow and restricted objectives, and to be essentially subordinate in role.

At the same time, however, the treaty conceded that there might be special circumstances in which a wider conception of transport policy might be appropriate. Thus, for example, Article 77 permitted the continuation of state subsidies for the purpose of transport coordination or as compensation for public service obligations, whilst Article 78 stated that any control of rates or conditions should take into account the circumstances of the carrier. Moreover, in Articles 74, 75 and 84 the treaty encouraged such a wider conception by empowering the Council of Ministers to lay down common rules for international transport within the Community and by establishing institutional procedures for the formulation of these rules. In particular, the role of initiating a common transport policy was given to the Commission.

The Commission took up this role by the production, in April 1961, of the Schaus Memorandum, a document that was to be the blueprint for transport policy for more than a decade (EEC, 1961).

The memorandum took as its starting point the general Community objective of a freer and more competitive market. But it identified four special characteristics of the transport sector, namely:

(i) a high degree of public intervention in the provision of infrastructure;
(ii) large, traditional public service obligations;
(iii) complex relationships between transport and other sectoral objectives;
(iv) low supply and demand elasticities, leading (supposedly) to unstable prices.

The Commission argued that, since these special aspects all hindered the normal play of competition, action must be based on removing them or on neutralizing their effects.

The policy framework which this suggested to the Commission incorporated three major objectives:

(i) to eliminate obstacles which transport puts in the way of the establishment of the common market as a whole;
(ii) to integrate transport provisions at the Community level to assist the free movement of international transport services within the Community;
(iii) to produce a common general organization of the transport sector within the Community.

3.1. The elimination of discrimination

The first objective presented no great difficulties. Action under Regulation 11 of July 1961 brought about the elimination of most transport rates involving conscious national discrimination. Where support tariffs were allowed to continue for regional development or similar reasons, their application was both restricted and monitored. Physical difficulties of frontier crossing were also rapidly eliminated so that by the mid-sixties this objective had been substantially achieved.

3.2. Integrating international transport

The second objective was to provide more positively for an integrated international transport system within the Community. The initial impediment to this was the existence in the various member states of different regulatory systems for road haulage, which made international operations particularly difficult.

To overcome this impediment two types of action were considered necessary. Firstly, the conditions of operation needed to be made sufficiently similar in the member countries for there to exist a fair basis for a freely competitive international road-haulage market. For this reason the Commission proposed a programme of measures of technical, social and fiscal harmonization. Secondly, the old system of bilateral arrangements allowing the entry into a country of foreign haulage vehicles had to be replaced by a multilateral control system so that haulers could engage in international transport within the Community with the minimum amount of administrative impediment.

On both fronts progress has been slow. Although regulations have been adopted on the crucial issues of drivers' hours and conditions of employment there is still no Community regulation on weights and dimensions of vehicles. On the licensing front a multilateral "Community" quota was first introduced, on an experimental basis, in July 1968. This was finally confirmed as a permanent system at the end of 1976 but the rate of expansion of the quota is very slow, only a 20 percent increase having been agreed in December 1977. It is estimated that about 95 percent of international road freight movement within the Community is still dependent on the bilateral arrangements.

For rail and waterway transport, technical and regulatory incompatibilities have been less of a problem because of the longstanding existence of arrangements such as the Berne Conventions and the Act of Mannheim. Only in respect of the financial arrangements for railways has the Commission felt that there was a major problem, and even here it has been the competitive position between modes, rather than the effect on the development of an international transport network, that has motivated the concern of the Commission. This issue will be discussed later.

3.3. Organization of the national transport markets

The third objective set out in the Schaus Memorandum was to secure a common system for the general organization of the transport sector. The memorandum envisaged a high degree of intervention including common rules on tariffs and entry to the national road-haulage markets; common conventions to apply to the relationship between transport operators (particularly the railways) and the states; a common infrastructure policy; and common social policies in the transport sector. This very wide-ranging set of interventions seems to have stemmed directly from the belief that harmonization must precede liberalization and that before such harmonization had been achieved it would not be possible to make any real progress towards the ultimate objective of fair competition between countries, between modes and between operators.

On transport rates the Commission thought that the elimination of conscious national discrimination was not enough and that for all transport, both national and international, rates should be "transparent" and controlled. The specification of upper and lower limits in the bracket tariff was thought of as a way of preventing either the instability of conditions of excess supply or the exploitation of dominant positions in particular transport markets. But even the limited application of this principle under Regulation 1174/68 to international haulage of goods by road proved unworkable and in 1975 the mandatory tariff was replaced by a reference tariff.

Similarly, the agreement to introduce a common domestic licensing system, reached in 1965 and embodied in a draft regulation in 1967, was abandoned in 1975. In both of these respects the Commission, partly as a result of the intransigence of the new members, and partly as a result of the great difficulty of implementing detailed measures of control over such a disaggregated industry without the wholehearted commitment of the member states, has modified its principle of harmonization before liberalization, almost beyond recognition. In its 1975 report to the Council of Ministers the Commission commented, "The view may be taken, however, particularly in order to take account of features inherent to each member state, that Community regulations may do not more than lay down the general principles on which national regulations are to be based, while leaving the member states the necessary latitude to choose the means used."

Two major planks of the initial philosophy seem to remain. In respect of railways the Commission has secured the introduction of three Regulations, 1107, 1191 and 1192, which in principle require the railways to operate as financially autonomous agencies, except in the specific respects provided for in the regulations. These cover the special social obligations of the railways, obligations to provide minimum levels of social service and the need for subsidies to ensure proper coordination between modes, given the differences in cost structures. In principle the railway managements are required to limit the level of subsidy to that justified on these grounds and to adjust their prices, outputs or costs to eliminate subsidies resulting from any other cause. But, in fact, the vagueness of the limiting regulations and the immense difficulties of interpreting railway costs has meant that the regulations have not been effective. In most cases deficits are allocated between the regulations *ex post* to exhaust the total deficit emerging rather than *ex ante* as a management guide.

The final area of policy, that relating to infrastructure, has not yet been overtaken by the same disillusionment that we have noted in most other areas. Previous failure to produce an effective procedure for consultation on infrastructure investment has produced a new determination in this area. A regulation has already been adopted for a standing committee on infrastructure, through which information on plans can be exchanged and coordination pursued. In addition a draft regulation is now before the Council to provide a modest transport infrastructure fund. The existence of such a fund would, of course, be a powerful inducement to further "coordination."

Similar enthusiasm appears still to exist for a common infrastructure pricing regime. The idea that prices should cover marginal social costs and should also be sufficient to produce budgetary equilibrium, sector by sector, has a long history. It was selected as the most appropriate general pricing policy (Allais et al., 1965), and shown to be theoretically capable of application at a more disaggregate level (Malcor, 1970; Oort and Maaskant, 1974). The latter particularly discussed the structure of optimal diversions from marginal cost pricing where such diversions were dictated by the budgetary equilibrium requirement. A proposed directive is now before the Council of Ministers which embodies broad agreement on this principle for pricing the use of road infrastructure by heavy-road-goods vehicles.

These changes of emphasis,* and particularly the less ambitious aims of the Commission, have been set out in Reports to the Council of Ministers in 1973 and 1975. The philosophy no longer seems to be unambiguously that of harmonization before liberalization. But the changes appear to owe more to disillusionment with the past failure to implement that philosophy, and pessimism about the political viability of any attempt to develop it further, than from the conversion to any other integrated, well-articulated, basis for policy. It is to the kinds of conflicts that have produced this situation that we now turn.

4. INCONSISTENCIES BETWEEN NATIONAL AND COMMUNITY POLICY

National policies, as exemplified by the U.K., and EEC policies, as described, differ substantially in each of the policy dimensions discussed in Section 1. It is by examining the nature of these differences in style, objectives, instruments and administration that we lay the basis for identifying a division of function between the policy roles of the EEC and the member states, which we present as our concluding section.

4.1. Style

The difference in style of policy making between EEC and its member states is most striking. The member states, with a comprehensive responsibility, are engaged essentially in "reactive" policy making — gradually adjusting existing policies as problems change. The Commission of the EEC, in contrast, has attempted to engage in "active" policy making, trying to establish new, "rational," policies and structures (Mayntz and Scharpf, 1975). Despite the fact that the common policy as envisaged by the Commission had no urban dimension, and is still primarily concerned with surface transport within the Community, the task of reconciling the different national policies and adapting them to a common, logical basis is immense. Inevitably, in attempting to secure that adaptation the Commission finds itself proposing changes within the member states which do not reflect any immediately perceived problem. Thus, as Helen Wallace has observed, the Commission starts from a qualitatively different, and in many respects more demanding, position than member states' governments (Wallace, 1977).

4.2. Objectives

As we have seen, economic efficiency within the transport sector, subject to certain distributional and environmental constraints, occupies a central role in British transport policy. Indeed, whilst the relative emphasis of these elements may differ somewhat, the same range of objectives appear to be sought by all the EEC member states. Perhaps the most significant difference is the greater extent to which transport policy is expected to contribute to regional distribution and other macro-economic policy objectives in mainland Europe. But, in all countries the structural questions concerning the degree and nature of competition in transport are viewed as second-order questions concerning the most appropriate instruments to achieve the fundamental policy objectives.

Quite the contrary seems to be the case with respect to EEC policy. The Treaty of Rome defines the fundamental objective of transport policy itself in structural terms. Primarily, transport policy should be so arranged to contribute in the best possible way to the development of a free competitive market in goods and services. Secondarily, insofar as it is consistent with the primary objective, it is desired to achieve a free market in transport itself. Social, environmental, and even economic efficiency considerations appear as constraints on the ways in which the fundamental structural objectives can be attained, rather than as objectives in their own right.

4.3. Instruments

In the event, this has led to much of the effort of the Commission being devoted to the development of common measures such as price controls, controls on entry, and the conditions of operation in the transport market which have immediately been of a restrictive rather than a liberalizing nature. For the U.K. this has led to a number of major conflicts with the Commission concerning the instruments being promulgated. It is perhaps worth while to briefly set out some of the issues and the nature of the disagreement.

(i) On weights and measures of vehicles the U.K. has consistently refused to accept larger vehicles, on environmental grounds, or heavier single-axle loadings, on grounds of the effect that this would have on road maintenance and bridge strengthening expenditures.

(ii) On drivers' hours, though control is accepted in principle, the U.K. has been particularly concerned about the effects on the economy of the bus industry in particular. This appears to be an example of a situation where a measure proposed for one reason is resisted because it threatens to upset a very delicate and particular balance in urban and suburban transport arrangements.

(iii) On entry to the road-haulage market, U.K. policy has not, since 1968, contained any general quantitative control. This is based on the belief that the industry is not inherently as unstable as previously thought (and as suggested in the Schaus Memorandum). This matter has recently been reviewed by the Foster Committee and there is little evidence in the U.K. to justify re-adoption of quantity control.

(iv) On price controls in transport, the U.K. has reviewed pricing freedom as an essential part of the strategy of securing coordination of transport through the market mechanism. It has been felt that cost structures are so complex and differ so much between modes and locations that any attempt to exercise price control would be economically inefficient and counterproductive. In any case, with so many small road-haulage operators it is doubtful whether price control could be implemented in road haulage. Here again is a situation where the introduction of the measure might upset the balance of competitive advantage between the modes in unplanned and uncontrolled ways.

(v) On railway policy, the U.K. presently takes the view that decisions have to be taken at a global level about the size of the subsidy. Because of the problem of the allocation of joint costs this does not permit the kind of specific attribution of subsidies that is implicit in the principles adopted (though not effectively implemented) by the EEC.

(vi) On infrastructure investment, the U.K., like all other member states, has been jealous of its power to control the allocation of national resources. This means that, whilst better consultation between member states may be acceptable, any stronger and more directive relationship would only be accepted in the context of a community transport infrastructure budget which the transport ministers of the member states thought to be an addition to, rather than a diversion from, the funds presently in their control.

4.4. Administration

The administration of transport policy differs as between the U.K. and EEC in two important respects. Firstly, it must be noted that the Commission as the body responsible for the formulation of policy and drafting of regulations has a degree of independence of the Council of Ministers, which is responsible for adopting regulations; this is quite different from that of a national civil service. Thus, it is possible for the Commission to spend a great deal of time and effort on the development of policies and strategies which in the event will never be implemented. Indeed, that is exactly the history of the development of the common transport policy. Moreover, because of its peculiar institutional responsibilities the Commission is inherently more likely to pursue elegant theoretical constructs in the search for an integrated policy than a national administration which is more closely subject, at the design stage, to the pressures of political reality.

The second point of importance is that even when regulations have been adopted it is at the national administration level that they have to be implemented and enforced. This means that if a member state has accepted a regulation without enthusiasm it is likely to operate it in the same spirit. For this kind of reason a number of policies have become dead letters (e.g. the bracket tariff).

The conflicts can be summarized thus. The Commission of the EEC has been attempting to engage in an "active" policy-making role to achieve the essentially structural objective of a transport framework which is transparently incapable of causing any distortions in the free market for goods and services. In contrast the member states, exemplified in our discussion by the U.K., have been "reactive policy" makers, responding to perceived problems, particularly in the transport sector itself, and generally unwilling to upset long-established arrangements and balances where short-term costs or problems will result.

5. TOWARDS A REALISTIC COMMON TRANSPORT POLICY

Our consideration of the common transport policy has shown that the Commission has tended to mimic the national governments' wide and eclectic use of policy instruments without having either its direct sensitiveness to the effects of policy or its direct responsibility for the administration of policy. As a result there has been little community of interest between the Commission and the member states.

Unfortunately, the Commission, though exclusively responsible for proposing legislation at the Community level, has little leverage to ensure its adoption by the Council of Ministers. Consequently the Commission is constantly engaged in the wasteful process of "preparatory" legislation, trying to get a foot into doors that the member states wish (and have the power) to keep closed, without being explicit concerning their intentions. Thus Regulations 1107, 1191 and 1192 are preparing for a control of the relationship between the railways and the state; the present draft regulations on heavy-goods-vehicle taxation are preparing for a common infrastructure pricing regime; and the proposed programme for the newly-installed infrastructure committee is preparing for an EEC-determined infrastructure investment plan. In each of these instances it is clear that at least some of the member states have no intention whatsoever of relinquishing their own powers to the EEC institutions. The outcome is frustration for the Commission, associated with a great deal of wasted time and effort in the development of procedures, analyses and proposals inevitably doomed to be fruitless.

The flaw in the arrangements would appear to be the absence of any statement in the Treaty of Rome of a clear division of function between the Community institutions and those of the member states. Article 2 of the treaty, having set out in very general terms the economic and social objectives of the Community, specifies two means whereby the objectives may be achieved. The first is the establishment of a common market; the second the progressive approximation of the economic policies of the member states. A similar distinction is contained in the transport chapter of the treaty which contains specific injunctions on discrimination on the one hand and more general permissive powers to develop a wider transport policy on the other.

On this basis, the Commission was encouraged to interpret "the progressive approximation of the economic policies of the member states" as requiring a set of common rules for the structuring and operation of the transport sector. But it is not under any obligation to make this interpretation. The disappointments of the last twelve years have already caused the Commission to withdraw from some areas of proposed Community legislation. Implicitly it has already accepted that a *de facto* division of function exists which, at the very least, reserves some matters for the member states. A realistic common transport policy, we would argue, can only emerge if the Commission accepts that fact explicitly and directs its attention to defining not, as it has tended to do in the past, an ideal transport policy for a unitary European state, but a rational basis for defining the division of powers in a loose federation.

What remains is to show that some basis can be found for separating the functions of the Community from those of the member states. There are, of course, many dimensions in which the line could be drawn; four are deserving of specific mention before we attempt to synthesize our own "solution."

5.1. *Principles v. regulations*

The Community might seek to restrict itself to defining, and agreeing upon, the principles on which the legal arrangements in the member states should be based. "Policy" in this sense would be separated from implementation and there would be no body of Community legislation beyond that contained in the Treaty of Rome, or possibly the regulations presently existing and not subsequently rescinded. The role of the Commission would then be primarily to appraise the consistency between the operation of member states' transport arrangements and the agreed principles. The difficulty about this "solution" is that it might prove extremely difficult to formulate principles with sufficient precision to allow this function to be performed.

5.2. National v. international traffics

A second way of separating functions might be to limit the Community interest to matters directly related to the international movement of goods and services within the Community. Thus the whole area of regulation envisaged under the third objective of the Schaus Memorandum would be abandoned. It may be argued that, with the possible exception of some measures of social harmonization, all of the attempts of the Commission to develop common policy in this area have either failed to secure adoption or have been dead letters in effect. The difficulty about this prescription is that it does not preclude the use of policies relating to internal traffic which have the effect of discriminating against international movements within the Community (as for example through transport subsidy policy).

5.3. Conscious national discrimination

A third possibility is to define the role of the Community as being that of identifying, and proposing to eliminate, any conscious discrimination in trade exercised through the conditions of transport. This would include the generally successful action taken under the first of the Schaus objectives but would put the onus on the Commission to demonstrate, with respect to structural, pricing, or infrastructure policies, that the fundamental objectives of the treaty were in jeopardy before a basis for Community action was established.

5.4. Operations v. infrastructure

Recent policy memoranda from the Commission have suggested one other dimension. Since 1973 the Commission has argued that much more emphasis should be put on infrastructure policy, which is the direct executive responsibility of member governments, rather than on controlling the large numbers of operators in any complex way. The Commission appears to concede that this change of emphasis is partly a result of its recognition of failure in controlling operations. Cynically one may interpret this as little more than a continuation of the "foot in the door" approach enlightened by the experience of those circumstances in which the foot gets crushed! In any case, infrastructure policy, as presently conceived by the Commission, is likely to yield as much disappointment in the next fifteen years as the control of operations has suffered in the last fifteen.

Our own inclination would be to a basis derived directly from the two "means" set out in Article 2 of the treaty. This would give a Community transport policy two main functions:

(a) Establishment of the common market.
  (i) To identify specific impediments to the establishment of the common market.
  (ii) To propose regulations to eliminate those impediments.
(b) Progressive approximation of the economic policies of the member states.
  (i) To identify the main dimensions of transport policy in the member states.
  (ii) To seek, by consultation with the member states, acceptable general principles in each of these dimensions.
  (iii) To promulgate those measures which have to be entirely common, or can only be promulgated centrally, in order to implement the general principles.
  (iv) To appraise and organize consultation on general transport measures in the member countries in respect of their consistency with the agreed general principles.

What this kind of programme does is to move the emphasis of the Commission away from its policy-formulation role and towards its roles of steering and stimulating the policy-making functions of the Council and the member states, administering those regulations which did exist and supervising the observance by members of agreed principles. (Kapteyn and Verloren van Themaat, 1975). In particular the Commission would be seeking to identify areas where the member states wanted common rules rather than trying to foist common rules upon them.

On this basis the more successful of the Commission's activities (the elimination of discrimination, the promulgation of an unimpeded international road-haulage capacity) would stand. Some of the moderately-successful activities would be given a new life and extended (consultation on infrastructure programmes and on aids would be extended to general consultation on all transport policy changes). But, above all, many of the more detailed attempts at standardization would have to be subject to reappraisal and would only be pursued if it was demonstrably the case that they eliminated significant obstacles to the common market in goods and services or were required to be standardized by the common wish of the member states. It is doubtful whether much of the control of operations area, or even the infrastructure pricing area, would survive that kind of scrutiny. The common transport policy would be a smaller policy, but it would be a more credible and realistic one.

REFERENCES

Allais, M., Del Viscovo, M., Duquesne de la Vinelle, L., Oort, C.J. and Seidenfus, H.St. (1965). *Options de la politique tarifaire dans les transports*. CEE Etudes. Série Transports no. 1, Brussels.

Beesley, M.E., Gwilliam, K.M. (1977). "Transport policy in the United Kingdom," *Journal of Transport Economics and Policy* 11:209–223.

Cmnd 6836 (1977). *Transport Policy*. London: HMSO.

Dept. of Transport (1976). *Transport Policy: A Consultative Document*. London: HMSO.

E.E.C. Commission (1961). *Memorandum on the General Lines of the Common Transport Policy*. Brussels.

Gwilliam, K.M. (1976). "Appraising Local Transport Policy: The New Regime," *Town Planning Review* 47:26–42.

Gwilliam, K.M. (1977). "Urban Road and Rail Policy," *The Chartered Institute of Transport Journal* 37:336–339.

Kapteyn, P.J.G. and Verloren van Themaat, P. (1975). *Introduction to the Law of the European Communities after the Accession of the New Member States*. London: Sweet and Maxwell.

Lindblom, C.E. (1968). *The Policy Making Process*. Eaglewood Cliffs, New Jersey: Prentice Hall.

Malcor, R. (1970). *Problèmes posés par l'application pratique d'une tarification pour l'utilisation des infrastructures routières*. CEE Etudes. Série Transports no. 2, Brussels.

Mayntz, R. and Scharpf, F. (1975). *Policy Making in the German Federal Bureaucracy*. Amsterdam: Elsevier.

Nash, C.A. (1978). "Management Objectives in Bus Transport," *Journal of Transport Economics and Policy* 12:70–85.

Oort, C.J. and Maaskant, R.H. (1976). *Study of Possible Solutions for Allocating the Deficit which May Occur in a System of Charges for the Use of Infrastructures Aiming at Budgetary Equilibrium*. Brussels: CEE.

Wallace, H. (1977). "National Bulls in the Community China Shop: Role of National Governments in Community Policy Making," in H. Wallace, W. Wallace, and C. Webb; eds. *Policy Making in the European Communities*. London: Wiley.

SPATIAL DEVELOPMENT, DEVELOPMENTS IN TRAFFIC AND TRANSPORTATION, AND CHANGES IN THE TRANSPORTATION SYSTEM

R. HAMERSLAG

1. INTRODUCTION

Traditional transportation models calculate transport volumes (passenger flows, etc.) given the geographical distribution of places of human activities (housing, employment, markets/shops, recreation grounds, etc.). However, the future geographical distribution of places of human activities is not given, but interacts with the transportation system.

By introducing elastic instead of fixed constraints, the interdependence of physical planning parameters and the transportation system is mathematically modelled. Some experiments with this model have shown that a realistic description of long-term developments can be obtained.

2. THEORY

2.1. The gravity model

For thousands of years people have been making observations of phenomena connected with the functioning of the solar system, such as the length of day and night, summer and winter, the dry and wet season, sometimes an eclipse of the moon, without being able to explain them. One felt at the mercy of the phenomenon and its nature. The Greeks were the first who tried to explain these facts by means of theory. Newton should be credited with elaborating, in 1687, the experimental law of Kepler and thus developing the gravity theory, which could explain the facts conclusively.

An analogy exists here with problems in traffic engineering, and one solution is the gravity model.

Two bodies, i and j, attract each other with a power which is directly proportional to the mass of these bodies and inversely proportional to the square of the distance. The bodies now are not celestial bodies, but towns. The number of trips between two transportation zones P_{ij} (a zone is a part of an area under study) is proportional to the polarities, Q_i and X_j (often the number of inhabitants of the zone), and inversely proportional to the square of the distance, R_{ij}:

$$P_{ij} = \rho \frac{Q_i X_j}{R_{ij}^2} \tag{2.1}$$

in which ρ is a constant chosen in such a way that there will be optimal adaptation to the trips observed.

2.2. The distribution function and travel resistance

It is not self-evident at all that people will behave in traffic like celestial bodies (Volmuller, 1971). However it is possible to justify the gravity model as well as what later is called the entropy model (Wilson, 1968) by means of utility theory (Golob and Beckman, 1971; Nijkamp, 1975, 1978). Thus, the mathematical forms of these two completely different phenomena correspond.

However, it appears that the mathematical form of the gravity model does not adequately describe reality anyway. In particular in the fifties the correctness in equation (2.1) of R_{ij}^{-2}, the so-called distribution function, has been questioned.

For a general view the reader is referred to Carrothers (1956), whose results can be summarized. R_{ij}^{-2} was replaced by the distribution function F_{ij}. The meaning of this function in the model is that, as the effort or resistance between zone i and zone j increases, the number of trips decreases.

For the case that in a certain relationship several means of transport can be used, in several studies the average resistance weighed according to the use of the various means of transport has been determined. This proved to produce faulty results. It appears to be much better to use certain distribution functions simultaneously for all means of transport (Hamerslag and Dersjant, 1976). The distribution function for every means of transport for a certain relation is thus equal to the sum of the functions for the individual means of transport.

$$F_{ij} = \sum_v F_v (Z_{ijv}) \tag{2.2}$$

In this equation (Z_{ijv}) is the effort or resistance (the disutility or cost) for the means of transport v.

In earlier studies distance was used for expressing resistance. But, by means of the theory of the individual consumer's behaviour it can be concluded that if time and cost budgets are used, the resistance consists of time and cost. Besides, effort also has its influence on the resistance (think of a trip by bike). There are two approaches now to the expression of resistance. In a number of studies, resistance is translated into a money value, the sum of trip cost and the product of trip time and the value of time. The value of time is often directly proportionate to income. The thus-calculated resistance is called "generalized cost":

$$Z_{ijv} = a t_{ijv} + k_{ijv} \tag{2.3}$$

in which

Z_{ijv} = the generalized cost from zone i to zone j by means of transport v.
t_{ijv} = the journey times from zone i to zone j by means of transport v.
k_{ijv} = the cost of a trip from zone i to zone j by means of transport v.
a = a coefficient, often directly proportionate to real income.

The generalized cost has the disadvantage that the resistance increases with increases in income. It leads to less trips with an increase in real income, which is not very logical.

In the second approach resistance is equated to travel time to which is added the income-related trip cost. The thus-calculated resistance is called "generalized time":

$$Z_{ijv} = t_{ijv} + \frac{k_{ijv}}{a} \tag{2.4}$$

If generalized times are used, the generalized time, and consequently the resistance, decreases as real income increases. The number of trips increases in that case. These results correspond more with expectations. Therefore, it is generalized times that are generally applied in traffic engineering.

3. GEOGRAPHICAL CONSTRAINTS IN THE TRANSPORTATION MODEL

3.1. A set of fixed constraints

The complete model for forecasting transport flows consists of a production model, a distribution model, a model for the choice of mode, a model for determining routes and times, and an assignment model. The gravity model can best be recognized in the distribution model. There too, however, there are many fundamental differences, because it appeared to be necessary to add a set of constraints to the original model. This will be illustrated by two examples.

Example 1
    Consider an island with three housing areas (A, B and C), with working

populations of equal size, and one place of employment, D. The values of travel resistance are AD = 1, BD = 2 and CD = 3 respectively.

Using the gravity model and again with P_{ij} indicating the number of trips between any given pair of zones, the proportion between the number of trips is $P_{AD}:P_{BD}:P_{CD} = 1:(1/4):(1/9)$. So in this example of the gravity model the calculation shows that the number of people living in A that actually find employment is nine times that in C. This is not logical, because in the example it is assumed that the working population is the same in A, B and C.

Therefore, it is more plausible to assume that in all three housing areas the number of workers is the same. Evidently, the working population of C will have to make a greater effort for a trip in order to be able to work at all than the working population in A or B.

In the distribution model this is realized by the addition of constraints. The number of departures in each zone (now equal to that of the working population) is added to the model as a constraint. This is possible only if at the same time for each equation a factor (called the "equilibrium factor") is added. *The size of this factor is a function of the extra effort needed to satisfy the constraint.* A poorly accessible zone has a higher value of the equilibrium factor. Consequently, the inverse of this factor is sometimes used as a measure of accessibility (e.g. Fortuijn, 1976). The mathematical form of the model is:

$$P_{ij} = \rho l_i Q_i X_j F_{ij}; \text{ for all i's and j's} \tag{3.1}$$

with the constraint

$$\sum_i P_{ij} = P_{.j} = A_j; \text{ for all j's} \tag{3.2}$$

if only the arrivals (working population A_j) are given in each zone j, or:

$$P_{ij} = \rho m_j Q_i X_j F_{ij}; \text{ for all i's and j's} \tag{3.3}$$

with the constraint

$$\sum_i P_{ij} = P_{i.} = V_i; \text{ for all i's}$$

if the departures (work places) are given. The meaning of the symbols used is as follows:

P_{ij} = the number of trips from i to j;
ρ = a constant (this constant is of little relevance in the model with one or two fixed constraints);
l_i and m_j = the equilibrium factors;
Q_i and X_j = the polarities;

F_{ij} = the value of the distribution function for the relation ij (see also Section 4.3.);

$P_{.j}$ and $P_{i.}$ = resp. the added columns and rows; they are resp. endo-geneously-defined arrivals and departures.

The models with one set of constraints are often named after Voorhees (1955), although Overgaard (1966) reports that these models were already used in Copenhagen in 1945. Other examples are the land-use models of Lowry (1964) and Wilson (1970).

3.2. Two sets of constraints

The model with a fixed constraint has a considerable disadvantage. This will be illustrated by an example.

Example 2

Consider housing areas A, B and C, with equal working populations, and work places D and E, having an equal number of work places. The situation of the areas is given in Figure 1. The resistances are given in Table 1 and the work trips, calculated on the basis of a single set of con-straints, in Table 2.

Summing of the rows of Table 2 produces the number of work places in D and in E, 131 and 169 respectively. It had been assumed, however, that an equal number of people are working in D and E. By introducing an extra set of constraints, this assumption is complied with. This is possible only if at the same time an extra set of equilibrium factors is added to the model. A high value of equilibrium factors indicates a poor accessibility.

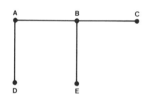

Figure 1. Example of Network.

Table 1. Resistances for Figure 1.

	A	B	C
D	1	2	3
E	2	1	2

Table 2. Trips calculated with one set of constraints (resistances from Table 1).

	A	B	C	Work places (calculated)
D	80	20	31	131
E	20	80	69	169
Working population (defined)	100	100	100	

The model with two sets of constraints is fairly commonly used and has superseded the model with one set of fixed constraints. Hamerslag (1961) has introduced the model in the Netherlands. Furness (1963) uses two sets of fixed constraints in the so-called time function iteration model. The entropy-maximization method of Wilson (1968) also uses the two fixed constraints mentioned.

The mathematical form of the model as it is used by the author and many others follows below. Two or more trip purposes are often distinguished. For each trip purpose the model is described by the following equations:

$$P_{ij} = \rho l_i m_j Q_i X_j F_{ij}; \text{ for all i's and j's} \tag{3.5}$$

and

$$\sum_{.i} P_{ij} = P_{.j}; \text{ for all j's} \tag{3.6}$$

$$\sum_{j.} P_{ij} = P_{i.}; \text{ for all i's} \tag{3.7}$$

In the models with two fixed constraints further applies:

$$P_{.j} = A_j; \text{ for all j's} \tag{3.8}$$

$$P_{i.} = V_i; \text{ for all i's} \tag{3.9}$$

V_i and A_j resp. are the exogeneously-determined departures and arrivals.

In the following sections arrivals will be dealt with as being equal to the working population and departures equal to the work places for the evening rush hour. It may already be noted that arrivals are often distinguished according to whether trips are made by persons having or not having a private car at their disposal.

4. SPATIAL DEVELOPMENT IN RELATION TO THE TRANSPORTATION SYSTEM

4.1. Spatial development in the past

By spatial development we mean the growth or reduction of activities considered in their situation in a certain geographic area (housing, working, recreation, etc.). For the proper understanding of the concept of spatial development it may be added that a certain spatial development need not necessarily be a planned development and that therefore the concept should be distinguished from town and country planning. In this section spatial development in its relation to the transportation system will be discussed.

In the previous section the models without or those with one or more fixed constraints were described. In these models the spatial distribution of activities was included in the polarities or in the constraints. Consequently, this distribution was assumed as not to be influenced by the transportation system, which includes roads, cycle paths, railroads and other public transport services. This is not correct theoretically; it does not correspond with reality and it also limits the applicability of the models. For instance Tissot van Patot (1975) has put forward that spatial development can only be fully explained if the transportation system is included in the model as an explanatory variable. However, he warns that there are other influencing factors too. To explain spatial development exclusively from changes in the transportation system leads to an over-estimation of this influencing factor. In itself an improvement of the infrastructure will not affect the geographical activity pattern. However, the degree to which potentially present possibilities can be utilized depends upon the extent and quality of the transportation system.

The above-mentioned theory appears to be confirmed by observations. For instance, the influence of the construction of railroads on the development of the population of the United States is generally known. The influence of the opening up of the hinterland by means of ports, roads and railroads in under developed areas is more recent. Similarly the development of commuter suburbs has been the result of, among other things, the development of railroads (Lowe and Moryades, 1975). In these cases the mutual influence should be pointed out. On the one hand, the spatial development is stimulated by the construction of the transportation system. On the other hand, the spatial development affects the growth of transportation and consequently the construction and improvement of the transportation system.

An interesting analysis of the development of towns was also given by Leibbrand (1957). In antiquity the greater part of the population could only make trips on foot. Goods were also transported by foot or sometimes on wagons. As a consequence the size of towns was limited. For instance, the biggest city in antiquity, Rome, had about 800,000 inhabitants in an area of 1,230 hectares.

In the Middle Ages the biggest cities were situated on the waterfront, which made the transport of goods considerably easier. From 1400 to 1600 the towns barely grew in size. As centres of the region of influence they had reached a limit. However this changed with the discovery of trade routes to the Indies. The function of Venice and Genoa in the Mediterranean was taken over by the Spanish, Portuguese, English and Dutch cities on the Atlantic.

The construction of railroads caused a big change in the transportation system. Thus a further growth of the cities became possible (when rail travel began, London had about 950,000 inhabitants, so just a little more than Rome in antiquity). On account of the construction of railroads the area of influence of the cities has grown a great deal. Increasing transport needs also resulted in a greater density of the rail network, in a higher frequency and an increase in speeds.

People and goods are transported in large quantities simultaneously by rail. As a result, the growth of towns and villages concentrated especially around the stations. Because of the increased importance of private means of transport this limitation has now disappeared. In certain countries the use of the bicycle has enlarged the sphere of influence of the stations. The increase in car ownership has made development possible in places, especially in towns and villages, without a railway station. Suburbanization, at first limited to places with a railway connection, now also takes place outside that immediate area.

4.2. The traditional transportation models

The traditional transportation models, i.e. the models described in the preceding paragraphs, take the geographical distribution of activities as given. It is introduced into the model through the polarities or through the constraints as an exogeneous quantity. Given the developments described, this is not in accordance with reality. Of course, this would be less serious if one could forecast the spatial development reasonably well, and in practice it appears to be possible to get reasonable results. It is also possible to use fixed constraints in the model in order to calculate the transportation implications of spatial planning. The transport flows to be calculated are rather sensitive to the constraints and thus to the assumed or planned spatial development. If the actual spatial development takes place in a different way, the reliability of the transport flow calculations may be affected adversely.

This type of model has another important disadvantage. Because the geographical distribution of activities is taken as given, one cannot see by means of these models what the consequences of transportation measures are on spatial development. The extent to which the transportation planning influences spatial development cannot be quantified. Yet, the assumption of a given geographical distribution of activities, presently under discussion, is an enormously important assumption which returns again and again. Furthermore, the implicit neglect of the influence of the construction of transportation provisions on spatial development may lead to an underestimation of the transport volume.

In order to meet the above-mentioned limitations of the model, it is necessary to take into consideration on the one hand spatial development as it is affected by transportation planning and developments in the transportation system, but also the influence on transport flows of spatial planning and other factors affecting the setting up, expansion and cutting down of industries, services and institutions.

5. THE MODEL WITH ELASTIC CONSTRAINTS

5.1. The constraints

In order to co-ordinate spatial planning, transportation planning, spatial development and development of traffic and of the transportation system, the model with elastic constraints was developed.

This model is a transportation model and has been tuned to this purpose regarding its degree of specification. Because in the past many transportation models were used as models for the spatial allocation of activities, the application of the model in this respect is not precluded either. It seems a good idea not to run ahead at this moment and to limit the discussion to the abstraction level necessary for a transportation model.

The transportation model contains equations in which equilibrium factors occur. The value of the equilibrium factors is a function of the extra effort needed to comply with the constraints. In poorly accessible areas the value of the equilibrium factor is high and, inversely, in easily accessible areas its value is low. Using a number of exogeneously-defined arrivals and departures the model with elastic equilibrium conditions is corrected by the equilibrium factor.

The effect of introducing the equilibrium factor is that in easily accessible zones (small equilibrium factors) the number of departures (work places) is raised. The same is true for the number of arrivals (working population). If the accessibility is poor, the number of arrivals or the number of departures is reduced. This is done by replacing the equations (3.8) and (3.9) with the following equations:

$$P_j = m_j^{-h} A_j; \text{ for all j's} \tag{5.1}$$

$$P_i = l_i^{-g} V_i; \text{ for all i's} \tag{5.2}$$

and besides P is determined for that purpose by

$$\sum_i \sum_j P_{ij} = \sum_i V_i \tag{5.3}$$

The mathematical form presented here is the simplest. In practical applications two or more trip purposes are used, and a subdivision can be made in different categories of the working population and possibly in different categories of work places too.

Thus the number of arrivals and departures becomes dependent, though not exclusively, on the degree of accessibility. Because the degree of accessibility is dependent on the quality of the transportation system, the number of arrivals and departures, and consequently the geographic distribution pattern of activities, also become dependent on the quality of the transportation system. If (3.5) is substituted in (3.6) and this again in (5.10), the following equation results:

$$\sum_i \rho \, l_i \, m_j \, Q_i \, X_j \, F_{ij} = m_j^{-h} A_j \tag{5.4}$$

Some conversion produces:

$$m_j = \left\{ \frac{A_j}{\sum_i \rho \, l_i \, Q_i \, X_j \, F_{ij}} \right\}^{1/1+h} ; \text{ for all j's} \tag{5.5}$$

If (3.5) is substituted in (3.7) and this in turn in (5.2), we get, after some conversion:

$$l_i = \left\{ \frac{V_i}{\sum_i \rho \, m_j \, Q_i \, X_j \, F_{ij}} \right\}^{1/1+g} ; \text{ for all i's} \tag{5.6}$$

$1/(1 + h) = s$ and $1/(1 + g) = r$ are defined as elasticities of the constraints, because different values are used for this purpose instead of the single values one or zero as was the case in the earlier studies. The model discussed here is therefore called the *transportation model with elastic constraints*.

The degree of accessibility, the quality of the houses and the housing area play a part in the choice of where to live. If the market mechanism were free, houses would be built in places where people would like to live. However, this desire for a certain place may be contrary to wishes concerning spatial planning.

The model with elastic constraints calculates the solution in which the views concerning spatial planning will be reconciled with the wish to settle

in a certain place. Employment in a certain zone is determined by industries, institutions and services such as the labour market, the transportation system and the land available. The degree to which people want
to work in a certain geographical zone is determined by the accessibility.
The attractiveness of the work offered will also influence choice. The
model with elastic constraints calculates the equilibrium between work
places, determined by industries, institutions and services (supply) and
the wish of people to work at a certain place (demand).

The degree of accessibility of the work places (the inverse of the equilibrium factor, see section 3.1) is a factor in the supply function. The
model with elastic constraints differs principally from the transport models
discussed earlier because an elastic constraint is used instead of a fixed
one. So spatial development is not assumed, but it is influenced by transportation planning, spatial planning and changes in the resistance experienced by the traffic participants.

5.2. The dynamic model

In transportation models with elastic constraints a static version is distinguished from a dynamic one.

The dynamic version of the model is to be preferred. This dynamic model
calculates the transport flows in the future situation by defining the changes
in the situation of the transport flows over one or more previous years. A
considerable advantage of this model is that time-dependent influencing
factors can be introduced into the model. Some examples are:

— The transport flow affects the development of infrastructure.and the
   latter in its turn affects the size of the transport flows.
— By means of the polarity the individual preference for certain activities,
   for instance housing, is also expressed. It is reasonable to assume that
   in general it is more attractive to live in new houses than in old ones.

Areas in which economic growth in previous years has been above average
will normally have a greater number of new houses. Consequently, it may
be assumed that the magnitude of the polarity is a function of the growth
or decline of the previous years. In a dynamic model the magnitude becomes dependent on the calculations from a previous period. Another
characteristic of the dynamic model is that influencing factors that are
hard to determine can sometimes be eliminated if it may be assumed that
they do not change with time. This leads to a considerable simplification in
the application of the model.

Besides, application of these models has the advantage that the occur-
rence of boundary values can be better anticipated. For instance, if a
transportation capacity is exceeded, it affects the development. In dynamic

models it makes a difference whether the capacity is exceeded at the beginning or at the end of the period under consideration. In the static version of the model this is generally not taken into consideration.

In order to use a dynamic model it is necessary to have available an origin and destination table of trips that is representative of the present situation: the base matrix. In the past, observed relation matrices were often used for this purpose. However, these matrices appeared to consist mainly of zero-observations. Still base matrices are defined by calculation. This is done on the basis of mathematical estimation theory and the assumed mathematical form of the transportation model.

Hamerslag (1972) has made up a base matrix by means of optimal adaptation to census data. It is also possible to construct base matrices by means of optimal estimation of coefficients in the transportation model while using home interviews (Hamerslag and Dersjant, 1976) or adaptation to home interviews, measurements of distances, traffic censuses, etc. (Hamerslag and Huisman, 1978).

6. EXPERIMENTS WITH THE MODEL WITH ELASTIC CONSTRAINTS

6.1. No distinction in means of transport

A new model can have certain characteristics which may surprise even the designer of the model himself. Therefore, it is to be recommended always to perform calculations with a new model in order to check whether the model functions in accordance with our expectations.

In order to be able to perform calculations, assumptions have to be made regarding size of population, work places, networks, polarities, etc. It is advisable to keep these assumptions as simple as possible so as to be able to follow the calculations properly.

The networks used in this section are rendered in Figures 2 and 4. They are made up of links which together form a number of equilateral triangles. The links all have an equal resistance. An exception are the heavily-drawn links, which have a resistance equal to one-fourth of the thinly-drawn links. From both figures it appears that in the course of the calculation process the resistance (W) in both networks is highly reduced (from 20 to 1). Thus expression is given to the fact that the resistance between two areas, with distances unchanged, has diminished in the course of years and is still diminishing.

In the nodes of a network the population and the work places are allocated. The line has been taken that in the initial situation the working population and the work places are equal to each other.

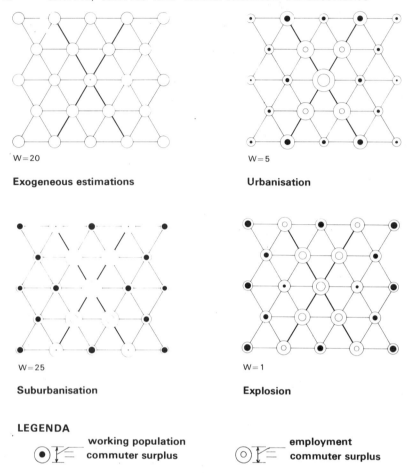

Figure 2. The influence of changes in resistance (W = 20, W = 5, W = 2.5 and W = 1) on the spatial distribution of population and work places in an X-shaped network.

The size of the working population and the number of work places are shown in circles. The surface of the black-shaded small circle is proportional to a residential-commuter surplus. The large circle belonging to it is proportional to the working population. The surface of non-shaded small circles is proportional to the work-commuter surplus. The large circle belonging to it is proportional to the work places.

If the values used for the elasticities of the constraints are for r from −1 to −2 and for s from 0.2 to 0.5. realistic descriptions of the spatial development can be obtained. These will be discussed below. In Figure 2 the consequences of the reduction of the resistance for the calculation are shown. At a resistance of 5, concentration takes place for the towns situated on the heavily-drawn links. One might define this phenomenon as urbanization. A reduction of the resistance to 2.5 makes the commuter surplus grow, on account of which both housing and working areas arise. Reduction of the resistance to 1 also causes a drawing-away of the working population.

An important arithmetical advantage of the model is that it is not necessary to distinguish *a priori* work places of a type that give an impulse to economic activity and those that are of a servicing nature, as is done with the allocation model developed by Lowry (1964). Quite often this distinction is hard to make and besides it is one that changes with time. Steigenga (1954) made a distinction between employment which is of a type giving impulses to separate urban districts but of a servicing nature with

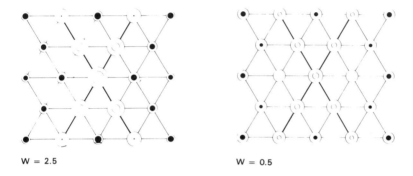

W = 2.5   W = 0.5

Distribution of working population and of work places. W is the value of the resistance on thinly-drawn links; the value of the resistance on heavily-drawn links is $\frac{1}{4}$ of it.

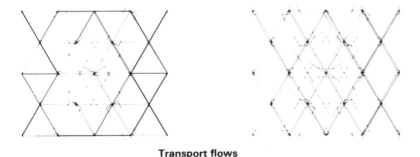

Transport flows

Figure 3. The influence of changes in travel resistance (W = 2.5 and W = 0.5) on the spatial distribution of working population and work places and on the size of transport flows.

respect to a town as a whole, the same as employment providing impulses for a town but being of a servicing nature as far as an entire region is concerned. In the model an indication about this distinction is obtained endogeneously. Evidently towns with a large commuter surplus have work places which will provide impulses to activity in the zone itself but which are of a servicing nature in relation to the area as a whole.

In Figure 3 the relation between spatial development and the size of the transport flows is shown. In this figure, a reduction of the resistances shows a reduction of the commuter surpluses. It is often assumed that if the surpluses are smaller there will be less transportation and that the reduction of commuter surpluses should therefore be used as a planning instrument to restrict the transport volume. In contrast with what is assumed in practice, it may be seen from Figure 3 that a reduction of the commuter surpluses involves larger transport flows. This means that a reduction of the resistance leads to smaller commuter surpluses, but causes larger transport flows at the same time.

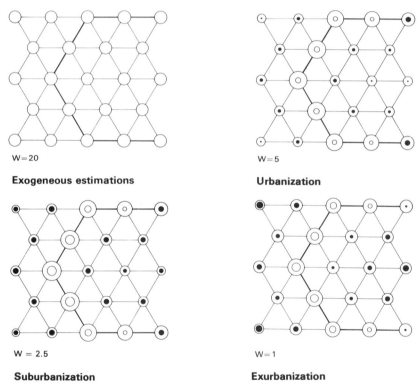

W=20

Exogeneous estimations

W=5

Urbanization

W = 2.5

Suburbanization

W=1

Exurbanization

Figure 4.   The influence of changes in travel resistance (W = 20, W = 5, W = 2.5 and W = 1) on the spatial distribution of population and work places. Horseshoe-shaped structure of networks.

The results mentioned urge caution in planning policy regarding the reduction of commuter surpluses. If the reduction of the surpluses is a result of trends of growth and not of spatial planning, it does not necessarily involve a reduction of transport flows.

In the network shown in Figure 2 the greatest development arises at the crossing of two routes with low resistances.

In Figure 4 the links with low generalized times are situated on a horse-shoe lying on its side. This is a schematic picture of the conurbation "Randstad Holland" ("Rimcity," the urbanized western part of the Netherlands). At a further reduction of the resistance (W = 2.5 and W = 1) suburbanization takes place, spreading into the so-called "Green Heart of Holland."

Thus it proves to be possible by means of simple assumptions about generalized times to describe spatial developments as they occur in cities like Paris and London or in the conurbation "Randstad Holland."

6.2. Car ownership and spatial planning

In order to examine whether the development of a central city could be influenced by the planning of the geographical distribution of housing and work places, calculations have been made relating to a Dutch city with 13 districts, in one case in combination with 2 satellite towns, each consisting of 4 districts, and in a second case in combination with 8 villages (see Figure 5).

In the calculations a distinction was made between car, bicycle and public transportation networks. The calculations were made for a low and for a high car availability.

The results show a strong influence of the increase of car ownership on spatial development. At the same time the impact of this increase can be seen on the development of the centre of the city. The villages situated along the railway do not develop centres of their own. The activities are found more in the central city. This stands in contrast with the development of the two satellite towns. Employment in these towns is withdrawn from employment in the big city.,

As a result of the assumed growth of car availability, the number of activities in the centre of the city decreases. In the case of a city with 8 villages the centre of the city maintains its position much better than in the case of a city with 2 satellite towns. One should take note that transportation flows are larger in the first case.

The above-mentioned changes indicate that it is probably possible to influence the geographical distribution of activities and transport volume by means of spatial planning. As an actual example the spatial

2 SATELLITE TOWNS   **8 VILLAGES**

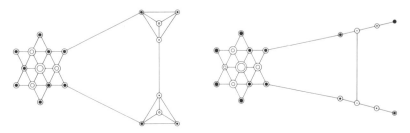

low car availability

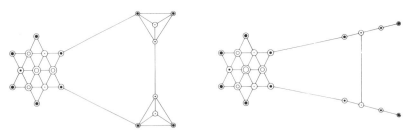

high car availability

Networks for car and bicycle

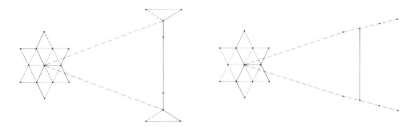

Public transportation networks

(bus connections are solid lines; the railway is shown by means of a dot-dash line; the dotted lines are pedestrian connections)

Figure 5. A comparison of the development of a city with two satellite towns with a city together with 8 villages, at a high and a low car availability.

development of Munich under the influence of the S-Bahn system may be mentioned (Kreibich, 1978).

Another insight, obtained through the studies described above, shows the influence of the public transportation system. In the year 2000 significant groups in the Dutch population still will not have a private car at their disposal all the time. According to Mulder (1973) they are:

— 100 percent of persons under 18
— 70–80 percent of married women
— 25 percent of the unmarried or divorced women and widows
— 40 percent of the men between 18 and 24 and 65 and 75
— 10 percent of the men between 24 and 65
— 80–100 percent of all persons older than 75.

The public transportation system needed for these groups of the population will also have the effect that certain zones become more easily accessible also for those having a private car at their disposal. Consequently urban zones which are also accessible by public transportation will have a better chance of development than those zones which can only be reached by private car.

6.3. The use of the model

In this section some results of experiments with the model with elastic constraints are described. If we take spatial development no longer as given, but as being open to the influence of transport planning, environmental planning and the change of the perception of travel resistance, it can roughly be described on an urban level.

Phenomena like urbanization, suburbanization and exurbanization can be explained on the basis of the change of resistance.

It is possible to explain both phenomena which occur over a very long period within a given geographical region and phenomena which can be seen as different phases of development in different parts of the world. Thus, in less-developed areas, where the limited individual income is an important check on long-distance trips, concentration takes place. In Europe, where the average income is higher, suburbanization is found. In the U.S.A., with an average high income and low trip cost, with a very good car system and a neglected public transportation system, an exurbanization is found.

For calculations on the level of city districts it is necessary to distinguish different means of transport. It is clear that in this case one should include in the model the choice between different means of transport. Thus it is possible to explain the developments in the centres of the cities, in particular the diminishing importance of the centre of the cities, also on the ground of the increase in car ownership.

The model indicates that there are possibilities to influence developments. One might mention the quality of public transportation as well as spatial planning.

The results achieved so far with the model are acceptable in every respect, in particular if one takes into account the global set-up of the experiment. The value of the model will have to be proved in more concrete situations. Because in the past other influencing factors have also made themselves felt regarding spatial development and the volume of transport, a further evaluation of the model might prove to be necessary. This is true in particular for the factors which have influenced spatial development.

These factors are taken as external explanatory variables in the transportation model presented. If one should want to use the model for describing, explaining, or influencing physical processes, these factors will have to be integrated in the model.

As yet it seems significant to use the model in the first place as a transportation forecasting model, i.e. for those cases in which a proper forecast of the transportation demand in relation to the development of the transportation system is required first.

7. CONCLUDING OBSERVATIONS

It should be stressed that in the model with elastic constraints which has been described, the use of certain values for the elasticities means implicit assumptions about the influence of spatial planning and transportation planning on traffic and transportation developments and on spatial developments.

Fixed constraints involve assumptions about arrivals and departures, as well as about the population in the work places from which they are deducted. Thus the model calculates transportation implications of assumed planning developments.

If no secondary constraints are used, arrivals and departures are calculated in the model. It is assumed that the population in the work places is determined exclusively by a priori assumed values of the polarities and of the resistances and consequently of the quality of the transportation system. The model calculates implicitly the spatial development based upon present transportation systems and thus without considering other influencing factors (e.g. planning). ·

In using for elasticities values not equal to zero or to one, one implicitly assumes that interdependence exists between transportation planning, spatial planning and transport developments. The value for the elasticities can be determined on the basis of historical developments. A change in these values, e.g. by choosing an elasticity closer to one, will show to what extent these developments are affected if the spatial planning policy has more effect than it had in the past.

The approach in this article was from the traffic-engineering point of view. By means of some examples which were kept simple on purpose, the working of the model was shown. It appears that spatial and transportation development and transport flows can be roughly forecasted over rather long periods on the basis of facts and theory and that this forecast corresponds reasonably with the actually occurring phenomena of growth. It is recommended to test this in more concrete situations.

It is also possible to use elastic constraints regarding the road infrastructure. This means that road capacity is adapted during the calculation process and will come to depend on the needs of users on the one hand and on the extent of the social efforts connected with construction on the other. Such a procedure would mean an integration of the ideas about optimization of road networks (Steenbrink, 1974) and those about equilibrium models (e.g. Ruiter, 1974, or Florian, 1974). The importance of the model in its present form is in the first place the improvement it offers in the reliability of the results of transport flow calculations, so that the effect of possible bad estimations in planning activities will be reduced.

The model is also of importance in enabling a better insight into the nature and interdependence of the development processes described above regarding traffic, transportation and spatial structure. It will enable us to foresee undesired developments and thereby to intervene, or otherwise to react expertly on those developments which cannot be controlled.

REFERENCES

Carrothers, G.A.P. (1956). "A Historical Review of the Gravity and Potential Concepts of Human Interaction," *Journal of the American Institute of Planners* 22:94-102.
Furness, K.P. (1965). "Time function iteration". *Traffic Engineering and Control* 6:458-460.
Florian, K. and Guyen, N. (1974). "A new look at some old problems in transportation planning," *PTRC Summer Annual Meeting,* University of Warwick.
Fortuyn, L.G.H. (1976). "De bereikbaarheid als vestigingsfactor: Een alternatieve notatie voor Hamerslags model," *Colloquium vervoersplanologisch Speurwerk*. Delft.
Golob, T.F. and Beckman (1971). "A utility model for travel forecasting," *Transportation Science* 5:79-89.
Hamerslag, R. et al. (1961). *Enkele beschouwingen omtrent de verkeersvoorziening in het Zuidhollandse Zeehavengebied*. Rotterdam: Stichting Verkeerswetenschappelijk Centrum.
Hamerslag, R. (1972). *Prognosemodel voor het personenvervoer in Nederland*. The Hague: A.N.W.B.
Hamerslag, R. (1974). "Transportation model with elastic constraints," *PTRC Summer Annual Meeting*, University of Warwick.
Hamerslag, R. and Dersjant, A.W.D. (1976). "The multiproportional estimation method for the simultaneous determination of the value of the deterrence function by mode," PTRC *Summer Annual Meeting*, University of Warwick.
Hamerslag, R. and Huisman, M.E. (1978). "Binaire kalibratie," *Verkeerskunde* 29:166-168.
Kreibich, V. (1978). "The successful transportation system and the regional planning problem. An evaluation of the Munich Rapid Transit system in the context of Urban

Planning Policy". *PTRC Summer Annual Meeting*, University of Warwick.

Leibbrand, K. (1957). *Verkehrsingenieurswesen*. Basel: Birkhäusen.

Lowry, I.S. (1964). *A model of Metropolis*. Memorandum R.M. -4035-RL. Santa Monica: Rand Corporation.

Lowe, J.C. and Moryades, S. (1975). *The geography of movement*. Boston: Houghton Mifflin Company.

Mulder, K. (1973). "De verspreiding van het autobezit in Nederland". *Intermediair* 9, no. 41:15–19.

Nijkamp, P. (1975). "Reflections on Gravity and Entropy Models," *Regional Science and Urban Economics* 5:203-225.

Nijkamp, P. (1978). "Gravity and Entropy Models State of Art," *Colloquium Vervoersplanologisch Speurwerk*. Farnborough: Saxon House.

Overgaard, K.R. (1966). "Traffic estimation in Urban Transportation Planning," *Acta Polytechnica Scandinavica*, Series Civil Engineering and Building Construction, nr. 37. Stockholm.

Ruiter, E.R. (1974). "Implementation of operational network equilibrium procedures," *TRB Record* 491. 40–51. Washington D.C.

Steenbrink, P.A. (1974). *Optimization of transport networks*. London, New York, Toronto: John Wiley.

Steigenga, W. (1954). "Het vraagstuk der regionale bevolkingsprognose," *Tijdschrift voor sociale en economische geografie* 45: 80–88.

Tissot van Patot, J.P.B. (1975). *De functie van het vervoer in de regionale economische groei*. Amsterdam: Vrije Universiteit.

Volmuller, J. (1972). *Algemene verkeerskunde-ell*. Technische Hogeschool Delft, Afd. Civiele techniek, 2–3 (no publication).

Voorhees, A.M. (1955). "A general theory of traffic movement," *Proceedings of the institute of traffic engineers*. New Haven.

Wilson, A.G. (1968). "The use of entropy maximizing models," *Journal of Transport Economics and Policy* 3:108-126.

Wilson, A.G. (1970). *Generalizing the Lowry model*. Working Paper 56. London: Centre for Environmental Studies.

Provinciale Planologische Dienst en Provinciale Waterstaat Zuid-Holland (1977). *Vervoers- en verkeersstudie Zuid-Holland. West en Oost*. The Hague.

SOME REMARKS ON TECHNICAL CHANGE AND TRANSPORT

A. HEERTJE

1. INTRODUCTION

In this article we shall examine technical change and its impact on the transport industry. Our intention is to discuss some developments in the technology of transport against the background of the heterogeneous and pluriform character of technical change in general. The broadness of the subject necessarily restricts us to general observations. We start with a description of the many aspects and effects of technical change in general, and then turn to some examples from the field of transport that are specific illustrations of the main theme of our contribution. Then we shall draw the appropriate conclusions in a closing section.

2. THE GENERAL PHENOMENON OF TECHNICAL CHANGE

Technical change is a many-sided phenomenon. It implies the development of new technical possibilities, the application of new technical methods and the diffusion of technical knowledge. The introduction of new products is just as much a feature of technical change as is the emergence of new methods of production. Invention and innovation are both aspects of the whole process of technical change, and though it can be a long way from the original new idea to its full-scale application in the market, there are cases in which the period that elapses between the invention and the innovation is quite short.

A new technique may be embodied in new capital goods or may require a new quality of labour, but it is also possible that a higher productivity of the factors of production is obtained without any physical change taking place in capital goods. Moreover, new technical methods may worsen or improve the environmental conditions on earth.

The disappearance of certain types of labour may be the inevitable consequence of technical change, but because it is a dynamic force it may also lead to a demand for more highly qualified labour. Furthermore, a new technical method may be accompanied by huge capital saving and may also require important investment in new equipment. There is no reason to expect mass unemployment due to technical change, but nevertheless important shifts in the labour market may occur.

We can think of spectacular new inventions of a kind that change the world and daily life, such as the light bulb, the motor car, the aeroplane. In these cases technical change has a rather disontinuous character, and is associated with the name of somebody who became famous. We may also think of technical change in the continuous sense, where in a given fixed equipment minor changes are introduced that raise productivity or improve the quality of the product made. In these cases technical change is mostly anonymous.

The process of diffusion of a new technique may differ from time to time, or from country to country, and may depend on the character of the new device. Also the process of adoption of a new product is complicated and does not fit into a uniform and homogeneous pattern.

Although the production of new technical knowledge in research laboratories has a more programmed and organized character than in earlier times, it is still the individual inventor who plays an important role. The man without much money and equipment is still able to invent new methods and new applications of old methods. His work contrasts with the teamwork of those who do their research in big companies or organizaions.

Technical change may both create and destroy monopolistic positions in business life. New technical methods often require large-scale operations, but small business is still conductive to a creative attitude and, therefore, towards innovation and invention. On the other hand, large-scale production provides a better starting-point for the development and application of new technical methods. Technical change may lead to a concentration of market power, but it may also reshuffle market conditions. In some cases competition will be strengthened through innovation, and in other cases competition is weakened by technical change. In the first days of the computer a centralization of the process of decision making did result, but today the computer can help to decentralize the decision-making process, both in the private and the public sector.

Successful technical applications are mostly demand-orientated: necessity is the mother of invention, but it also happens that technology promotes new methods and products, an actual and very spectacular example being the development of the micro-computer.

Preferences of consumers are not only influenced by expensive advertising but also by new products that are the fruit of technical change. This suggests that the demand and supply sides of the economy cannot be separated too clearly, as is usually assumed and practised by economists.

Technical change is both friend and enemy of mankind. It causes people to feel unhappy or uncertain, but it also creates new possibilities and the prospect of a better life. It can have autonomous features that control our behaviour, but it may also be directed in accordance with our wishes and preferences. It influences the rate of growth of the economy and the quality of production, the labour market, and the power structure. On the other hand it is influenced by a certain growth rate of the economy, changes in the labour market and the pattern of production, especially concerning the size of firms and the rate of concentration.

With respect to technical change one cannot think of any statement that is generally true. But we can try to see this dynamic force in a proper perspective. We now therefore turn to technical developments within the field of transport, in order to see how our general view about technical change applies to this particular and very important case.

3. TECHNICAL CHANGE IN TRANSPORT

Probably the most important contribution made by our forefathers to technical change has been the invention of the wheel. Even today the process of innovation continues, because applications of the idea of the wheel have still not been fully exploited. It would be difficult to think of any other idea for which the time lag between invention and innovation has been so long.

Both classical and radical political economists have always recognized that transport is a major and permanent feature of social and economic development. Writing in *The Wealth of Nations* in 1776 Adam Smith says:

Good roads, canals, and navigable rivers, by diminishing the expense of carriage, put the remote parts of the country more nearly upon a level with those in the neighbourhood of the town. They are upon that account the greatest of all improvements. They encourage the cultivation of the remote, which must always be the most extensive circle of the country. They are advantageous to the town, by breaking down the monopoly of the country in its neighbourhood. They are advantageous even to that part of the country. Though they introduce some rival commodities into the old market, they open many new markets to its produce.

While in 1867, in Volume I of *Capital*, Karl Marx puts it:

Hence, apart from the radical changes introduced in the construction of sailing vessels, the means of communication and transport became gradually adapted to ,the modes of production of mechanical industry, by the creation of a system of river steamers, railways, ocean steamers and telegraphs. But the huge masses of iron that had now to be forged, to be welded, to be cut, to be bored, and to be shaped, demanded on their part, cyclopean machines, for the construction of which the methods of the manufacturing period were utterly inadequate.

Modern industry had therefore itself to take in hand the machine, its characteristic instrument of production, and to construct machines by machines. It was not until it did this, that it built up for itself a fitting technological foundation and stood on its own feet. Machinery, simultaneously with the increasing use of it, in the first decades of this century, appropriated, by degrees, the fabrication of machines proper. But it was only during the decade preceding 1866, that the construction of railways and ocean steamers on a stupendous scale called into existence the cyclopean machines now employed in the construction of prime movers.

Thus both the classical and radical political economists have seen the importance of changes in the methods of transport in terms of welfare, though Marx is more critical and does also stress that technical changes do provoke a need for further change.

The steamboat, the locomotive, canals and railroads are all parts of the process of production of transportation, which had a tremendous influence on the emergence of the Industrial Revolution.

As so often in history it has been war which has most stimulated technical change, and this in the field of transport as much as elsewhere. The jet engine, for instance, was developed more or less simultaneously by Britain and Germany under the most intense pressures of war. Yet the jet engine has served humanity in the next generation in areas far removed from any theatre of war. And the progress continues. A more modern equivalent might be the challenge of space exploration, and the subsequent diffusion of the technology of space.

Today, technical change in transport is proceeding very rapidly, and is showing itself particularly in improved productivity. Several studies indicate a permanent rise in productivity, in the sense that both ton-miles and passenger-miles per man are higher (Deakin and Seward, 1969). These figures only describe the quantitative outcome of the changes that have taken place and of course important qualitative modifications in the process of transportation have been experienced at the same time (Nelson and Johnson, 1961). Marchefert Tassin (1975) demonstrated that important energy and time savings are associated with new and rapid ground transportation systems. Within a specific framework, the effects of technical change on production can be measured. Holzbaur (1972), who for the German airline Lufthansa viewed technical change as the residual after the contribution of capital and labour had been deducted, reached the conclusion that in the years between 1950 and 1970 the average rate of technical change was 9.8 percent. He also established a positive relationship between this rate of technical change and the rate of profits. A similar kind of research has been carried out by Vernon L. Smith (1957), who studied the trucking industry. For the railroad industry, Mansfield (1965) has placed the whole process of technical change in a wider perspective by making a clear distinction between invention, innovation and diffusion within the industry. Further, he has given a qualitative description of the improvements made by electronics to railroad operations (see also Aldcroft, 1969). Then the specific role that patents have played in the production of new technical knowledge in the railroad industry has been studied very carefully by Dick (1970).

The "demand-pull" side of the process of technical change can be illustrated by the problems of urban congestion. These problems are such that
the need for invention and innovation is obvious. New solutions have been
developed and applied, which also try to cope with the "costs of economic
growth." These environmental aspects also come to the fore if the pros and
cons of supersonic transport are considered. The relevant studies in this
field indicate that it is very difficult for governments to direct and influence
the process of technical change, even if the necessity to do so in view of all
externalities is very urgent (Bouladon, 1972; Felix, 1972). It is interesting
to note in this respect that Walgreen et al. (1973) reach the conclusion
that in the case of the United States supersonic programme positive externalities were "non-existent or were being purchased at too high a price
relative to alternative means for attaining them." Woolley (1972), who
made a cost-benefit analysis of the Concorde project, also concluded that
absolute and relative externalities in the operation of Concorde may be
disregarded. These conclusions are in striking conflict with the general
feeling of unease about several side effects of these developments. If, however, only those aspects are taken into account that can be expressed in
terms of money or are otherwise of a quantitative character, it may seem
that the positive effects outweigh the (measurable) negative aspects. A
wider view linked with a long-term perspective may change this conclusion.
A uniform economic policy does not fit the heterogeneous character of
technical development and its consequences. Decisions about the extension of technical knowledge and about its diffusion and application have
far-reaching consequences for the number and type of jobs available, the
environment, real income per head and the welfare of future generations.
The assessment of all these effects requires a micro-economic approach
to do justice to the variety of welfare effects which differ with time
and place.

4. CONCLUSIONS

Technical change in the particular field of transport shows the whole range
of the possible effects of technical change in general. The relation between
transport as a service and the factors that provide that service is constantly
shifting, and these shifts have both a qualitative and a quantitative com-
ponent. A simple production function is apt to deal with the quantitative
relationship between production and the factors of production, but a
qualitative change does lead to a new production function. The new
production function then is more then just the outcome of the shift of the
old one. The introduction of the container in shipping for example
implies a major change in the process of production of transportation,

to such an extent that the new production function cannot in a simple way be derived from the previous one, without ignoring important qualitative changes. So far, in the literature on transport the emphasis has been more on the quantitative effects of new methods and means of transport than on the qualitative causes of technical change in this field. This is partly due to the difficulty of giving any real meaning to the explanation of technical change, and partly to the circumstance that most transport economists are so-called practical men, who often do not have a general, up-to-date knowledge of economic theory and its development. As practical men they are inclined to think that economics as a science is restricted to the market mechanism and the calculation of pros and cons in terms of prices and money. The idea that economics is concerned with the (subjective) satisfaction of wants, related to the allocation of scarce resources, does not seem to have much influenced them until now. This may not only lead to a neglect of possible negative side effects of technological change that operate outside the market, but also to an underestimation of the endogeneous character of technical change in this field. New methods of transport not only influence the economic process as it stands, they are also the result of internal economic forces. The development and structure of a specific subway system may be caused by the character of industry and trade in a certain area. The huge increase in the number of motor cars on the roads produced negative external effects that partially destroy the original benefits brought by this popular method of transportation and creates the need for new developments. This example also illustrates a point made by Hirsch (1977) that besides the problem of physical scarcity we face social scarcity: what is possible for the individual and should be attainable for everybody, on grounds of social justice, cannot be attained by everybody because of the cumulative effect of the satisfaction of their wants. Social scarcity seems to demand collective action in order to cope with it. More research by transport economists, it seems, could usefully be devoted to these aspects of technical change.

Furthermore, it may be suggested that a careful study should be made of the influence of new technical methods of transport on the demand for and the composition of labour and on the market structure. Does technical change in this field lead to a reduction in unskilled labour and a demand for skilled labour? And does it lead to more or less monopoly on the market?

Also the problems in reverse are important. In what way does the structure of the labour market influence the development of new technical methods and what is the relation between already existing monopolistic positions and the introduction of technical change?

The development of new methods and products in the field of transport seems to be more intensively associated with an inter-linking of private and public welfare effects than is the case with technical change in general. Noise, air pollution and traffic congestion are all consequences of the massive application of new technical possibilities. This may explain the paradoxical combination of the urgent demand for freedom by individuals to do what they want to do, and the need for governmental action to reduce the damage resulting from that freedom, and the negative external effects of the proliferation of transport services. In view of this paradox economic theory may be on the brink of a breakthrough of the analysis of the optimal allocation of resources.

The study of technical change has been too much neglected in economic theory, and only in recent years have attempts been made to fill the gap (Heertje, 1977). The emphasis has been mainly on macro-economic contributions on the basis of aggregated production functions in which the effect of technical change is measured. In order to understand the process of technical change and especially its creative background and imaginative basis, more micro-economic analysis is needed. The study of the mutual relationship between technical change and transport seems a very promising area for this development. New technical methods in this field are called for by intensive pressures of a private and a public character. The development of new methods of transport is more or less directly pointed to the application on a full and large scale. Also in this field necessity is often the mother of invention and it is therefore possible to look carefully at the creative process that brings about the new methods and products. Do patents play a role or not? Is the diffusion of new technical methods hampered by market structures in the field of transport? The contributions of Dick and Mansfield, mentioned above, are illustrative of how this kind of questions can be tackled, but both authors are more recognized as general economists than as transport economists. If our remarks should stimulate transport economists to devote more time and energy to the significance of technical change in their field, the modest task we have set ourselves will have a successful outcome.

REFERENCES

Aldcroft, D.H. (1969). "Innovation on the Railways," *Journal of Transport Economics and Policy* 3:96–107.
Bouladon, G. (1972). "The Introduction of Innovation in Urban Transport," *Transport Planning and Technology* 1:3–9.
Deakin, B.M. and Seward, T. (1969). *Productivity in Transport. A Study of Employment, Capital Output, Productivity and Technical Change.* Cambridge: University Press.
Dick, T.J.O. (1970). *An economic theory of technical change: the case of patents and the U.S. railroads from 1871 to 1950.* Ann Arbor, Michigan: University Microfilms.
Felix, B. (1972). "Perspectives de techniques nouvelles dans le domaine du transport urbain," *Transports* 17:1–17.

Heertje, A. (1977). *Economics and Technical Change.* London: Weidenfeld and Nicolson.

Hirsch, F. (1977). *Social limits to growth.* London: Routledge and Kegan Paul.

Holzbaur, M. (1972). *Die Berechnung des technischen Fortschritts bei einer Luftfahrtgesellschaft.* Reinheim: Universität Freiburg (Switzerland).

Mansfield, E. (1965). "Innovation and Technical Change in the Railroad Industry," in National Bureau Committee for Economic Research, ed., *Transportation Economics — a conference of Universities.* New York–London: Columbia University Press.

Marx, K. (1967). *Das Kapital.* Berlin: Dietz. English translation (1967) of 3rd German edition, *Capital.* New York: International Publishers.

Nelson, R.S. and Johnson, E.M. (1961). *Technological change and the future of railways.* Evanston, Ill.: Transportation Centre at Northwestern University.

Smith, A. (1776). *An inquiry into the nature and causes of the Wealth of Nations.* Reprint 1976. Oxford: Clarendon Press.

Smith, V.L. (1957). "Engineering data and statistical techniques in the analysis of production and technological change: full requirements of the trucking industry," *Econometrica* 25:281–301.

Tassin, Y.M. (1975). "Energy and Time Savings Associated with Rapid Ground Transport Systems," *The Logistics and Transportation Review* 10:327–334.

Walgreen, J.A., Rastatter, E.H. and Moore, A.B. (1973). "The Economics of the United States Supersonic Transport," *Journal of Transport Economics and Policy* 7:186–193.

Woolley, P.K. (1972). "A cost-benefit analysis of the Concorde project," *Journal of Transport Economics and Policy* 6:225–239.

TOWARDS A NATIONAL MODEL FOR PASSENGER TRANSPORT POLICY

A.A.I. HOLTGREFE

1. THE PROVINCE OF WORDS IN A COUNTRY OF MODELS

Mathematical models are widely used as expedients to solve transport and traffic problems. Models are used to predict the number of cars (University of Amsterdam, 1973), to determine the transport production and attraction of a region, to calculate the distribution of transport between regions and to determine the division of transport among the different modes (Hamerslag, 1972, 1978). The results in their turn are the input to models which determine the optimum size of the transport networks (Steenbrink, 1974). Each of these models can be very complex and can consist of thousands of variables. Because of the existence of necessary feed-backs between these models, the size of what may be called the envelope model becomes so huge that even large-scale studies (such as the integrated transport study in the Netherlands in 1972 and the North-East Corridor Transportation Study in the U.S.A. in 1970) cannot comprise it. So the intention of such a study, being the determination of an optimal transport system consistent with a specific spatial structure of a country, cannot be realized.

The complexity of arithmetics in transport models and the inability to approximate a general optimum might be reasons why policy makers remain afraid to use mathematics in their plans. Even transport plans which are of a recent date, such as those of the U.K., are entirely verbal (Department of the Environment, 1976; Department of Transport, 1977). The medium-term plan for passenger transport in the Netherlands for the period 1976–80 (Meerjarenplan Personenvervoer, 1975), also consists of an entirely verbal description of transport policy. The report states that, it being impossible that all effects are valued or measured in a single dimension, the final product is not the result of arithmetical operations but of political weighing and considerations.

This renouncing of using arithmetics as a tool for the determination of a policy is in contrast with a long tradition in general economic policy. Economic models have been and still are to be considered the most powerful tools for economists. Convincing examples are to be found, among other places, in the work of Tinbergen (1964) and of Theil (1964). Therefore, it is hardly believable that a model of the transport sector cannot be used in the determination of a transport policy. Such a model would have to be on a more aggregate level than the existing transport and traffic models. In fact, the verbal descriptions of transport plans contain the logic of a policy model.

The aim of this contribution is to show that it should be possible and useful to construct a national policy model for passenger transport. Section 2 describes the steps to be taken, starting from a plan which is wholly in words, up to the optimal policy as the outcome of a mathematical model. The medium-term plan for passenger transport in the Netherlands (MPP), already referred to, is used as an example to try out the first steps between the words of the plan and the complete calculations of pros and cons of several policies. Sections 3 and 4 describe the situation and policy before and after the appearance of that medium-term plan. Some conclusions are presented in Section 5.

2. MARKING THE WAY FROM WORD TO MODEL

A verbal plan contains implicitly or explicitly a reasoning leading to a policy. It can be useful to map this reasoning according to logical steps resulting in a mathematical counterpart. In this context it will be necessary to take the following steps:
(a) enumerate (the) relevant magnitudes in a (transport) policy;
(b) indicate the magnitudes that can be determined by the policy maker (the instruments);
(c) indicate the magnitudes that are objectives of the policy maker;
(d) construct a flow scheme, indicating the interactions between the magnitudes;
(e) attach a plus or minus sign to each of the flows in the scheme;
(f) determine the units in which the magnitudes can be measured;
(g) quantify the boundary conditions;
(h) quantify the interaction between the magnitudes;
(i) determine the desired values of the objectives;
(j) determine the relative importance of the objectives, resulting in an objective function;
(k) determine the optimal solution.

These (a–k) steps result in an operational model of mathematical shape. A planning model for the Netherlands Railways has been constructed along the same lines (Holtgrefe, 1975).

The earlier steps (a–e) are very important to explain the reasoning leading to a proposed policy. Moreover, the consequences of that policy can be shown more clearly by a flow scheme (product of step e) than by a verbal explanation only. Therefore, it is meaningful in developing a transport policy to take these first steps towards a model, even if that model is not the final goal.

The later steps (f–k) can be used to specify the verbally-expressed policy and to verify its consistency. The MPP will be used as an example in showing the results that can be obtained by applying the earlier steps.

3. DEVELOPMENTS AND POLICY IN THE PASSENGER TRANSPORT SECTOR BEFORE THE MPP

The accelerated growth of the number of private cars is the main phenomenon in the passenger transport sector of the last decades. The increase in the number of cars, initially caused by the rise of national income, gives people the opportunity to spread their activities, like working and living, over an extended area. This dispersion causes in its turn an increase of the utility of owning and using private cars and consequently an increase in the number of private cars. The increase in the number of private cars causes a shift from travelling by public transport to travelling by car. The increase in travelling by car, however, mainly arises from "new" trips. By the enormous increase in private transport the car owners bring pressure to bear upon the authorities to adapt the road infrastructure.

Travelling by public transport is negatively influenced by the scattering of working and living activities of people. The continuous rise in national income, though having positive effects on travelling by public transport, is not sufficient to compensate a decrease in demand for public transport. The financial profits of the public transport companies deteriorate. This deterioration could be prevented by substantial increases of rates in public transport, coupled with decreases in the quality of public transport (determined by the size of the public transport networks, the number of stations and stops, the frequency, and the level of comfort). These rate increases and quality decreases would cause a decrease in travelling by public transport. The costs of owning and using a car influence the number of private cars and the extent of travelling by car and by public transport. The authorities can partially determine these costs.

The objective of transport policy in the Netherlands in the last decade was: "Meeting the demand for transport of passengers, given the spatial and financial opportunities." Apart from this general objective it was attempted in the early seventies to stimulate the use of public transport by increasing its quality. This description of the transport sector is illustrated by the flow scheme (giving the results of the steps a–e of Section 2) in Figure 1. The policy objective "meeting the demand" adds the two dotted arrows to the flow scheme. It gives rise to four multiplying effects in the

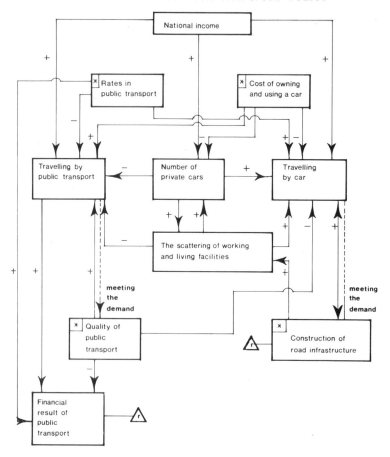

$\boxed{\text{x}}$ = instrument of policy maker

+/− = the magnitude from which the arrow originates changes in the same (+) or in the
      opposite (−) direction as the magnitude in which the arrow enters

⚠ = spatial and/or financial restrictions

Figure 1.   Flow scheme of the passenger transport sector.

passenger transport sector:
— As a result of a decrease in travelling by public transport, the quality of
  that transport is reduced. This measure causes in its turn a decrease in
  travelling. It is a description of the well-known imminent downward
  spiral of public transport.
— When the continuous rise of car travelling is followed by construction of

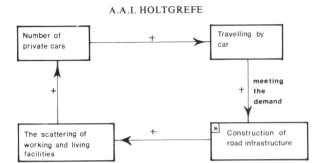

Figure 2.   A loop of causes and effects initiated by new road infrastructure.

a new road infrastructure, the utility of — and consequently the demand for — travelling by car is increased.

— Construction of a new road infrastructure initiates another loop of causes and effects. This loop is shown in Figure 2, which is part of the flow scheme of Figure 1.

— A decrease in the quality of public transport would initiate a loop as shown in Figure 3.

Only the restrictions on spatial development and financial results might stop or slow down these chain reactions.

The first and the fourth multiplying effect have not been passed through in the Dutch situation of the last decades. Travel by public transport remained fairly constant because the quality of public transport has remained constant or even increased.

The conclusion is obvious: the transport policy of meeting demand, given the spatial and financial opportunities, would ultimately lead to a society dominated by the private car system in passenger transport. This would not be too serious if there were no or few negative effects owing to the private car system. However in actual fact a whole series of negative externalities would arise.

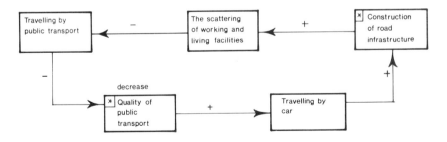

Figure 3.   A loop of causes and effects initiated by a decrease in the quality of public transport.

4. THE OBJECTIVE AND POLICY IN THE MPP

The scattering of working and living facilities caused by the growing number of private cars does not fit in the spatial structure desired by the government. Stationary and moving cars cause such inconveniences as visual intrusion, noise and pollution. Private car traffic also is not considered very safe. These negative externalities become highly perceptible in urban areas. Moreover, the private car uses a lot of scarce natural resources, while public transport needs a considerable expenditure of public money.

Therefore, the medium-term plan mentions as the new objective of transport policy: "Meeting the demand for transport of passengers and goods as far as the net contribution to the welfare of the community shows a surplus. This policy has to be carried out in such a way that the negative effects, especially in urban areas, are limited."

Figure 4 shows a flow scheme for the new relevant magnitudes for the subsector of private transport. The flow scheme shows that the negative externalities caused by private car movements in cities increase the scattering of working and living facilities and initiate a multiplying effect. In order to limit the negative externalities in urban areas, physical restraints are put on car travelling in those areas. So, travelling by car becomes, as far as urban areas are concerned, an instrument of the policy maker. It is hoped that, by means of putting restraints on private car travelling and parking in urban areas, the city, or at least part of it, regains its attraction to live in.

A decrease in negative externalities in the urban areas can influence spatial developments: the continuous scattering of working and living facilities is seen as an undesirable spatial development that has to be reversed, stopped or slowed down.

The construction of road infrastructure is still an instrument to meet demand; but in the revised policy it is also directed, by means of restrained building of new roads, to limit undesirable scattering of working and living facilities.

A third instrument of the policy maker is the determination of the cost of owning and using a car. This instrument is, according to the MPP, considered to be less effective than the other two. There is a strong necessity, however, for further detailed study of the quantitative effects of cost increases.

Other instruments, not mentioned in Figure 4, are the quality and rates of public transport. An increase in the quality or a decrease in rates would negatively affect travelling by car (see Figure 1). An element of the quality instrument, the construction of new rail infrastructure and of bus lanes, would slow down the scattering in working and living.

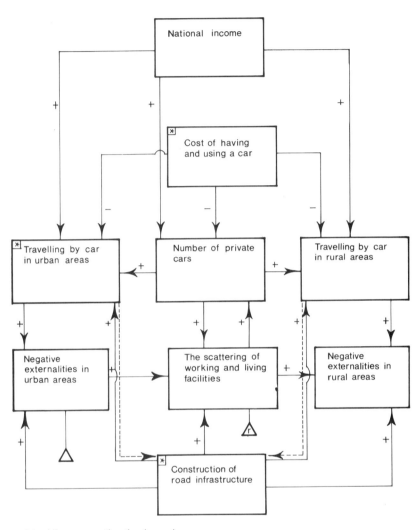

Figure 4.   Flow scheme of the MPP policy concerning private transport.

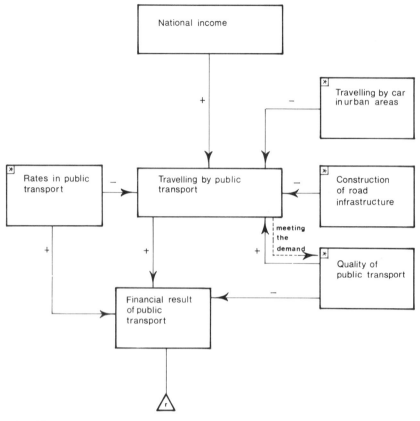

Figure 5.   Flow scheme of the MPP policy concerning public transport.

Figure 5 shows a flow scheme for the new relevant magnitudes for the subsector of public transport. It is the intention of the policy maker to stimulate travelling by public transport by means of keeping cars out of some urban areas and by a limitation on the road construction program. If that would result in an actual increase in the use of public transport, the policy maker is prepared to adapt the quality of public transport in a positive direction.

Autonomous quality improvements are only accepted if the financial results of public transport remain within predefined limits.

5. CONCLUDING REMARKS

Even the extremely simplified flow schemes in Sections 3 and 4 give more insight into the interaction between passenger transport and spatial development than verbal descriptions can. Especially the multiplying effects caused by circular interdependencies can be shown easily by flow schemes. The essential task of the policy maker is to break through undesirable multiplying effects. The flow schemes also show that a passenger transport policy can easily add undesirable multiplying effects instead of stopping them.

Finally, the conclusions from the flow schemes and from the verbal descriptions seem to be very sensitive for the size of effects. Therefore it is necessary to take the further steps towards a mathematical model. First of all attention has to be paid in future studies to the quantification of the interaction between the magnitudes. Surprise is not out of the question.

REFERENCES

Department of the Environment (1976). *Transport Policy, a Consultation Document.* London: HMSO.
Department of Transport (1977). *Transport Policy.* London: HMSO.
Hamerslag, R. (1972). *Prognosemodel voor het personenvervoer in Nederland.* The Hague: ANWB.
Hamerslag, R. (1978). *Voorspellen over modellen.* Delft: Delft University Press.
Holtgrefe, A.A.I. (1975). *An optimizing medium-term planning model for the Netherlands Railways.* Rotterdam: Rotterdam University Press.
Meerjarenplan voor het personenvervoer 1976–1980 (1975). Report presented to the second chamber of Parliament by the minister of Transport and Public Works. The Hague: Tweede Kamer, zitting 1975–76, 13711, nrs. 1–3.
Nederlands Economisch Instituut (1972). *Integrale Verkeers-en Vervoersstudie.* The Hague: Staatsuitgeverij.
Steenbrink, P.A. (1975). *Optimization of transport networks.* London: John Wiley.
Theil, H. (1964). *Optimal Decision Rules for Government and Industry.* Amsterdam: North Holland.
Tinbergen, J. (1964). *Economic Policy: Principles and Design.* Amsterdam: North Holland.
Universiteit van Amsterdam, Instituut voor Actuariaat en Econometrie (1973). *Het aantal personenauto's in Nederland.* Amsterdam.
U.S. Department of Transportation (1970). *North-East Corridor Transportation Project Report.* Washington D.C.

OPTIMUM USE OF TRANSPORT NETWORKS AND ITS POSSIBLE CONTRIBUTION TO WELFARE MAXIMIZATION

L.H. KLAASSEN

1. INTRODUCTION

When discussing the optimum use of transport networks one is inclined to focus on the question of how given transport networks for public as well as private transport can be used in an optimum way. Almost naturally one then thinks of such solutions as freight transportation during the night and passenger transport in the daytime, charter flights from airports during the very early and very late hours of the day, and regular flights during normal hours, park-and-ride systems, etc. In these cases one considers the networks as given and tries to distribute the traffic that has to be accommodated over the existing network(s) in such a way that some sort of an optimum is reached.

Another, more general approach could be, however, to start from a given spatial structure of a country, i.e. a given distribution of activities and population across space, and to design on the basis of the traffic supposed to result from that spatial structure a network or networks that serve this traffic in an optimum way (Steenbrink, 1974). Although the latter approach has not dealt satisfactorily with either the existence of several sorts of networks, or the multiple use of one and the same network, e.g. the use of roads by buses and private cars, it does provide us with a great deal of insight into the need for extending particularly the road networks in order to assure that spatial structures foreseen as needed for the future will coincide with actual future structures.

In particular the last-mentioned point is important, first and foremost in urban areas. If the networks designed influence the location of people and business activities, it may not be possible to solve the transportation problem in the sequential way indicated above, i.e. by designing first a spatial structure and proposing then a network that meets the demand of traffic resulting from it.

Rather the problem would call for a simultaneous solution, i.e. the simultaneous designing of the spatial structure and the networks in such a

This article is an adapted version of a report prepared earlier for the European Conference of Ministers of Transport (London, 1977).

way that some sort of general optimum is achieved. It should be added immediately that such an optimum should not be defined as an optimum existing at a given moment of time but as a design that guarantees an optimum situation for an essentially infinitely-long future period.

It is particularly the nature of the sought optimum that should interest us. Obviously a general optimum could never be reached with a solution that minimizes total traffic flows. Traffic flows reflect the desire of people to optimize their well-being in view of the location of their desired destinations and the quality of the network that enables them to reach these destinations. A network of lower standard could force them to limit their total effective demand for travelling, but thus their well-being would certainly not increase as a result. Travel time is one of the sacrifices that have to be made in order to reach a certain degree of well-being. Less travel time, as such, could be considered a benefit, but would have to be weighed against the disadvantage of reaching fewer destinations or reaching destinations less frequently.

An individual household's well-being depends on the attraction of the different destinations as well as on the travel costs or travel sacrifices. The household determines its location by maximizing the difference between the two in such a way that marginal benefits caused by a shift in location equal marginal travel costs from such a shift. In order to give a more suitable analysis of the problem, it seems useful to consider the nature of the costs and benefits involved in some more detail.

2. TRAVEL COSTS

Travel costs are defined as the costs that have to be made to bridge a certain distance. Costs in this sense are to be interpreted as sacrifices to be made. These sacrifices consist of money costs, time and risks involved. Other elements such as resistance due to the "strangeness" of the destination, and the psychological distance to be bridged, could also be mentioned here, but will be left out of consideration. It follows that generalized transportation costs can be defined as the weighted sum of the three elements first mentioned, or as:

$$D_{ij} = \alpha_1 C_{ij} + \alpha_2 T_{ij} + \alpha_3 R_{ij} \tag{2.1}$$

in which D_{ij} = total generalized transportation costs between i and j;
$\quad\quad C_{ij}$ = total money costs (or perceived money costs);
$\quad\quad T_{ij}$ = total time costs;
$\quad\quad R_{ij}$ = total risks (or perceived risks);
$\quad\quad \alpha$'s = weights of different cost elements.

Evidently, costs, time, and risk can also be expressed per unit of physical distance (f_{ij}). (2.1) then becomes:

$$D_{ij} = \alpha_1 c_{ij} f_{ij} + \alpha_2 t_{ij} f_{ij} + \alpha_3 r_{ij} f_{ij} \tag{2.2}$$

Since $t_{ij} = f_{ij}/v_{ij}$, in which v_{ij} is the average speed, we may write:

$$D_{ij} = (\alpha_1 c_{ij} + \alpha_2 \frac{f_{ij}}{v_{ij}} + \alpha_3 r_{ij}) f_{ij} \tag{2.3}$$

The expression between brackets represents the generalized transportation costs per unit of distance between i and j.

A few remarks concerning the coefficients in equation (2.3) seem in order.

In many transportation studies an attempt is made to choose one specific dimension in which to express the generalized transportation costs; often the monetary unit is chosen. In that case obviously $\alpha_1 = 1$, α_2 reflecting the money value of one unit of time. According to economic theory the marginal value of one unit of time equals the value of net earnings per unit of time minus the disutility of labour experienced during a marginal time unit. α_3 expresses the sum of money that could be looked upon as the trade-off of one unit of risk, this expressed as the probability of an unfortunate event taking place per unit of time.

An internationally more comparable unit would be the time unit. In this case $\alpha_2 = 1$, α_1 expressing the number of time units per unit of money, and α_3 the trade-off between one unit of risk and the number of money units.

Whatever unit is chosen, D_{ij} expresses the total generalized transportation costs to be made if one individual decides to undertake the trip from i to j.

It should be mentioned here that all the coefficients in the equation are certainly not equal for all individuals. If the monetary unit is chosen as the basic unit, α_2 represents the translation of time costs into money costs, and the value of one unit of time having been defined as the earnings per time unit, corrected for the disutility of labour per time unit, it seems reasonable to assume that this value is an increasing function of income. A similar reasoning holds for α_3: if the risk of an accident is defined as the sum of the human suffering, the money costs of the accident, and the earnings lost, α_3 becomes a function of income too. On the other hand, α_3 might be a function of travel experience, decreasing with experience for air travel and increasing for car travel.

The foregoing leads us to the extremely important conclusion that generalized transportation costs are in fact a function of an individual's specific situation regarding his income (Institut d'aménagement et d'urbanisme de la Région Parisienne, 1966) and travel experience. It seems reasonable that also the socio-economic characteristics of the household he belongs to affect the weights in the generalized costs function. Of course, even for individuals in the same situation as far as income and household characteristics are concerned, subjective evaluation of time costs and risks might differ considerably. It is assumed, however, that such random differences cancel out one another when groups of individuals are considered.

It is not a new but still a valid assumption that the individual's (or household's) income level is one of the most important factors when it comes to explaining the distribution of traffic among the different transport modes. Leaving aside for a moment that a traveller will consider not only overall travel time but also the manner in which that time is spent (in waiting, changing, actual travelling, etc.), we may state that certain modes involve considerably less expenditure but also considerably more time than others. Comparing the generalized transportation costs of private car and public transport, we observe that, particularly for smaller distances, the private car is preferred to public transport, because of its low time costs and in spite of its high money costs, while for long distances public transport is often preferred (Klaassen, 1969) because it is cheap in relation to travel time. The higher the income, the heavier the time costs will count, and the more readily an individual will shift to the most time-saving transport mode. Or, in terms of the above argument: the higher a person's income, the higher the value he attaches to time, and consequently, the longer the distance for which he will be inclined to use his car, and the shorter the distance for which he will prefer to take an airplane. The train, as the intermediate mode, will, for as long as conventional speeds are maintained, lose at both ends as income rises.

3. TRAVEL BENEFITS: ACCESSIBILITY

In the previous section we treated the concept of generalized transportation costs, defined as the sacrifices in money, time, and risk the individual has to make in order to reach a certain destination. Now it is time to turn to the benefit side of travelling, on which depends how heavily the individual will count the travel costs.

Let us consider a specific case. An individual living in a region i considers visiting a recreation area of given quality and size in region j. In order to do so he will have to bridge the physical distance f_{ij} and sacrifice generalized transport costs to the amount D_{ij}. Furthermore he will have to pay an entrance fee of P_j so that his total costs will amount to $D_{ij} + P_j$. In this case it is, of course, assumed that D_{ij} is expressed in monetary units. The attraction exerted by the recreation area is now determined by two factors: on the one hand the benefits derived from the visit and on the other hand the costs of the trip, or, more exactly, the perception of the benefits and the perception of the costs of the trip.

Starting with the latter, it seems reasonable to assume that the perception of the costs is an increasing function of the costs themselves, so that:

$$p_{ij}^c = \varphi_c (D_{ij} + P_j) \qquad (3.1)$$

in which p_{ij}^c = perception of costs.

$$\frac{d\varphi_c}{d(D_{ij} + P_j)} > 0, \qquad \frac{d^2\varphi_c}{d(D_{ij} + P_j)^2} > 0$$

The last expression indicates that marginal costs are assumed to be increasing with "distance" and entrance fee.

The benefits depend on the "quality" and size of the recreation area x_j:

$$p_{ij}^b = \varphi_b (x_j) \qquad (3.2)$$

in which p_{ij}^b = perception of benefits;

$x_j = q_j s_j$;
q_j = quality index of the recreation area;
s_j = size of the recreation area;

$$\frac{d\varphi_b}{dx_j} > 0, \frac{d^2\varphi_b}{dx_j^2} < 0$$

These expressions indicate that it is assumed that benefits are an increasing function of the size and quality of the recreation area, but that marginal benefits are a decreasing function of these two variables.

It seems logical to define the attractiveness of the recreation area as the ratio between perceived benefits and perceived costs, in other words to define:

$$\Pi_{ij} = \frac{\varphi_b(x_j)}{\varphi_c(D_{ij} + P_j)} \qquad (3.3)$$

A specific example of (3.3) could be $\varphi_b(x_j) = x_j^\beta$ in which $0 < \beta < 1$ and $\varphi_c(D_{ij} + P_j) = e^{\alpha(D_{ij} + P_j)}$ so that (3.3) can be written as:

$$\Pi_{ij} = x_j^\beta e^{-\alpha(D_{ij} + P_j)} \qquad (3.4)$$

Equation (3.4) has a number of important features which need further attention. The coefficient α represents the friction a consumer experiences in making the sacrifices $D_{ij} + P_j$ for visiting the recreation area, or, rather, *a* recreation area. It is therefore *activity-specific*. The element $e^{-\alpha(D_{ij} + P_j)}$ may be said to represent the *accessibility* of the recreation area in j for an individual living in i.

If we consider not only the recreation area in j but all recreation areas, we obtain a variable describing simultaneously the accessibility and the size and quality of all recreation areas seen from the region i. We then arrive at defining the *recreation potential* for i.

Obviously:

$$\Pi = \sum_i \Pi = \sum_{ij} \Pi = \sum_j x_j^\beta e^{-\alpha(D_{ij}+P_j)} \tag{3.5}$$

in which Π_i is the recreation potential for i.

The next step is to assume that the number of trips originating from i to a recreation area anywhere is a function of this potential and of the income level of the individual (household). To that end we write:

$$n_i = \gamma_0 \Pi_i^{\gamma_1} y^{\gamma_2} p_i \tag{3.6}$$

in which n_i is the number of trips to recreation areas, y the average income, and p_i the size of the population in i. From equation (3.6) it follows easily that it is reasonable to assume:

$$n_{ij} = \frac{\Pi_{ij}}{\Pi_i} n_i \tag{3.7}$$

This equation together with (3.6) determines the number of trips to each recreation area.

It should be mentioned here that the potential as defined is not uniquely determined. Usually there are different ways to make a trip from one place to another; consequently there are as many potentials as there are ways to make the trip. With two possibilities, e.g. by public and by private transport, there are two potentials. In that case it can reasonably be assumed that the fraction of total trips made by public transport equals:

$$\varphi_{ij}^{PV} = \frac{\Pi_i^{PV}}{\Pi_i^{PV} + \Pi_i^{PR}} \tag{3.8}$$

and the fraction performed by private means of transportation:

$$\varphi_{ij}^{PR} = \frac{\Pi_i^{PR}}{\Pi_i^{PV} + \Pi_i^{PR}} \tag{3.9}$$

If both potentials are equal, 50 percent of the trips will be made by public and 50 percent by private means of transportation.

A similar reasoning to that developed above for recreation can, of course, be made for shopping, job opportunities, and environmental qualities. For each of these a potential can be defined from which, in the way indicated in the former paragraphs, trip creation can be derived.

4. A SPATIAL WELFARE FUNCTION

The theory so far presented can be extended by assuming that from a total set of potentials that could be derived, three main potentials can be determined:

(a) a potential describing the living conditions (Π^L);
(b) a potential describing working conditions (Π^W);
(c) a potential describing the availability of amenities (including recreation areas) (Π^A).

A social (spatial) welfare function could then be defined as:

$$\omega_i = \omega_i\,(\Pi_i^L,\,\Pi_i^W,\,\Pi_i^A) \tag{4.1}$$

(Van den Berg et al., 1975) or, more specifically:

$$\omega_i = (\Pi_i^L)^{\delta_1}\,(\Pi_i^W)^{\delta_2}\,(\Pi_i^A)^{\delta_3} \tag{4.2}$$

It is important to note that the δ's in this function will be mostly *household-specific*. If there are children in the household the availability of schools will play an important role. If the household consists of a pensioned husband and a housewife, job availabilities become unimportant and δ_2 will become zero, etc.

Since (4.2) describes the satisfaction that a given individual household derives from its location in i, the same function could be used to explain the movement of households from one region to another. This could be done in the following way. The absolute attraction the welfare of region j exerts on an individual living in i could be defined as:

$$a_{ij} = \omega_j e^{-\epsilon f_{ij}} \tag{4.3}$$

The attraction of the welfare levels of all regions to a household in j could consequently be defined as:

$$a_i = \sum_j \omega_j e^{-\epsilon f_{ij}} \tag{4.4}$$

so that the relative attractiveness of j can be written as:

$$\frac{a_{ij}}{a_i} = \frac{\omega_j e^{-\epsilon f_{ij}}}{\sum_j \omega_j e^{-\epsilon f_{ij}}} \tag{4.5}$$

The factor f_{ij} is introduced into these equations in order to express that the "strangeness" of a region—the lack of familiarity with conditions prevailing in that region—creates a resistance which assumedly will increase with physical distance f_{ij}. ϵ expresses the intensity with which this factor works.

Now assuming that migration between regions takes place according to the relative attractiveness of regions, we may write:

$$\frac{m_{ij}}{m_i} = \frac{a_{ij}}{a_i} \qquad (4.6)$$

in which m_{ij} is the number of individuals or households migrating from i to j, and m_i represents all migrating individuals or households, including those migrating from i to i. This means that:

$$m_i = p_i \qquad (4.7)$$

Accordingly, we may write:

$$m_{ij} = \frac{\omega_j e^{-\epsilon f_{ij}}}{\sum\limits_j \omega_j e^{-\epsilon f_{ij}}} p_i \qquad (4.8)$$

This expression, together with (4.2), allows us to estimate the size of the δ-coefficients.

5. GOVERNMENT POLICIES

5.1. Introduction

One could question the type of functions chosen and even fortify one's arguments with some statistical evidence. That has been done in, e.g., a study about commuting in the north ring of the so-called "Rimcity" (the urbanized western part of the country) in the Netherlands, in which it has been shown that there is no evidence of an influence of distance on commuter behaviour for journey times less than 30 minutes (De Langen and Verster, 1976). A reasonable explanation has not yet been found, but one of the reasons could well be that people derive certain benefits from travelling over a small distance; that many people actually like to drive some distance (particularly with their car) between work hours at their job and leisure hours at home. If this were true, it would change the shape of the job-potential function, at least for the short distance. A similar reasoning could hold for recreation, where part of the benefit might also be the enjoyment of the trip itself, again, of course, only as far as the shorter distances are concerned.

Future studies will have to show to what extent the individual functions will have to be corrected. For the following it suffices to assume that the general framework of the theory remains upright.

It now will be assumed that the general welfare level of a country can be defined as:

$$\omega = \sum_i \omega_i\, p_i \qquad\qquad (5.1)$$

i.e. as the sum of the individual welfare levels of households in all regions. Now it is the task of the government for a given budget year to spend the budget in such a way that the increase in welfare of the country as a whole is maximum. Of course, in doing so, the government could attach more importance to a certain increase in welfare of a poorer region than to the same increase in welfare of a richer region. Such a policy could easily be taken into account if the government were able to specify the weights involved.

It is important that several ways are open to the government for pursuing a welfare policy. In principle the government can influence each element of the welfare function, and accordingly, there are at least five different policies:

1. amenity policy,
2. industrial location policy,
3. housing policy,
4. infrastructure policy,
5. pricing policy.

Let us dedicate some attention to each of these policies.

5.2. Amenity policy

Amenity policy is a policy that influences the quality, size, and location of so-called social amenities, such as schools, theatres, recreation areas, health facilities, etc. If we consider the amenity policy in isolation from the other policies, government expenditures would have to be distributed in such a way that:

(a) the marginal contribution of one additional amenity to social welfare in a given region equals that of any other additional amenity in the same region;
(b) the marginal contribution of one given amenity in one region equals that of the same amenity in any other region.

These first-order conditions are in fact similar to those in consumption theory, where a consumer spends his income in such a way that the marginal utility of a given money unit spent in one direction equals that of a money unit spent in any other direction. The difference is, of course, that in our case the spatial element, usually absent in consumer theory, is introduced.

Many decisions in this field are taken on the lower level of the province or the municipality. In these cases the central government pursues its amenity policy in an indirect way, through subsidies for specific purposes, or through subsidies that municipalities are entitled to if given conditions are fulfilled (as often happens for educational purposes).

Whatever the way in which the policy is carried out, it is evident that it influences the traffic flows in the country. Amenities cannot and will not be made available irrespective of the consequences for the traffic flows and thus for the use that is made of the infrastructure network.

5.3. Industrial location policy

A similar reasoning as has been presented for amenity policy can be given for industrial location policy. That is particularly true as far as the location of business activities within urban areas is concerned. A simple example can make this clear.

Suppose we have two centres, one of them an employment centre and the other a residential centre (Figure 1).

Suppose 20,000 people are living in centre I and are working in centre II. Every morning there will be a flow of 20,000 people moving from I to II and every evening the same people will move back from II to I. As far as road traffic is concerned, each car will need two parking places, one in I and one in II. Public transport will suffer from one-sided traffic both in the morning and in the evening.

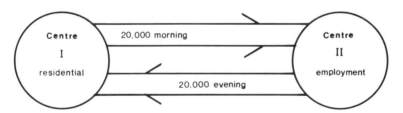

Figure 1. Traffic flows between separate residential and employment centres.

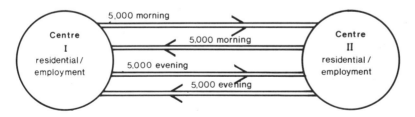

Figure 2. Traffic flows between mixed residential/employment centres.

Now consider another case, in which both centres are mixed employment/residential centres (Figure 2). Assume that each centre has a mixture of 10,000 work places and 10,000 active residents, 50 percent of whom work in the other centre, the remaining 50 percent in their living zone.

It appears then that the total traffic flow reduces to one half of that in the first case, while the number of parking places required can also be reduced considerably (by 50 percent at the most). The required capacity of the road infrastructure is reduced by 75 percent.

So, by influencing the location of industry, the government is able to diminish the traffic flows, to reduce considerably the need for infrastructure, and to cut the need for public transport at peak hours while achieving a much better general occupancy rate.

Of course, the example presents an extreme case. Still, it demonstrates that within certain limits, industrial location policy might make for smaller traffic flows as well as for better use of the existing networks, both for private and for public transport.

5.4. Housing policy

In many cities local government is promoting the development of residential areas in city centres, although the possibilities are often limited. Still, rehabilitation of older houses, re-destining buildings to residential purposes, prohibiting the construction of further offices, etc., all this is becoming more and more common in Western European cities. By policies to that effect a more reasonable balance between working and living is being obtained, and a balanced use of the infrastructure network achieved in much the same way as was contrived by industrial location policy. The construction of systems for rapid public transportation connecting city centres with suburbs works contrary to the trend towards balanced spread of working and living and the balanced use of infrastructure. Although the main purpose of such systems is to facilitate existing traffic between the suburbs and the centres, they tend to create new traffic in the same directions, since they make it considerably easier than before to reside in the suburb and work in the centre. As far as these systems are "successful," they promote the increase in distance between work and residence by shifting the latter outwards.

5.5. Infrastructure policy (I)

Infrastructure policy may be regarded as a complement to amenity policy, industrial-location policy and housing policy. The degree to which infrastructure policy is connected with, for instance, amenity policy may be demonstrated by the example of pedestrian zones.

In Section 3 we indicated the attraction of a recreation area in j exerted on an individual living in i as:

$$\Pi_{ij} = x_j^{\beta} \, e^{-\alpha D_{ij}} \tag{5.2}$$

(the price level—entrance fee—is left out of the equation).

We now interpret x_j as the size and quality of a shopping centre and write again:

$$x_j = s_j \, q_j \tag{5.3}$$

in which s_j indicates the size of the shopping centre and q_j is the "quality" determined by, among other things, the assortment of goods offered by the centre. We may then write:

$$\Pi_{ij} = s_j^{\beta} \, q_j^{\beta} \, e^{-\alpha D_{ij}} \tag{5.4}$$

Now q_j may also be interpreted in a much wider sense than the goods assortment offered by the centre. We might include in the quality index the atmosphere of the centre, its quietness, the cleanliness of the air, the street decorations, and the traffic risks; many of these factors depend on the amount of traffic passing through the streets of the centre, the speed of the traffic, and the number of cars parked there.

Turning the centre into a pedestrian zone contributes to its atmosphere and thus raises its quality. Simultaneously, however, D_{ij} will rise because of the decreased accessibility by car. Whether or not the transition of the centre into a pedestrian area will prove a success depends, then, on the trade-off between the two factors mentioned, the increase in q_j and the increase in D_{ij}. Parking facilities close to the centre will limit the increase in D_{ij}, and the set of improvements in the centre itself will, together with the absence of traffic, determine the increase in q_j. Careful planning of both might make the operation successful.

So far we have treated the creation of the pedestrian zone as the outcome of simultaneous infrastructure and amenity policy measures. Evidently, one could also see it as the result of two different but well-coordinated infrastructure policies, one decreasing accessibility by car, the other increasing accessibility for pedestrians.

The interwovenness of infrastructure policy with other policies, including the pricing policy to be discussed later, will be our main consideration when dealing with the central theme of this article, the optimum use of infrastructure networks.

The foregoing may have shown that this interwovenness is not inherent to the policies mentioned, but simply stems from the fact that the search for optimum use of infrastructure networks is just one facet of the universal search for maximum welfare.

Solving the problem of maximizing a country's social welfare, given the conditions prevailing in that country, would implicitly solve the problems of optimum size and quality of the network and of its optimum use. Because a proper pricing system is a condition for such optimums to be achieved, we will now dedicate some attention to pricing policy before returning to our main theme.

5.6. Pricing policy

A consumer may easily make decisions which he would certainly have avoided if, from the first, he had been familiar with the costs of the external effects involved.

Many efforts have been made to translate noise nuisance and air pollution into money terms. The study of the Third London Airport is only one example of many in which certain rules were proposed for treating such factors in such a way that they would neatly fit into a regular cost-benefit analysis. It remains to be seen, however, whether or not these efforts will in the end prove successful. The procedure described in the first section of this article does not leave much hope for a favourable outcome. The essential point presented there was that social welfare is not a cardinal but an ordinal variable. In equation (4.2) the constant was deliberately left out because it would be impossible to attach any fixed value to it; in other words, any value would do. It was assumed that the government would spend its budget in such a way that the increase in w, whatever the unit in which w is measured, would be maximum. This means that the government would apply the principle of cost-effectiveness analysis rather than that of cost-benefit analysis. For the latter benefits must be measurable. Since evidently they are not, the next-best procedure is that of a cost-effectiveness analysis, the effect to be considered being the increase in social welfare resulting from spending the available means in an optimum way.

But if that is true, then it is also true that the only way to measure the damage to the scenery or noise nuisance is the indirect way of assessing how they affect people. People will react to infringements on their social welfare, and their reactions are an indication of the degree to which social welfare is diminished by environmental factors. However, it is hard to see how the indication thus derived could be translated into money terms.

The conclusion must be that although in principle it would be right to charge everyone for the direct costs as well as for the external effects of policy measures, translation of the effects into money terms remains a doubtful procedure, fraught with more or less arbitrary decisions and estimates. The principle of charging a fee thus becomes somewhat shaky and the only thing that can be said is that we know, or at least think we know, what effects are positive and what effects are negative; and that charging some fee for negative effects is in any case better than charging nothing at all.

The former considerations apply to the pricing system that was already proposed at an earlier stage for traffic, viz. the *road* pricing system. This system was in fact limited to the external effects of one's participation in traffic on the other participants. Obviously, road pricing should be one of the elements of a general pricing system in which all external effects are to be incorporated, not only of activities in the sphere of traffic but of all activities. The negative effects on the surrounding scenery of a hypermarket built in the country should be charged for as well as its contribution to congestion, and so should the adverse effects of intensive recreation on the ecology of the recreation areas. To what extent charges should be made remains an open question. It seems likely that the complete pricing system just proposed would end up in an extremely complicated and arbitrary set of rules according to which everybody is charged for something — everybody in fact paying everybody else, via the government, for the damages they inflict on general social welfare. Moreover, it can hardly be expected that every goal set by the government can best be achieved by pricing measures. If, for instance, the government aims at rehabilitating the centres of our cities, or protecting the scenery and nature, pricing measures may be of some help, but direct physical planning measures might prove much more efficient and immediately successful. It seems reasonable, therefore, that some measures are direct planning measures and others pricing measures. Road pricing seems a good example of the sort of pricing measures that could be effectuated rather efficiently, while protection of the environment calls, rather, for direct planning measures.

5.7. Infrastructure policy (II)

We may now turn back to infrastructure policy. From the preceding paragraphs we may derive that there are three important elements of infrastructure policy, viz.:

1. the planning of traffic-creating elements;
2. the planning of the infrastructure itself;
3. the pricing system.

These three elements, their interrelations taken into account, will in the end determine the volume and nature of actual traffic flows.

Figure 3 indicates what the interrelations are, and how accessibility, and hence the actual traffic flows, in the end are influenced by the measures the government is able and willing to take.

Through the planning of traffic-creating elements and the application of a pricing system, the government is able, given the level of income, to

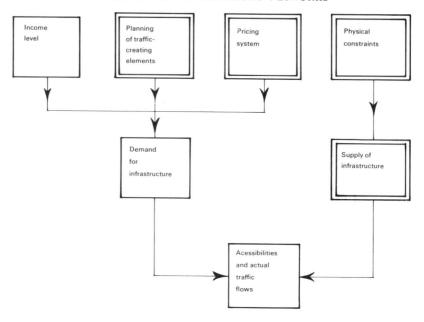

Figure 3. Impact of elements of infrastructure policy on volume and nature of actual traffic flows.

influence the demand for infrastructure. Physical constraints, such as preservation of nature, and preservation of historical city centres, determine the willingness of the government to provide infrastructure. The infrastructure supplied determines, when confronted with the demand for infrastructure, the volume of traffic on the network and simultaneously the costs of using the infrastructure. The latter are decisive for the accessibility of jobs and amenities to the population. If the planning in this scheme takes place according to the rules laid down, it may be said that:

(a) the infrastructure network is an optimum network,
(b) the use of this network is optimum.

The important questions that remain to be answered are how the planning of traffic-creating elements must be effected in practice, what pricing system is to be used, and what physical constraints should be imposed in order to reach what might be called a societal optimum.

6. PRACTICAL CONSIDERATIONS

6.1. *Introduction*

The analysis so far has been general in nature. It has considered the behaviour of individuals in all their activities in relation to their social and economic situation as well as the characteristics of their environment in the broadest sense of the word. It would be easy to argue that such a general analysis, though perhaps interesting from a general societal point of view, is not operational enough for one thing, and for another, not of immediate relevance to transportation in the narrower sense. It seems worthwhile to dedicate some attention to the points thus raised, particularly as, in the eyes of the author, transportation analysis has already suffered too long from an all too narrow engineering approach that is a far cry from the behaviouristic approach that is, in fact, required (Bonnafous and Gerardin, 1976).

When individuals go shopping, they do so in various ways, showing different behaviour for different goods; when they go to recreation areas, they may go to the beach, to the woods, etc., whatever their region has to offer; they will sometimes go for sporting, at other times for resting or enjoying the scenery. People also go to school or to their jobs. They choose a place to live in an area where there are proper houses and which offers them the highest access to the kind of jobs and amenities they prefer. From their choice it follows what their transportation behaviour will be, taking into account the available infrastructure and superstructure. As a matter of fact, if they have chosen their location well, they will have taken the infrastructure into consideration when making the location decision. A government that understands its task well will try to help individual citizens in their locational choice by improving local amenities and infrastructure, thus bringing about comparable welfare situations in all regions.

That, as simple as it may sound, is the theory presented in the first four sections. This theory is difficult to relate to transportation, not so much because it would be too complicated to be properly tested, but rather because each element of the theory, though simple enough in its set-up, requires elaborate testing with data that are not generally available. Testing of the whole theory will be so time-consuming and call for so much intensive research that there is a great temptation to fall back on much simpler solutions of the gravitation type. Such solutions demand not much more than a proper computer for finding the optimum network, if there is a given, "reasonable," spatial distribution of activities and population to start from. Probably the pitfall hampering the development of transportation theory has always been the need for the proper integration of such a theory in a multidisciplinary approach to spatial consumers' behaviour.

An example may elucidate the point made here. If one wants to analyse the direction and extent of trips made for shopping, the analysis should be placed in the framework of a general study on shopping behaviour. Such a study requires at least:

(a) information per zone about shopping facilities in the study area, dif-

ferentiated according to categories of goods supplied, size of the shops, assortment, and prices;
(b) information per zone about residential households, their composition, income, social status, car ownership, age structure, etc.
(c) information (sample) on shopping behaviour, number of trips made, amount of money spent in each zone.

If all this information is available, the testing can be performed. Testing is needed to measure distance friction per category of goods bought, for car-owning households and non-car-owning households, to measure the attraction of the various shopping centres as a function of their size, assortment, parking facilities, etc., etc. A team of the Netherlands Economic Institute has over a period of about two years gone through this whole procedure and succeeded in estimating the most important coefficients (distance-friction coefficients) as well as in deriving from the material important conclusions relevant to shopping-centre policy in an area close to the city of Amsterdam.

What they could not do is to take into account sales to people living outside the study region, the amounts spent on trips originating from the work place of the consumers, the extent to which multi-purpose trips play a role in shopping behaviour (Hensher, 1976), etc.; although some of these were provided for in the theoretical model underlying the analysis (Klaassen, 1974).

That the fruits to be picked from such studies in the narrow field of transportation alone are small, is unimportant in view of the wealth of information they produce. What counts is that a full analysis of people's behaviour as regards shopping seems the only way to provide transportation experts with information on shopping trips that is based on actual shopping behaviour.

Analysing commuting behaviour appears even more complicated. This complexity is, in fact, the dilemma that confronts us: should we continue to work with simple models by which potentials for all activities are calculated according to the same principles, deriving traffic flows and "optimum" networks from them, or should we take the long road along which we shall find much more, and much more detailed, information, but which keeps us going for many years to come? Years during which, after all, decisions will still have to be made. If for fear of doing wrong nobody makes any decisions at all, we are heading straight for one gigantic traffic chaos.

To this dilemma the next sections will be devoted.

6.2. Towards better use of the transport networks

Hopefully, in the preceding sections we have succeeded in showing that the optimum use of transport networks can in principle only be accomplished along the road of optimizing the spatial structure of social welfare. The use of the transport network resulting from such optimization analysis is automatically the optimum use. It is the author's conviction that this road should be followed, however long and painful it may be. If in the following a different procedure is proposed, it is done for pragmatic reasons. The pragmatic approach is, rather than trying to find the optimum use of an as yet unknown network, to settle for a more effective use of the existing network.

The matter can be further simplified by defining a bad use of the infrastructure network as a degree of utilization far below its capacity.

Now that is a definition that seems to represent a shift from the approach adopted so far in this chapter, by which under-utilization in certain circumstances could be considered the best possible use of the infrastructure network, rather than as a situation to be improved. However, in an attempt to reconcile the two approaches, we point out that at present the total volume of traffic is still growing, and that even if we accept that unlimited growth of what is called "mobility" should be considered undesirable, adequate infrastructure must still be provided. As an alternative to constructing new infrastructure we might consider using the existing infrastructure better; to a certain extent the same alternative would, as a matter of fact, be considered in the general solution. When a network is under-utilized, the marginal costs of new traffic are low. So, less investment will be needed for activities that create new traffic on under-utilized parts than for activities that create new traffic on other parts of the system.

Therefore, other things being equal, the former activities would also rank higher than those that require additional infrastructure on the priority list according to the general approach.

6.3. A profile approach

Let us now imagine that an integrated regional study (including a transportation study) is going to be undertaken for a certain region. The following steps could be conceived:

(a) investigating what potential growth possibilities the region has that would contribute to higher future incomes and to a more stable economy;
(b) making assumptions as to how far such growth potentials could be realized;
(c) planning, on the basis of the assumptions meant under (b), the social infrastructure needed:;

(d) drawing up a spatial plan in which population and activities are distributed across the region in an optimum, or rather, an acceptable way.

This approach would have been the obvious one until very recently. In the early sixties the main concern of the authorities in matters of regional development was to attract activities to a region that could contribute to growth and higher income as well as to the stability of the regional economy. The stability could be improved by diversifying the economy, avoiding the monostructures that have often shown themselves highly unstable foundations for a sound economy. However, of recent years other welfare elements have entered into the considerations about future development, and with them a different approach to the selection of activities to be attracted.

This new approach was understandably most popular during the years in which economic growth and full employment prevailed and confidence was strong that the situation would continue like that. The philosophy behind it was in fact that the regional governments (as well as the municipal authorities) could take their pick out of all applications of industrial firms that wanted to start in the region or extend their existing establishments. By imposing constraints in the above sense on those new activities, the government could contribute to the decrease of discrepancies in the labour market, improve the environmental conditions and limit the volume of traffic, while pursuing at the same time the old goals of economic policy: growth and stability.

Conditions have considerably changed since then, particularly as a result of the oil crisis, and it seems that the change has also altered the opinion of the authorities.

It does not seem unlikely that world economy will recover from the influence of the fantastic increase in energy prices, and will gradually find, together with the OPEC countries, a new equilibrium, with (probably modest) further economic growth. That will enable us to resume, perhaps on a more reasonable scale, the pursuit of a growth in welfare in which all five objectives, viz.:

(a) reasonable economic growth;
(b) stability;
(c) acceptable environmental conditions;
(d) acceptable discrepancies on the labour market;
(e) acceptable traffic conditions,

play their role.

If we go into somewhat more detail as far as the traffic conditions are concerned, we shall keep in mind that these represent only one objective out of five. Thus we shall remain in complete concordance with the point we stressed earlier, that the optimum use of infrastructure can never be considered on its own, but should always be defined within a more general social-welfare framework. Sometimes heavy congestion will have to be accepted, sometimes heavy under-utilization, if the conditions prevailing in other fields require it. In the following we shall have to keep that constraint in mind.

Let us assume that the regional study has been performed to the point where the potential new activities have been defined as calculations performed regarding the nature and quantity of amenities that will be needed in the future.

We will further assume that a number of possible and acceptable scenarios for the region's future will at this stage be designed. Each scenario will define a certain spatial distribution of population and activities.

At this point the behaviouristic approach should be introduced. From the distribution of employment, shopping centres, recreation areas and other amenities, schools, and population, we should be able, with the help of models that explain commuting behaviour, shopping behaviour, recreation behaviour, etc., to calculate the traffic flows created by each possible and acceptable spatial arrangement.

The additional traffic created, defined per direction, per hour, and per day, will then have to be compared with the non-utilized infrastructure per direction, per hour, and per day. If we denote the additional traffic by:

$$\varphi_t = {}^\delta t_{ij}^\tau \tag{6.1}$$

to be called the *new-traffic profile*, in which t is the number of passengers, δ the day of the week, τ the hours of the day, and ij the direction in which the traffic takes place, and the non-utilized capacity by:

$$\varphi_u = {}^\delta u_{ij}^\tau \tag{6.2}$$

to be called the *unused-capacity profile*, the plan should be chosen for which *for all* ${}^\delta t_{ij}^\tau > {}^\delta u_{ij}^\tau$

$$\sum_\delta \sum_\tau \sum_i \sum_j \left[{}^\delta t_{ij}^\tau - {}^\delta u_{ij}^\tau \right] f_{ij} = \text{min.}$$

f_{ij} representing the physical (or time) distance between i and j.

According to the principles laid down in the preceding section, the plan envisaged, wherever possible and acceptable, should imply:

(a) extension of the general use of under-utilized parts of the network;
(b) more balanced distribution of residential and employment areas;
(c) planning of recreation areas and residential areas in such a way that during the weekends those parts of the network are used for recreational and social-visit purposes that during weekdays are used for commuting and shopping;

(d) improvement of public-transport networks on parts of the road network where congestion prevails;

(e) in all other cases extension of the capacity of the existing network rather than the construction of new links.

7. FINAL REMARKS

In the foregoing a number of theoretical considerations were presented which were partly of a highly theoretical nature and partly of a somewhat more practical character.

For an elegant presentation, the more practical conclusions ought to have been derived from the theory presented first. However, in this article it has not been possible fully to meet that requirement, because testing the theory would have called for so much original research that only very partial results could have been presented now.

For that reason a simpler approach to the practical matters has been chosen, linked to the theory in many respects but certainly not making full use of its potentialities.

The dilemma in which transportation theory finds itself at this moment is certainly not typical of transportation problems. More than ever it is realized that all the major problems the world is faced with today are no more than facets of a much more general problem, the problem of how to find a societal optimum. In labour-market studies, environmental studies, economic studies, and physical-planning studies, the same problem arises. Improvement of the conditions on the labour market might create new traffic, and require the expansion of industrial production that harms the environment. Measures that promote the quality of the environment fast and efficiently could cause serious repercussions on the labour market and gravely infringe the individual's freedom to travel. To maximize economic growth has become as doubtful an objective as to minimize traffic flows and maximize the quality of our environment. All these objectives should get their proper weight in the social-welfare function in order to enable society to find a solution that is acceptable for most people as the best solution that can be reached given the prevailing conditions and financial and other constraints.

The procedure followed in this article finds its justification in the position in which most researchers in all the fields indicated find themselves. On the one hand they are inclined to concentrate on the general societal problem, on the other hand they are faced with the necessity to propose solutions for practical problems, solutions that have to be realized at short notice. Society cannot wait until the long-term optimum solution has been found, and many politicians are even far from convinced that it is right to go on searching for it.

It is, indeed, the author's conviction that two lines should be followed simultaneously. One line is the study of integrated models that, if made operational, could provide integrated solutions on many specific problems. The other line is to search for partial solutions, taking into account all external effects of any measure proposed, so that the solutions suggested are likely to fit into the framework of the general model.

Even a partial approach to each of the specific fields referred to above — including that of transportation — will require the formation of a multidisciplinary team. Compared to the general framework of societal models, every model, however complicated and sophisticated, be it a transportation model, or an economic model, or an environmental model, or a labour-market model, is a partial model, and not more than that. Practical solutions, however, require more than the solution a partial model is able to give. That's why we should try to walk along both avenues simultaneously, however difficult it may seem from a transportation point of view.

REFERENCES

Berg, L. van den, Klaassen, L.H. and Vijverberg, H.T. (1975). *Evaluation of governmental welfare policy by means of a social welfare function.* Foundation for Empirical Economic Research, no. 7. Rotterdam: Netherlands Economic Institute.

Bonnafous, A. and Gerardin, B. (1976). *Passenger transport demand in urban areas, Methodology for Analysing and Forecasting.* Paris: ECMT, Round Table 32.

Hensher, D.A. (1976). "The structure of journeys and the nature of travel pattern," *Environment and Planning* 8:655–672.

Merlin, P. (1966). "Les transports urbains et leurs usagers en région de Paris," in *Transports urbains*, vols. 4–5. Paris: Institut d'aménagement et d'urbanisme de la Région Parisienne.

Klaassen, L.H. (1969). "Voorkeuren in het personenvervoer," *Verkeerstechniek* 20:536–543.

Klaassen, L.H. (1974). *A shopping model.* Foundation for Empirical Economic Research, no. 13. Rotterdam: Netherlands Economic Institute.

Langen, M. de, and Verster, A.C.P. (1976). "Verband tussen bereikbaarheid en vestigingsgedrag," in J.P.J.M. van Est, G.R.M. Jansen, P.H.L. Bovy and S. le Clerq, eds., *Planevaluatie, vervoersmodellen en ruimtelijk keuzegedrag*, Colloquium Vervoersplanologisch speurwerk. Delft.

Steenbrink, P.A. (1974). *Optimization of transport networks.* New York: John Wiley.

TRANSPORT POLICY IN A SELF-MANAGEMENT SYSTEM: DEVELOPMENTS IN YUGOSLAVIA

V. KOLARIĆ

1. INTRODUCTION

Transport is a basic integrating factor of the economy and the society, connecting production, trade and consumption into an integrated process of social reproduction. Therefore the basic features of the development of the structure of the transport system, and thereby also of the conception of the transport policy of any country, depend on two basic elements: (1) the level of development and the structure of the economy and society and (2) the geographical situation of a country and the role of its transport system in international transport — the transport system being, on the one hand, a complementary part of the country's economy and on the other, a complementary part of the international transport system.

Our aim being to point out the essentials of the transport policy in the self-management system of Yugoslavia, the development of that policy and the role of scientific research in that development, we first concentrate on the two basic elements mentioned above and on the general principles and the institutions of the self-management system. We next will give an outline of transport policy in Yugoslavia, followed by a section indicating the relationship between transport policy and research in the self-management economy of Yugoslavia. Some final remarks refer to the needs for further research.

2. DEVELOPMENT OF THE ECONOMY AND SOCIETY

2.1. Structural development of the economy

Yugoslavia is a developing country which has had a very dynamic development as one of the countries with the highest economic growth rate. It has already achieved a level of development at which it turns from an agricultural to an industrialized country with a very developed international trade.

During the last two decades in Yugoslavia, and in all industrialized countries as well, significant demographic, geographic and economic structural changes have taken place. The population is steadily increasing whereas its density in the various parts of the country is always changing under the effects of changes in growth and structure of production and its geographical locations. The process of these changes is expressed in the forming of large densely-inhabited industrial zones and cities. In 1972 40 percent of the population lived in urban settlements against 21 percent in 1948. During the same period the absolute number of inhabitants living in towns increased from 3.1 to 7.9 million.

For the years to come (up to 1985) the economic development projections provide an average annual economic growth rate of 6.5 to 8 percent, industrial production being expected to grow by 9 to 10 percent per annum. In this orientation, the development policy will be focused on the production of energy, raw materials and food.

The further increase of the population (from 20 million in 1977 to 25 million in 1985), of the national income and of the average income per capita, will certainly imply a further increase in the mobility of people and the pace of motorization.

The rapid pace of modernization of the country during the last two decades has already resulted in an increased mobility of the population, in a process of decentralization of big cities and in the forming of new settlements in the vicinity of cities and industrialized regions. Under the influence of an increased motorization and a growing number of private cars, the distances between home and place of work have been growing longer. Changes in the structure of manufacturing industry and tertiary activities as well as the structure of production of large and small enterprises and goods exchange have instigated the development of motor freight transport. Changes in the production and consumption of liquid fuel, gas and electricity also have had their effects on traffic flows and on the roles of railway, road and air transportation. Those effects and their implications for transport policy will be set forth in more detail in Section 3.

2.2. The situation and role of Yugoslavia in the European transport system

Yugoslavia is one of the most transit-intensive countries in Europe. It is integrated in the European transport system with very intensively used through-routes in railway, air, road and river traffic.

In 1976 on the Western Europe/Near and Middle East route alone, 3.2 million tons of freight in 229,000 trucks, of which 97.6 percent had a foreign license, passed through Yugoslavia. In passenger traffic, the Yugoslav frontiers were crossed in the same year by 18.3 million passenger vehicles coming in and by 16.9 million going out, with 55 and 50 million passengers respectively. The freight transport by rail over JŽ transit lines was 7.9 million tons, or 38.5 percent of the total international freight transport of 20.5 million tons (Bulletin, 1977). The transit transport by air and by river counted for 6.4 million tons. Also in air transport Yugoslavia is a transit country. Its transit situation and its role in interconnecting the European transport system and the countries of the Near and Middle East indicate that Yugoslavia must follow the development trends and the conceptions of the transport policies (regarding especially the infrastructure policies) of the countries of Europe and of the Near and Middle East.

Those trends offer two essential elements for the international transport situation of the country. First: modernization and building of motorways which in the near future will bring to the Yugoslav western frontier considerable masses of passengers and freight, and secondly: the reconstruction and modernization of main through high-speed railway lines.

The Near East countries have adopted ambitious plans for enonomic development. They are facing today an important process of industrialization and growth in their standard of living. Therefore they keep increasing imports from the Western European countries. Due to the limited capacity of the Near East ports, the imports from Europe are directed to land routes. For these reasons and in view of the fact that in industrialized countries railways play an important role, the governments of Near East countries have accepted construction programs for their railway systems. Thus, in addition to the construction of motorways, the modernization and orientation to the construction and upgrading for higher speeds of main transit railway lines connecting the European and the Near East Railway systems, have become basic elements of the transport policy in Yugoslavia as a transit country.

The main changes in the structure of the transport system occurred by an exponential growth of road and air transport, which has substantially changed the shares of the various modes in the transport market (Table 1).

Table 1. Shares of rail and road transport in Yugoslavia, 1955–75.

	1955	1975
Rail passenger transport	80.5	13.9
freight transport	80.1	40.6
Road passenger transport	16.2	85.2
freight transport	8.8	40.2

These structural changes occurred as well in other countries with developed transport, partly as a consequence of the development of the economy and partly due to unequal competitive conditions in the transport market (Seidenfus, 1959; Kolarić, 1968a; Voigt, 1973).

2.3. The socialist self-management system

For a proper understanding of transport policy in the context of the self-management system existing in Yugoslavia a few words may be devoted to the characteristics of this system. The philosophy and general principles of the self-management system involve socialist market production organized under conditions of planned orientation of the economy. The functioning of the market mechanism is accepted, but its effects are governed and directed by social development plans and by instruments of the economic system in such a way that free initiatives of working organizations in production and exchange are encouraged, but at the same time an uncontrolled functioning of the market mechanism is prevented.

The working organizations independently approve their own plans on the basis of the medium- and long-term social development plans, which determine the basic lines of development.

In particular as regards the transport sector the role of governmental authorities has been changed. First, the function of governing the relations with the transport sector and the financing of transport development have been transferred from federal authorities to republics and provinces. Secondly, the functions of managing transport organizations have been transferred to the self-management authorities of working organizations in the transport sector. Governmental authorities are not entitled to interfere with decision-making within working organizations. Their role is brought down to enacting basic laws. Self-management communities have taken over the role of the governmental authorities. The assemblies of these communities consist of delegates from transport organizations and from economic and social organizations as users of transport services. The role of governmental authorities in matters like transport policy, transport development, etc. is in fact replaced by self-management agreements between working organizations and by the social agreements signed by the republics, provinces, chambers of economy and trade unions. Within this system of self-management agreements, social agreements and legal regulations of the government, transport enterprises appear in the transport market as independent self-management working organizations.

3. MAIN FEATURES OF TRANSPORT POLICY IN YUGOSLAVIA

3.1. Summary of developments

As a consequence of the situation of Yugoslavia in the whole of the European transport system, the transport policy of the country must mesh with the course of development of the European transport system. Because the international passenger, tourist and freight transport of the country and its inclusion in the international division of labour greatly depend on the efficiency of the system and on the co-ordination of its techniques and technology with the systems of other countries, the transit role of Yugoslavia in international traffic can best be achieved by a co-ordinated development of entire traffic flows. As for the railways, Yugoslavia is included in the "Plan Directeur" of the future European railway infrastructure — prepared by the International Union of Railways (UIC) — covering some 40,000 kms of main lines (of which 14,000 kms are to be up-graded and 6,000 kms to be newly built) in the total of 250,000 kms of railway lines in Europe.

The development trends will continue to enhance the problems of the transport system as it exists and will require a radical re-orientation and correction of errors which have arisen in development until now. One of those errors has been that road and air transport make the position of the railways deteriorate, not only as a logical consequence of the former's technical and economic advantages, but partly also because of unequal basic competitive conditions; railways lost transport for which they are more profitably suited from the point of view of society as a whole. As already indicated in Section 2.2., the share of railways is steadily decreasing, whereas the shares of road and air are increasing beyond the limits of social profitability and economic justification.

The forming of an irrational structure of the system results in a steady increase of the total costs of transport for the society and in an increased adverse effect of transport on the human environment. Serious social problems of spatial planning, urbanization and protection of human environment are arising, problems in which transport plays a decisive role. Its development requires more and more space. New investments in the road system are being undertaken, while the capacity of railways is not fully used. Space for recreation and diversion and green surfaces are becoming lesser and fewer; the human environment is more and more affected by noise, air pollution, constriction of living space and deterioration of traffic safety.

Society cannot passively accept all the consequences of the existing system. The system cannot be considered as a simple sum of the individual modes of transport. It must be seen as a technically, technologically and economically co-ordinated system, and, in the Yugoslav situation, as a complex self-management system for the arrangement and forming of the optimum structure to which at this "transport juncture" the social community must pay special attention.

3.2. Transport policy

Studies have been made of the trends, the consequences and the lines of further development and of the concepts to be prepared for the transport policy of Yugoslavia (Novaković et al., 1976). On the basis of these studies and of versatile discussions at all levels of the self-management organization of the transport system and economy, a Social Agreement on Transport Policy was enacted in 1977. This Social Agreement has not been enacted by any government body, however, as is normally the case in other countries. As already stated (see Section 2.3), in the Yugoslav system transport enterprises appear in the transport market as independent self-management working organizations and operate on the principles of economic organizations. The organs of the socio-political communities, the socialist republics, the provinces and the federation direct the development of transport by medium-term and long-term social development plans, by the policy concerning the construction and financing of transport infrastructure and by the instruments of the allotment of financial means and the regulation of the economic status of the modes of transport.

Within this institutional framework, all specific measures of orientation and regulation of certain problems of the economic position and the development of individual modes of transport are taken on the basis of self-management agreements and social agreements.

The Social Agreement on Transport Policy is signed by the Federal Executive Council, all executive councils of republics and provinces as representatives of the social community, the Chamber of Economy as a representative of associated labour in transport and the economy, and the Association of Trade Unions as workers' representatives. The essentials of the decision-making process concerning transport policy can briefly be indicated as follows:

— selection of objectives for further development of the transport system structure;
— establishment of priorities in development policy relative to the individual modes of transport;
— elimination of conflicting relations in the development of individual modes of transport and co-ordination of targets of transport development with the targets of medium- and long-term development plans of the economy of Yugoslavia.

Actually, the substance of transport policy as such is the changed relationship in the development of individual modes of transport, viz. with the aim of ensuring a faster development and modernization of railway and river traffic, of increasing the share of public transport and decreasing the share of private transport and of transport by enterprises' own fleets, and of a more efficient co-ordination between the modes of transport, based on the comparative advantages and the social profitability of each mode. The investments needed for the realization of development plans are financed by the social funds of republics and provinces, the economy and the working organizations in the transport sector, by means of a social agreement for each mode or sector, according to the priorities of development, provided that infrastructure projects are financed by the society, by the economy and in the form of loans. Investments in rolling stock and other facilities must be financed out of the funds of the working organizations themselves.

The expected result is a greater initiative of transport working organizations and of the economy for the modernization and the development of transport capacity, a more rational development of the transport system structure, reduction of transport costs for the society and a more adequate inclusion into the international transport system.

The basic strategy of the transport policy of Yugoslavia as specified in the Social Agreement of 1977 is contained in the following targets:

— changing the pace of development of individual modes of transport to reach an optimum structure of the transport system on the basis of comparative advantages and social profitability of each mode, thus eliminating disproportions in the development of transport and of other sectors, of public transport and private transport, resp. transport on own account, and of the various modes of transport;
— a more rational division of transport between the modes of transport for the purpose of reducing the total transport costs of the economy and society, and in that respect, the orientation of long-distance hauls to rail and river, and of short-distance hauls to public road transport; passengers on medium- and long-distance journeys to rail and air, and on short and medium journeys, as well as urban and commuter traffic, to road transport;
— greater orientation to a faster development of public transport and the restriction of private transport to a reasonable level;
— development of rapid rail traffic as a basis of transport in major cities and towns and of road traffic as a supplementary mode, thus forming a functionally co-ordinated transport system;
— orientation of the development of the transport system structure and of the process of modernization towards a more rational use of energy in transport and towards protection of human environment:
— orientation to integrated processes by the development of the self-management system and to the self-management principles for the purpose of rationalization of the entire transport system and improve-

ment of its efficiency by the development of integration of transport, common inland and port terminals, junctions, freight-distribution centres and an adequate inclusion of national transport into the international transport system.

For the achievement of this basic strategy for transport, the following criteria have a decisive effect:

1. quality of service, speed and regularity in particular,
2. functioning in relation to different distances,
3. accessibility and suitability for the broadest range of users,
4. traffic safety level,
5. possibility of using existing facilities, needs for new investments and space occupation and the social profitability of investments,
6. kind and quantities of energy consumption
7. possibility of increasing efficiency in the transport system as a whole,
8. reduction of total transport costs,
9. effects on human environment.

4. THE RELATIONSHIP BETWEEN TRANSPORT POLICY AND RESEARCH IN A SELF-MANAGEMENT ECONOMY

Scientific research in Yugoslavia in the field of transport actually dates from the past 10–15 years. Organized scientific research started at the beginning of the last decade with the forming of the Transport Institutes at Beograd, Zagreb and Ljubljana. Since 1955 transport has been studied as a scientific discipline at the Economic Faculties in Beograd and Zagreb through the subjects "Transport Economics" and "Economics and Organization of Transport Enterprises."

Nowadays transport faculties in Beograd, in Zagreb and in Rijeka exist. These faculties train an adequate number of specialists in the fields of transport economics, techniques and technology. Thus there are today solid scientific teams in all areas of transport science and an adequate number of young scientists.

In the process of taking over in the field of transport roles of former government authorities by the new self-management institutions, scientific research more and more takes a primary place. The final decisions for important self-management agreements and for social agreements in the transport sector are only taken on the basis of prior studies, and of investigations carried out by the institutes and emanating from symposia and discussions on the results of the studies. The scientific workers and university professors in the area of transport participate in almost all commissions and working groups for transport of federal and republican authorities in drawing up the self-management agreements and the social agreements governing relations in the transport sector.

The interrelation between decision making and research in transport is indeed very strong. Almost all important transport policy measures, reorganizations and the regulating of economic relations in transport taken since 1960 by federal, republican or provincial authorities, by committees of transport or by communities of railways and post, have been preceded by studies on specific problems ordered from transport institutes. We mention some of the most important problems.

(1) The development of the self-management system required substantial changes in the organization and in the management of transport, in particular regarding the large systems of railways and post. The heart of the problem was how to make the self-management authorities decide independently on their business policy, and in particular how the railways would appear in the transport market and compete, while on the one hand the government authorities still have a very strong influence on the development and the organization of the railways and on the other hand the latter are working under unequal conditions of competition. The railways have been treated dualistically, both as self-managing organizations and as services of special significance for the society.

The main features of the recommended solution were: equalization of conditions for the formation of tariffs, the financing of infrastructure (the railway infrastructure included) by the society, the creation of a self-management community of interest for transport and regulation of the relations within the joint self-management authorities of all modes of transport.

This is being achieved only now by the social agreements on development of individual modes, the bringing about of a solution for the economic position of the railways and the social agreement on transport policy (Kolarić, 1964; 1968b).

(2) The preparation of the long-term development plan for the economy and for the transport sector was preceded by an extensive study on the "Optimum Structure of the Transport System of Yugoslavia." The research work took 5 years and all institutes and renowned scientists and transport experts took part.

The main problem (and goal) relating to transport was to determine the requirements of the economy and of society as a whole as for the future development of all modes of transport. The main innovating elements of the transport policy were a detailed analysis of results of development to date and the determination of particular disproportions between transport and economic development against the background of modern transport development in Europe. Proposals for solutions given in the studies have been used as the basic assumptions for drawing up a long-term transport development plan.

(3) The regulation of economic relations between the modes of transport and the economic conditions of the operations of the transport enterprises were used as a basis for a special study in the areas of economic conditions of operations, the financing of investments, the system of allocating the transport infrastructure costs, etc. The main results of this study and its possible effects on the element of co-ordination in transport policy will be forthcoming only after implementation of the Social Agreement of Transport Policy.

(4) The tariff structure of the railways under the new conditions of rail-way operations under the self-management system asked for new approaches. Studies ordered by the Yugoslav Railways were carried out and possible solutions given.

The problems emanated from the fact that the railways saw themselves faced with technical obsoleteness and low tariffs which are imposed on the railways on the basis of general interests of society. The main features of the proposed solutions were an accelerated modernization of railways and a tariff system which is differentiated according to individual lines (Novaković, et al., 1974a, 1974b, 1976).

Further research is now under way at the institutes in behalf of the federal authorities and of the Community of the Yugoslav Railways, concerning the socio-economic principles of the financing of transport infra-structure; road-user charges; railway costing; the optimum structure of the transport system in Slovenia; freight transport flows, etc.

It should be remarked that the research work undertaken in Yugoslavia, of which some examples have been given above, is not carried out in isolation. An active part is taken in the work of international organizations (e.g. the International Railway Union, UIC, and the International Association of the Railways Congress, AICCF) and their committees, and especially in the research work of the European Conference of Ministers of Transport. In many respects this work appears to be of both theoretical and practical use also for the situation and the transport policy of Yugoslavia.

5. SOME ISSUES FOR FURTHER RESEARCH

In view of the conditions in which both theory and practice of transport economics and transport policy in the self-management society of Yugoslavia are developing, there still remain in our view important questions to which research has not yet given satisfactory answers. We will conclude this article by mentioning what we feel are the most pressing of these questions.

(1) One of the fundamental problems of modern society is the protection of human environment, which is more and more affected by the structure of the transport system. Therefore important questions must be answered relating to the criteria which have to be taken into account when striving for an optimum structure of the transport system from the standpoint of social profitability, including the methods of evaluation of indirect effects of transport and its infrastructure. The methods of measuring the social profitability resp. the effectiveness of investments in transport which are extensively elaborated in both socialist and capitalist countries cannot be the last word in this matter. In Yugoslavia policy making needs more sophisticated evaluation methods especially as regards the social profitability of the transport system.

This is of particular interest for decisions on investment projects like the construction of motorways and the modernization and reconstruction of railways for high speeds.

(2) A very important issue for transport co-ordination and for a socially-rational division of transport among the modes of transport, especially between railways and roads, is the problem of the system of infrastructure financing and the methods of charging each mode with the costs of the use of infrastructure. In Yugoslavia this issue has a special importance in view of the changed position of the social-community authorities in transport co-ordination and of the economic independence of transport organizations in the self-management system. Government is no longer entitled to intervene directly in the transport market in order to regulate relations between transport enterprises. However, competition is still developing under unequal conditions. The railway tariffs include the full costs of railway infrastructure, being 28 percent of the total of railway costs, whereas road transport and inland shipping bear only partially their costs of infrastructure; taxes on road transport and inland shipping amount respectively to 6 percent and 1 percent of their total costs. Consequently ways must be found for creating a policy and methods of financing infrastructure (extensions as well as replacements) and for achieving a balanced allocation of the costs of infrastructure to the users.

(3) Related to (1) and (2) is the problem of pricing system and pricing policy in the transport sector. From the first classical theories of Emil Sax (1918–22), through more recent marginalist theories (Oort, 1961) to up-to-date theories of costs and prices (Riebel, 1975), there still remain

unanswered questions regarding the formation of prices. In Yugoslavia different views exist on matters such as the formation of prices of railway services: could and should the current prices of railway services cover all infrastructure costs? How to ensure the financing of expanded reproduction under conditions of economic and self-management independence of the railway enterprise, taking into account the changed role of the social community? These are still open questions; answering them cannot be postponed too long.

(4) The Yugoslav self-management system produces another open question: the relationship between the social community and transport. From earlier theoretical discussions on the relationship between the government and the railways (Witte, 1932) to the more recent extension of this issue (Schroiff, 1961) connected with the systems and methods of transport co-ordination, theoretical views have crystallized into the notion that the relations in the transport market cannot be simply left to the sole effect of the market mechanism and that intervention of society is essential. On the other hand, the process of commercialization of the railways is a must and the application of marketing methods is underway in the whole field of transport. The conflict between these two "principles" cannot be ignored. Intervention of the social community in the transport market aims at the provision for social interests. The marketing concept aims at ensuring the economic interests of each transport enterprise, which supposes as much independence as possible.

An optimal system of social intervention must be found which ensures maximum incentives for initiatives and competition in the transport market and which at the same time ensures a rational utilization of transport facilities according to the social profitability of each mode of transport. Evidently the problem is common to the transport policy of nearly every country. So far the problem still awaits a satisfactory solution, in Yugoslavia as elsewhere.

REFERENCES

Bulletin *"Transport and Communications"* 1977. Savezniravod za Statistiku 17:51, 163.

Kolarić, V. (1964). *Transport organization and the problems of self-management in transport enterprises.* Beograd: Transport Institute.

Kolarić, V. (1968a). "Eigenarten des Verkehrsmarktes als eine der Determinanten der Verkehrspolitik," *Verkehrsannalen* 15: 353–364.

Kolarić, V. (1968b). *Railway Transport Economics;* volume 3: *Organization of railways as a complex technical and technological, economic and self-management system.* Beograd.: Press and Publicity Institute of YR (JŽ).

Novaković, S., Kolarić, V. and Savić, M. (1974a). *Transport development policy in Yugoslavia.* Beograd: Institut "Kirilo Savić".

Novaković, S., Kolarić, V. and Savić, M. (1974b). *Socio-economic Prerequisites for Optimization of the Transport System in SR of Serbia.* Beograd: Institut "Kirilo Savić".

Novaković, S., Kolarić, V. and Pavlović, T. (1976). *Criteria and Measures of Socio-economic Appropriateness of Development of the Transport System* — a study for establishment of the transport policy of Yugoslavia. Beograd: Institut "Kirilo Savić".

Oort, C.J. (1961). *Der Marginalismus als Basis der Preisbildung in der Verkehrswirtschaft.* Rotterdam: Verkeerswetenschappelijk Centrum.

Riebel, P. (1975). "Grenzkosten als Grundlage einer marktorientierten Preispolitik," *Verkehrsannalen* 22:451–459.

Sax, E. (1918/22). *Die Verkehrsmittel in Volks- und Staatswirtschaft*, 2nd ed. Berlin: Springer.

Schroiff, F.J. (1961). "Staat und Verkehr," in Zentral-Verein für Deutsche Binnenschiffahrt, ed., *Verkehr und Wirtschaft*, Festschrift Otto Most. Duisburg-Ruhrort: Binnenschiffahrts-Verlag.

Seidenfus, H. St. (1959). *Verkehrsmärkte.* Basel/Tübingen: Kyklos/J.C.B. Mohr (Paul Siebeck).

Voigt, F. (1973). *Die Theorie der Verkehrswirtschaft*, Erster Band—Erste Hälfte, *Verkehr.* Berlin: Duncker and Humblot.

Witte, B. (1932). *Eisenbahn und Staat.* Jena: Gustav Fischer.

TRANSPORT STATISTICS IN A CHANGING TRANSPORT PROCESS: THE YEARS AHEAD

H.C. KUILER

1. INTRODUCTION

Today many countries have at their disposal a complete set of statistics for inland transport. The mode of transport forms the primary criterium for the organization of the statistical material. The relation between points (or districts) of loading and unloading comes in the second place and the type of commodity in the third.

In contrast to the period when transport statistics were first established on a more systematic basis (during the Depression of the thirties), enterprises, governmental agencies and research workers now show great interest in these statistics and they often press for more information. For transport models the available information is essential as a basic input into these models.

Nevertheless, the question can be raised of whether the kind of information as is presently being provided is the best that can be made available. This question should be seen against the background of developments during the sixties, when the character and structure of the transportation process changed fundamentally.

In the following we shall first look into the changes in the statistical requirements as a consequence, among other things, of the fact that more and more industrial enterprises organize their transport in a more or less integrated way; we are faced with a concept in which each link of the transport chain can only be seen as a part of the chain as a whole: quantities, type of product, choice of the modes of transport, all are dependent on the process of the complete chain.

Next, we will try to envisage the consequences of these developments for the process of getting adequate statistical information. Then, some difficulties will be dealt with in the field of statistical methods and techniques. Concluding, some attention will be paid to the years ahead.

Based on a study which had been previously undertaken by the author to improve the quality of information given by transport statistics, a special study has been executed by the Netherlands Central Bureau of Statistics in which transport chains and transport links within and beyond the frontiers of the Netherlands' economy were analyzed by bringing together information from statistics of production, international trade, consumption and transport. The spatial distribution of these transport chains and transport links got special attention. The results were very promising and will certainly show in the years to come their influence on the statistics already available. Especially an integration of the statistical information will give a very intensified view on the Dutch economic process.

This article gives a comprehensive idea of the lines along which the study has been built up. The reader will do well to keep in mind that the subject matter is in a new field which has not yet been thoroughly explored.

2. CHANGES IN STATISTICAL REQUIREMENTS

Transport flows are a function of the relation between economic activities and their spatial distribution. From this results a first requirement which transport statistics will have to fulfill: they should be an aid in showing the relations between economic activities. These relations can be of a rather complex character. To start with, there are the inputs in the production processes of raw materials. Furthermore there exists an exchange of semi-finished products between various production processes and thirdly the final products are brought to the markets where the final consumers pick them up. Of course this process is spatially distributed, sometimes in a small region, in other cases world-wide.

Is it possible to show at least for groups of homogeneous products the complete spatial transport pattern, with the relevant modal splits, in any case at least as a function of total production or consumption? Is it possible to give also in these respects a statistical reconstruction of the national economic processes as seen by transport economists?

The most extensive example of transport chains as organized by industrial enterprises is perhaps the transportation of crude oil and of oil products by the "majors" in the oil industry. Crude oil is, for example, transported from several oil-wells by relatively small pipelines to a loading port at the Persian Gulf, from which the crude oil is brought by VLCC (Very Large Crude Carrier) to Rotterdam. After storage and processing, oil products are brought by inland-waterway transport to inland depots or by big pipelines to industrial centres in the hinterland of Europe. From the depots the oil products are distributed by trucks to the selling points, where the final consumer buys the products in small quantities (see Scheme 1, structure of a transport chain). Can a complete statistical reconstruction of this whole process, together with the spatial effects, be given?

For many other products, chain integration has also taken place, partly or completely. One can think of iron ore/pig iron/metal semi-finished pro-

Scheme 1.   Structure of a transport chain.

| Winning of raw materials | 1st transport link
Type of commodity: raw materials; transport technique: e.g. rail |

| Transport terminal | 2nd transport link
Type of commodity: raw materials; transport technique: e.g. bulk carrier |

| 1st technical production process | 3rd transport link
Type of commodity: semi-finished product; transport technique: inland waterway |

| 2nd technical production process | 4th transport link
Type of commodity: final product; transport technique: truck |

| Distribution point | 5th transport link
Type of commodity: final product; transport technique: private car |

| Household |

ducts/metal final products. Cereals can also be an example. But even when the transport chain is not integrated (partly or completely) by one enterprise, the links of the chain are interdependent. Mostly a relation exists between quantities transported in each link, though the type of product is quite different. Each type of product in its turn — together with the spatial aspects — is relevant for the modal choice.

With an advanced statistical system it must be possible at least in theory to reconstruct the most important of these transport chains, links, intermediate processes and their spatial distribution.

As has been indicated in our Introduction, many transport statistics are related to the special characteristics of a specific transport technique or are established for pure ad hoc, often non-economic reasons. Product statistics were built up in which a regional breakdown in the figures is lacking, while many production quantities are not given in tons but in other units; foreign trade statistics always bear the characteristics of custom requirements, etc. We are in need of a general concept behind all these different statistics. For the present, a complete reconstruction of transport chains in the above-mentioned sense involves the difficulty of a certain inconsistency between the various kinds of statistics. Nevertheless the study made in the Netherlands mentioned above has shown that the existing statistical material enables us to reach interesting results. (Some examples are given in an Annex to this article.) In describing transport as an intermediary in connecting different economic activities, we have approached closely the method by which the economic process is described in a statistically-consistent way: the national accounts and the input/output table. In the following we look at the possibilities that can be derived from the input/output table for the aims as mentioned in this section.

3. STATISTICAL PICTURE OF THE STRUCTURE OF THE NATIONAL ECONOMY

The main sectors of a national economy to be distinguished from the point of view of a transport economist are: enterprises, government, private households and the rest of the world. The relations between these sectors — in most cases given with a further breakdown to branches of industry — can be found in an input/output table (see Scheme 2, commodity flows in an input/output table). From a transport view these relations can be analyzed in two different ways. Macro-economically one can analyze the importance of transport in a national economy: contribution to national income, effects

Scheme 2. Commodity flows in an input/output table.

Types of activity 1 2 3 4 .... m	Final deliveries Export Households Government
Types of *activity* 1 2 3 4 : : n	row ⟶ column outputs inputs INTERMEDIARY DELIVERIES	row ⟶ final deliveries according to type of buyer· FINAL DELIVERIES
Imports row ⟶ imports for the various types of activity IMPORTS	

on the balance of payments, etc. In a more micro-economic sense the table allows an analysis of the sectors, respectively branches of economic activities, between which flows of goods must take place. In this respect the use of an input/output table offers new perspectives for a future development of transport statistics.

Analysing an input/output table along these lines, one finds that in the quadrant of the table which represents the intermediary deliveries a strong clustering of transport flows exists between the different phases of a production column. In general, all other intermediary deliveries on a certain row are — in relation to these clusterings — of relatively minor importance. In this way a number of important transport chains may be constructed. They give an indication of the area to which the transport economist must direct his attention in the first place. Of course, the information gives no insight into the volumes transported: the sector/branch relations are only indicated in terms of the monetary value of the transactions. Even in those cases in which it is possible to calculate a relation in volume terms or to derive information from production or consumption statistics one has no information on the quantity transported in reality. This quantity can be equal, bigger or even smaller than that calculated from the input/output table. For this phenomena we have to direct our attention to the characteristics of a transport chain from a transport point of view.

A second restriction of the input/output table for the transport statistician is the fact that the table gives no spatial distribution of the sector/branch relations. Here the transport statistics must give another stepping stone. The transport relations analysis of the input/output table not only gives the links between two sectors/branches, but also the whole transport chain which must be used before the product reaches the final consumer.

When the most important transport chains and links in a national economy have been identified with the help of a monetary input/output table, a second step can be made, namely the tracing of the relevant goods flows in the transport statistics. For that purpose we need matrices per type of commodity showing within the cells of the matrix the quantities of goods (measured in tons) transported between or within regions. Where (in many cases) a transport from origin to destination passes through two or more links of the chain with different transport techniques, separate matrices for the different techniques for each commodity will have to be built up as well. Statistical information in this form is not readily available; in many cases it will have to be reconstructed out of the basic statistical material.

Working per commodity with four matrices (one for the total volume transported, three for rail, inland waterway and truck transport respectively) a good picture can be given of the transport structure of each commodity. In many cases one will find complementarity of transport techniques. For example, cereals are brought by bulk carrier from overseas. In order to preserve as long as possible these — or at least part of these — economies of scale of the bulk carrier, cereals are transported from the seaport to inland ports by inland waterway (up to 2,000 tons). From there, distribution is effected in smaller quantities by truck to the factories that have cereals as an input. The same quantity (say 50,000 tons) is on the continental trip transported twice. As a result the total of the cereals matrix will indicate a total of 100,000 tons.

Therefore the breakdown per transport technique is essential in order to bring the transport totals in accordance with (in this case) the imported total. The inland-waterway matrix now shows large flows from the seaport to the different regions in the country, the truck matrix shows the regional transport and will have no or at the utmost only a few minor interregional transports. This transport structure has been found for many products imported via seaports or with production strongly concentrated within a certain area.

Sometimes a complication arises from the fact that also between different production regions large transport flows exist. In these cases we are dealing with intermediary deliveries, for example between factories of chemical products. In such cases the transport total of the commodity is largely increased. For comparison with the real production total these intermediary flows have to be taken separately.

Another complication may arise when the commodity is not sufficiently homogeneous, e.g. when cereals are taken as a total. The deliveries from the seaport will for instance consist of wheat or maize, but in regional transport home-produced rye or barley is also included. In such cases one cannot work with cereals as one group of some kind of general goods classification system such as the NSTR (Nomenclature uniforme de marchandises pour les statistiques de transport); the basis then has to be the separate items (wheat, barley, etc.).

A statistical problem could also be the fact that road-transport statistics are made on the basis of a sample. When this method is used, it is theoretically possible that the cells of a rather disaggregated matrix are unreliable.

To complete the matrix analysis, one has to take into account the imports and exports of the commodities analyzed and especially those imports or exports that do not give rise to complementary inland transports. These direct imports and exports influence production and consumption directly but inland transport flows are only influenced indirectly or even not at all. After having analyzed the goods matrices along these lines, one will find transport patterns which are characteristic for each commodity separately. The knowledge of such transport patterns is, of course, of great use for the statistical input in transport models.

The most simple cases are those in which only one mode of transport is used; for example in the Netherlands the truck has more or less a transport monopoly for final chemical products such as dyeing materials, medicinal and pharmaceutical products, perfumery and cleansing preparations, etc. In these cases patterns exist like those described for cereals. Similar patterns exist for liquid fuels, animal foodstuffs, etc. We also meet situations in which all modes of transport participate in interregional long-distance transport. This is the case for instance with scrap iron: regional assembly of scrap iron by truck and interregional flows by rail and by inland waterway to two production plants that use scrap for an input; the explanation of the modal split between rail- and waterways being that one of the two plants has no rail connection.

4. PRACTICAL PROBLEMS

Each separate final product, however small it may be, has passed through a transport chain once it has reached the final consumer. In theory it could be possible to reconstruct in statistics such "micro-chains." In reality however, millions of these chains would have to be reconstructed. Statistically this would be impossible. Moreover, for transport policy, even on the level of a separate transport enterprise, such a micro-analysis would be of very limited use. Aggregation will therefore be inevitable. But on what level?

The type of goods, as a species, can be a first step in the aggregation process. A special type of goods (bread, cars, etc.) is produced in production units with a high degree of specialization. This leads therefore to the production unit where the ingoing and outgoing flow of a certain species of goods can be examined. At such a micro-level of the simple production unit we are still faced in many cases with a very detailed statistical problem of fact-finding and processing.

The next step in the aggregation process leads to the economic-activity branch. On this level of aggregation we have at our disposal a lot of information from existing statistical sources. This level also makes it possible to use the input/output table in order to reconstruct, be it only in a qualitative way, the major transport chains.

When taking the branch of economic activity as an aggregation level for production, we meet the problem of goods classification. The classification must be in accordance, or at least comparable, with the branches distinguished. A uniform classification for all types of statistics does not (yet) exist however. There are good reasons for taking the transport nomenclature (NSTR) as a starting point. Production and trade statistics in the Netherlands do not show a regional breakdown of the national totals, but transport statistics, in accordance with their nature, have a regional entrance. For the analysis of transport chains this is an essential prerequisite. The spatial distribution of the transport chains can be derived from the transport statistics together with the NSTR commodity classification. This classification gives a maximum breakdown according to 170 items, a small number in relation to trade statistics. It is therefore a classification that has to be accepted as a minimum. Each of the 170 items shows an acceptable level of homogeneity and in most cases can clearly be identified as an output of a certain branch of production. This last element is essential when forming links with certain branches of production and consumption. In the analysis of transport chains mentioned earlier, the 170 items proved to be a good starting point for establishing links with production figures. This can be seen as a great step forward in obtaining useful input material for transport models.

For the spatial distribution of the transport chains it appears that an already-existing regional division for transport statistics can be used as a starting point.

A disadvantage of the use of transport districts is that they are to a certain extent not comparable with those in use with, e.g, agricultural statistics. By grouping it is possible to obtain comparable results on a more restricted regional basis.

The choice of an optimal regional breakdown just for the analysis of transport chains appears to be irrelevant. In principle any regional breakdown is possible when analysing transport chains. This means that the choice of the regional breakdown can be made on other criteria, relevant to other purposes of the research worker.

5. TRANSPORT STATISTICS: THE YEARS AHEAD

Transport statistics still have a long way to go in order to be nationally complete, internationally comparable and for the transport economist an absolutely reliable basis as an input in his verbal or mathematical transport models. But the horizon widens.

An explanation of transport flows is only possible when they are seen as a link between two spatially-separated economic activities. Many attempts have already been made to explain transport flows in this way. Statistically the results were often not very satisfactory because the level of aggregation had to be too high. Combination of commodities which have only a certain homogeneity in their technical appearance (farm milk versus factory milk), or which have a similar final use (foodstuffs can be for consumption either by human beings or by animals) or forming the same input in an economic activity (sand and gravel are both destined for the building industry, but their transport flows are quite different) leads to statistical transport flows which cannot be interpreted in a meaningful way or may even lead to —far more dangerous — trivial or senseless conclusions.

To avoid these problems a way has to be found to come to a more consistent statistical presentation of transport chains and transport links as a function of economic activities.

The first attempt will have to be made on the basis of the statistics available. This is, of course, a restriction: they have not been set up for that purpose. But nevertheless, as was shown by the study made in the Netherlands, it is possible to reconstruct the most important transport flows in the national economy, in their relation with the real volumes of production and consumption and with their spatial distribution and modal split.

In some cases it was possible to reconstruct complete chains, from their primary origin to their final destination, including the intermediate technical processes, the transport terminals, the change in modal split and the change in the physical appearance of the commodity.

In other cases the results had to be — on the basis of the available statistical material — of a more restricted character: sometimes a relation could only be established with the inputs or the outputs of a certain technical process, in other cases the goods classification proved to be inconsistent or incomplete.

Anyhow the road for transport statisticians to follow in the years ahead is clear. The new method shows new possibilities, respectively purposes:

1. The relation between volumes of production and the incoming or outgoing transport flows, with their modal splits and spatial distribution, can be reconstructed.
2. The building of an input/output table for the national economy with the intersector relations expressed in physical quantities had as a first attempt a promising result.
3. For many homogeneous products spatial transport patterns with the relevant modal splits can be formed, in any case as a function of total production or consumption.

These purposes form at the same time the broad outlines for the transport statisticians in their future work of improving transport statistics. Once we have a certain set of statistics, as in the case with transport statistics, improvements are mostly related to more or less small items of a mostly technical character. When the horizon widens and new theoretical elements are brought into the picture, the improvements become more important and require a consistent view on the whole process of economic activities in which transport plays a role. It is this general economic approach which will cause the transport statistician to direct his view to statistics of production, consumption and trade. A new view on useful collaboration: that is the challenging future for the new generation of transport statisticians.

ANNEX

Some numerical examples of transport chains

A. *Example of a country-wide distribution from two import regions by inland-waterway transport (IWT), followed by a regional distribution by truck: cereals.*

In the Netherlands cereals are for the greater part imported; domestic production is relatively small. The import flows enter the Netherlands via two regions (Rijnmond and IJmond) and are distributed from these regions over the whole country by IWT. The regional distribution has a two-fold character: on the one hand it is complementary to the regional arrivals by IWT, on the other hand it consists of the local production of cereals. With the aid of transport and production figures a reasonable reconstruction of the complete transport pattern is possible. The main traits of the transport pattern appear from the tables below. In the IWT matrix the two rows from the seaport regions dominate (country-wide distribution); in the truck matrix the diagonal dominates (regional distribution).

Inland-waterway transport from district of loading to district of unloading.

CEREALS   Year: 1975 Unit: 1000 tons*

District of loading**	NN	EN	SL	District of unloading OSN	SWN	R	IJ	OWN	Total
NN	23	5	—	1	—	27	27	1	84
EN	8	13	—	9	3	49	19	5	105
SL	—	—	—	7	—	14	1	—	22
OSN	2	—	—	19	—	2	—	2	25
SWN	2	13	—	32	16	18	9	4	95
Rijnmond	172	519	12	495	251	37	237	263	1987
IJmond	40	101	2	142	15	30	123	77	531
OWN	3	9	—	14	4	26	27	13	95
Total	251	659	14	718	290	203	443	364	2944

* Differences between individual items and totals are due to rounding off.
** Abbreviations, see below.

Inland road transport (truck) from district of loading to district of unloading.

CEREALS   Year: 1975   Unit: 1000 tons*

District of loading**	District of unloading								
	NN	EN	SN	OSN	SWN	R	IJ	OWN	*Total*
NN	396	23	1	6	2	—	1	10	438
EN	12	443	3	8	2	1	18	20	507
SL	1	—	12	15	—	—	—	5	34
OSN	2	6	9	259	13	2	8	—	301
SWN	5	7	—	28	202	12	—	29	284
R	2	6	2	5	9	19	3	29	74
IJ	—	4	—	3	—	6	4	14	31
OWN	3	18	1	17	15	12	13	216	299
Total	424	507	28	343	244	52	47	322	1967

* Differences between individual items and totals are due to rounding off.
** Abbreviations, see below.

B. *Example of a complete transport chain:*

Crude oil and oil products.

Year: 1975   Unit: million tons

Deliveries by tankers of crude oil		109.8
Destined for other countries		57.9
		51.9
Production of crude in the Netherlands		1.5
Available out of imports and domestic production		53.4
Production out of reserves		3.6
Total available (excl. production losses)		57.0
Losses in the production process		2.9
Total available		54.1
Import of products	10.0	
Export of products	33.3	− 23.3
Final total available for home consumption		30.8
Deliveries to the chemical industry	4.9	
Deliveries to ships	12.1	
		− 17.0
Available for distribution in the country		13.8

Most of the quantity of 13.8 million tons was distributed by inland transport, a smaller part by pipeline.

Deliveries of oil products by inland transport:

To:				
NN	0.51	0.06	0.04	0.61
EN	0.92	0.19	0.11	1.22
SL	0.07	0.03	0.12	0.22
SN	0.84	0.16	0.15	1.15
WN	0.62	1.47	0.04	2.13
Total (appr.)	2.96	1.97	0.46	5.33 (B)
In and between production regions	5.2	0.3	1.7	7.3 (A) minus (B)

Regional distribution by truck:

NN	EN	SL	SN	WN
1.0	1.4	0.25	1.4	2.1

Abbreviations:

NN: Northern Netherlands
EN: Eastern Netherlands
SN: Southern Netherlands
OSN: Rest of Southern Netherlands
SWN: South-Western Netherlands
R: Rijnmond
IJ: IJmond
OWN: Other Western Netherlands

TRANSPORT POLICY AND POLITICS

G. Kuypers

1. PLEASANT ENCOUNTER

It may have been modesty. Or fear. Or aloofness. But the fact is, that, traditionally, many economists were, or still are inclined to stop short wherever "their" domain appeared to become "non-economic."

For example, when they meet an objective like "a fair income distribution." What is it? That is not for us to decide, so they reason. That is a matter for other people. For politicians, moralists and whoever else has a finger in the pie. Another example. "Income per capita" can certainly be used as an economic indicator of the prosperity of a population. Answers to the question of how prosperity, measured in that manner, can be increased, are logically two-fold: (1) by increasing the total income and (2) by reducing the number of souls. Economists have a lot to say about the former. Also about the latter?

Professor J.P.B. Tissot van Patot is an economist who did not show this traditional inclination (Tissot van Patot, 1972–73).[1] He started from the idea that "transport policy" is "economic policy" conducted in a sector of the economy, "transport." And, he said, economic policy is a special case of policy in general. A very simple idea indeed. Apparently unassailable. But an idea implying consequences. So many consequences that an economist who realizes them — as Tissot fully did — deserves our praise for his courage.

For what is the case here? An economist who conceives "transport policy" as a special case of "policy in general," when meeting an objective like "good public transport," will not shrug his shoulders. He will nor can stop short because of the term "good." Certainly, he also will point to politicians, moralists and whoever else has a finger in this pie, this time in deciding what is "good" in matters of public transport. Or, perhaps, he will refer to some indifference curve. But besides that, he will do another thing. An economist like Tissot will also point to a wholly different kind of people: political scientists. And that because political scientists are supposed

---

[1] I base statements like this one on a "syllabus," written by Professor Tissot van Patot for his students, not for publication. Its title: "Inleiding tot de vervoerpolitiek" ("Introduction to Transport Policy"), Amsterdam 1972/73.

to study "politics in general." In doing so he brings into the study of economics, a difficult-to-grasp type of practitioner, alongside a difficult-to-grasp type of theorist: the politician and, as if that were not enough, also the political scientist.

Political scientists: what are they? I do not want to say much about them. As far as Europe is concerned, they popped up only after the Second World War. A more long-standing and continuous tradition characterized "political science" in the United States. Suffice it to say that political scientists have their own history, their own organizations, boundless literature and periodicals. They know their own fights about methodology, trends, approaches, diverging frames of reference, changing main problems, jargon (Easton, 1965).[2] Political scientists had and still have to define their position not only towards economists (contacts, dialogues and even collaboration occurred intermittently throughout their past) (Bentley, 1949; Dahl and Lindblom, 1963; Wade and Curry, 1970), but also towards the jurists, psychologists, sociologists, historians ... particularly when the political scientist himself was such a person by training.

For the sake of making acquaintance with the breed, it might be interesting to indicate roughly what political scientists these days worry about. It is about subjects like:

— "What are the relations between the political system and the economic system?"
  Possible backgrounds: general systems theory; or neo-marxism; or welfare theory.
— "Political behaviour: can it be quantified or formalized?"
  Possible backgrounds: the need of social indicators; the ideal of a scholar to become a scientist.
— "Democracy: what is it, and how can we democratize?"
  Possible backgrounds: improving the society we live in; or rejection of that society as such; or power theory.
— "Are there methods or can methods be developed for designing a policy in general?"
  Possible backgrounds: dissatisfaction with the "behaviouristic" past of the discipline and/or the state of the society; or a cacaphony of planning techniques; or a theory about politics in general.

Well, an economist who wants to study economic policy as a case of policy in general and who, for that reason, wants to link up with political science, has many options. Tissot, for one, tried the approach laid down by this author (Kuypers, 1973). I am not the person to say even one word about the luckiness of that choice. I do say that I learned much from the daring

[2] A renowned approach in political science is that of Easton (1965). An interesting periodical is *The American Political Science Review*.

imagination with which he applied that approach. And the reason why I mention the fact is that what will follow shows the way in which not "political science" but "a" political scientist is dealing with a subject like the present one. So it is my way. My apology is that it is a way in which Tissot once joined me, so that now I can join him.

2. WHAT'S IN A DEFINITION

Let us define "transport policy" as a structure (brought about in some process) of ends, ways, means and points of time, chosen by an actor concerning the satisfaction of needs of movement of persons and goods with the help of a relevant system of means of production (Tissot van Patot, 1972–73).

What are the implications of such a definition? How is it justified? What does it lead to? What can one do with it? The first implication is that each transport policy is someone's transport policy. That is to say: there is no policy without an actor. By an actor we mean a choosing or acting person or organized group. Whose policy are we talking about? Who is "the actor of the policy"? There is a clear difference between studying the transport policy of the Dutch government and studying the transport policy of the city of Rotterdam. The transport policy of a multinational enterprise in electronics organizing its own transportation differs in kind from the transport policy of a shipping company or a trucking company. In the Netherlands a promotion group exists, called "Stichting Weg" ("Highway Foundation"), pleading for road construction whenever appropriate: it has its transport policy. Another example, seemingly trivial: we have in the Netherlands a radio programme called "Truck" serving the needs of teamsters and attracting them to the (socialist) broadcasting association in question: it also has a "transport policy" of its own. Nice to ponder over the character of all those different policies.

The second implication of the definition is that each policy is viewed as a "snap shot." What is the structure of choices at a given point in time?

It is clear that the "transport policy" of any government at a given moment may easily differ from its "transport policy", e.g. eight months earlier. If this is your notion of "a policy," then and at any rate you should not call it "a process" (i.e. a sequence of events over time). You should call it "a scheme" (i.e. a picture to be ascertained at a given point in time of actions and situations projected in the future).

A "policy" conceived as above does, of course, not fall from heaven. It came about over time. There was "a process." So we can and we do speak of "the" process of making "that" policy. But we have to distinguish "that policy-making process" very sharply from "the policy-making process" or just shortly "politics" in general. These are concepts which, in spite of their overwhelming popularity, deserve our extreme suspicion. For, if policies differ, why then should not also the processes of their coming about differ? Speaking in such general terms, which policies of which actors at which moments or over which periods are we talking about? Obviously, we then are generalizing, reasoning more or less inductively, but on which grounds?

Granted, in real life the formulation, acceptance, implementation, adaptation, adjustment, silent modification of "a" policy is a continuing story, difficult to analyze. But just for that reason, just to disentangle that confusing "process," science has to develop what many love to call "analytical tools." "Policy" and "the process of making a given policy" as defined above are such analytical tools. No more. But also: no less.

A third implication of the definition is what Lasswell once called "goal-thinking" (Lasswell, 1947). With that kind of thinking economists have been familiar for a long, long time. But political scientists — at least some of them — have spun that out in their own manner. Some characteristics to illustrate this:

Ends and means ("finality") are related (in many ways) to causes and consequences ("causality"). In fact an end is a special kind of consequence, namely an intended one. And a means is a special kind of cause, namely a chosen one, brought about by an actor. After saying "intended effect," you have to say "side effect." And after saying "end," you have to distinguish kinds of ends, such as: "ultimate ends" and "intermediate ends" (from the first to the n-th order). Also you have to relate your concept of "end" to notions like "objective," "norm," "motive," "Utopia," "ideal," "optimum," and so on.

After saying "means" you will discover very soon that in a policy there are more means than only goods and services. Or just "money," for that matter. You will recognize also that nothing is either "an end" as such or "a means" as such. What you end up with is the insight that the important things are not "the ends" and "the means," but the "end-means relationships" and the "means-end relationships" (Baker et al., 1975).[3]

So these are just implications of a seemingly very dull definition. They offer part of the justification for this definition. To repeat one thing: when you define "a policy" as a system of chosen elements (actions or situations), in which each element related to one or more other elements as a means to an end and/or as an end to a means, then you should stop using the term "policy" in the sense of, e.g. "guide-line" or "strategy" for action to be

---

[3] For instance: "significant reduction in gasoline consumption." Is it: "a means" or "an end"? Wrong question. It may be one of the "ends" of a public policy . . . serving the survival of mankind. It may be one of the "means" of the policy of a transport enterprise . . . to keep out of the red. Cf. Baker et al. (1975, pp. 200–201).

Scheme 1. Ends-means tree of a public transport policy (existing or conceived).

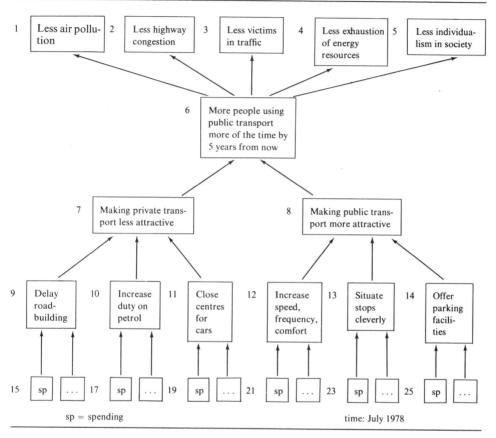

sp = spending

time: July 1978

Actor: the Government

specified later on. For us, a policy is, as of now, a specification of all the choices, not only of actions but also of situations, the actor has made at a given moment.

The rest of the justification of the definition may be presented in showing where that definition leads to, what you can do with it.

It leads to what we call "an ends-means tree." Scheme 1 is an example of a very partial "ends-means tree", a fragment taken from a (not so imaginary) "transport policy" of an imaginary national government.

No policy document, from which such a tree cannot be extracted. No policy design, which does not follow the structure of such a tree, whether upwards or downwards.

It should be noticed, therefore, that this scheme can be read as representing either an existing policy, in the sense that all the elements have been chosen by the actor and that the policy is in the process of being carried out, or as a conceived policy, in the sense that all the elements have been chosen by the designer but not yet by the "actor of the policy" on behalf of whom he is designing.

In both cases the abbreviations stand for more extensively and more carefully phrased formulations (often in quantitative terms), whereas the arrows represent means-end relationships (the point is always towards the "end"). Just for easy reference, the elements in the scheme bear numbers.

3. WHY PLANNING LOOKS WHITE

To begin with let us assume that the model represents a conceived policy. Call it "a plan." It has been designed by an actor, called "the planner," on behalf of an actor we have called "the actor of the policy" in question. In this case: "the Government." By "planning" or "policy development" we mean the process of designing this "plan" or "conceived policy."

The reader will surely be struck by the neatness of the scheme. Take for instance elements nrs. 1–5. Call them "ultimate ends," "concerns," "ideals," "motives" or whatever you like: can anybody be against any of them?

Then look at the causal relationships the planner has foreseen: aren't they plausible, all of them? Is not increasing the duty on petrol (nr. 10) an obvious way to make private transport less attractive (nr. 7)? Does not a change-over to public transport (nr. 6) lead to less highway congestion (nr. 2)? And so on. Pay attention also to the logic of the tree. Of course in order to induce more people to use public transport more often, you will have to do two things: make private transport less attractive (nr. 7) and make public transport more attractive (nr. 8). It is also perfectly logical that no end whatsoever can be achieved without spending at least a certain amount of money: see the elements nrs. 15, 17, 19, 21, 23 and 25 (marked "sp" for spending). The tree shows another remarkable point: it seems to refute any artificial distinction between so-called "economic policy," "social policy," "financial policy" or what have you. For even this very simple example illustrates clearly that policy elements of the most hetero-geneous kinds fall into one and the same self-evident "system."

Label, if you like, one particular policy element as "economic" (nr. 4) or "financial" (nr. 21) or "social" (nr. 5) or "juridical" (nr. 10) or "psycho-logical" (nr. 6) or "technological" (nr. 12) or "physical" (nr. 1) or "ethical" (nr. 3), the fact remains and the really important thing is that in a policy all such heterogeneous elements are united by a very special tie: "ends-means relationships." And that is what makes them "a system."

So the planner has done his work well. He has presented his government

a well-conceived, nice, intelligent, intelligible, logical, cautiously-formu-
lated, realistic, acceptable plan, showing common sense, systematic thinking, inventiveness, creativity and no traces of the (always too narrow)
discipline in which this planner accidentally got his training.

What kind of work did the planner do? It could be described as "an
intellectual kind of work." Dramatizing, you could call it "inventing the
future." Nevertheless, one man could do it. Superficially it seems not too
difficult. Use only your brains and let no one disturb you. Think first of all
in terms of ends and means. And in terms of (future!) causes and effects
immediately thereafter.[4] Estimate probabilities, calculate and weigh costs
and benefits (not only in the strictly economic sense!). Apply standards,
principles, norms. Hopefully, you will not have to choose them, but you do
have to apply them.

In short: how rational a plan can be! Reason seems to reign supreme
here. How enthusiastic a planner may become! Objectivity seems to be his
pillar. Planning, indeed, looks white.[5]

4. WHY POLITICS LOOK BLACK

Let us now assume that literally the same model (Scheme 1) represents an
existing policy. That means: we are now assuming that the plan (formulated
as in the "tree") has been accepted by the government; that the Government
got the approval of the plan from its Parliament. In other words: we now
have to sketch the history of "the process of the formation of this policy."
Or call it "the politics of this policy."

One supposition hidden in this exercise in imagination is highly unrealistic. That is: that the "plan" got off without a scratch. Such a thing almost
never happens. But that does not harm our present purpose. On the contrary, this simplification will be very useful for making my points.

First question: when and where did the politics of this policy begin? Let
us say: when a certain coalition government concluded its "agreement to
govern," one of the points in that agreement being "stimulating public
transport."

---

[4] Some authors claim that the social sciences are able to contribute to the forecasting
of transport needs and the planning of transport investments. See Foster (1968).
[5] It *looks* white. Baker et al. (1975, p. 226): "In the end, the policy analysis procedure
simply provides a method for combining a variety of basic elements of social policy making
in a common framework. Its value is that it provides comprehensive information and in a way
that allows the decision maker to understand and communicate the implications of his
choice-process. In this sense a good policy analysis is neutral and unbiased; it is a tool and a
resource for the policy maker."

Next question: was there any succession in time of "political processes" and "planning processes"? The answer is: no. As always, the designing of the plan was embedded in political processes all the time. Let us see how.

The planning process started with a political act: an instruction from the Minister of Transport to work out a public transport policy according to the coalition agreement. Instruction to whom? The "planner" was not a person but a committee. Because of the interdepartmental aspects of the subject this planning committee was perhaps manned by officials from several Ministries. The first draft however was offered by the member from the Ministry of Transport (see the "tree").

The following scenario will, to begin with, show that there is more politics involved than merely between government and parliament or between political parties or between interest groups.[6]

— The member from the Ministry of Finance: "The costs for improving the public transport system [nrs. 21, 23, 25] have been underestimated outrageously. Besides that, in the next five years there will be no room for additional expenditures in the sphere of collective goods, even on the estimated level."

— The member from the Ministry of Culture (suppose: the first Ministry to suffer cuts in its budget as a consequence of any new project of this kind and also the Ministry which considers fighting against the growth of individualism in society as its main task nowadays): "I firmly support the objections of our colleague from the Ministry of Finance. My Minister will not be misled by the fake of element nr. 5."

— The member from the Ministry of Economic Affairs: "I am strongly against delaying the road construction program [nr. 9]. We cannot afford another spectacular unemployment news item before the provincial elections of next May. Already the Road Builders Association has approached us with fierce warnings. And there is one essential point you have forgotten. Building no new roads will not only discourage the use of private motorcars [nr. 7], there are also trucks on the roads. It will harm the economy."

— The member from the Ministry of the Interior (charged with the relations between the Government and the country's municipalities: "Impossible for us to stress the relations further by asking our biggest cities to close their centres to private traffic [nr. 11]. You do know that we have no competence to oblige them to do that, don't you?"

Faced by so many objections and near-veto's the member from the

---

[6] "The attitude of a public official tends to reflect his office. (. . . .) Public officials of suburban communities perceive the urban mass transportation problem differently from the mayors of central cities": Schneider (1971, p. 250).

Ministry of Transport proposed to reformulate element nr. 6 into: "Less people using private transport more of the time." This principle was accepted by the planning committee. Some days later the designer, working out the necessary changes in the draft as a whole, got a telephone call from his Minister, saying that the Prime Minister had told him to stick to the coalition agreement.

So the original draft was reintroduced in the committee, adopted, sent to the Minister of Transport, accepted by the Cabinet and sent to Parliament. Here we pause for a moment.

Politics is omnipresent. Even in the "white" process of planning there are planning actors, who are playing politics and who are obliged to do so. That is to say: they have powers and use them, one being more powerful than others. The push and pull to defend the interests, or call it the "tasks," the "viewpoints," the "concerns" of the agency which sent them. Everybody tries to win something; nobody likes to loose something. It is difficult to separate the arguments from the use of means of power (promises, threats, warnings, non-coöperation, support, prestige, cleverness, withholding money, rights). Often the officials, rather than the politicians, in the "policy preparation," make the essential compromises. Often it is the official through whom all kinds of societal influences operate.

But politics may even be blacker than that. Let us continue the story, following the policy proposal through Parliament. Here, of course, we find political parties and interest groups.[7] Here we see the classic arena of politics in a pluralistic democracy. A short scenario again.

— The spokesman of the Liberal Party (opposition): "By preparing this policy, the Government only intends to wring still more money out of the citizens. Government knows perfectly well that car owners will pay duty on petrol [nr. 10] so that the congestion on our highway [nr. 2] will not be reduced at all. And if people were to make more use of the so-called 'public' transport [the warm feeling the term 'public' emanates to some people!], then it remains still to be seen whether there would be less air pollution [nr. 1], less victims in traffic [nr. 3] or less exhaustion [nr. 4]. I am not speaking about 'less individualism in society,' which is simply too ridiculous [nr. 5]. This proposal will not be my main argument for demanding this Cabinet to resign, but it certainly adds to my arguments."[8]

---

[7] The diversity of interests and of groups, involved in a policy-formation process on urban mass transportation is shown by a number of those testifying during hearings: Schneider (1971, pp. 255–256).

[8] A member of the American Transit Association: "The federal government gets its funds by coercion from people who live, work and are taxed in all parts of the nation. To force people in Blue Bump, Mississippi, to pay, in their taxes, for the failures of transit to break even or make a profit in Chicago, Milwaukee, Los Angeles, New York or else where . . . is immoral legalized robbery." Quoted by Schneider (1971, p. 257).

— The spokesman of the Center Party (coalition): "I suspect a contradiction in this policy. In general, a government profits heavily from all kinds of vices. The more people drink or smoke or drive, the more a government cashes in. Now, if the duty on petrol will be increased [nr. 10], does the Government then expect an increase or a decrease of the total receipt on this duty? I realize that this question has something to do with the point raised by the member of the Liberal Party, so I would like to hear an answer to his question too. And if the financial advantages from measures in this sector [nrs. 9, 10] are not so certain but have been weighed against the investments [nrs. 12, 13, 14] for the improvement of public transport, which are certain enough, what then will be the consequences for this scheme as a whole?

This brings me to my second question: can the Minister tell us whether any cost-benefit analysis has been made for this project? If so, can he present that to this House? And if not, will he explain why such an analysis was not really feasible in a case like this?"[9]

— The spokesman of the Democratic Party (independent, with some personal connections with the government-owned national railway company): "Public transport systems have not been distinguished clearly enough into urban systems, regional systems and national systems. If this had been done, it would have been evident that the investments provided in this scheme [nrs. 21, 23, 25] are blatantly insufficient for all of these systems. Making my own calculations I have concluded that with those amounts of money you can achieve the necessary minimum for extending and modernizing our present railway system. What I am proposing is to do just that. The argument is clear enough: the intercity highways are congested most and cost most and it is there that most of our quickly dwindling oil resources are being wasted".[10]

— The spokesman for the Socialist Party (coalition, promising freshman): "I support the policy as a whole on behalf of my group as a whole. Now is the time to push back this holy cow, this modern idol, this moving cave of individualistic man, the private motorcar, at least a little

---

[9] "Cost-benefit analysis" is becoming rapidly a fad with politicians and there are a lot of such studies in the field of transport policy. See for example: Morde and Bacon (1967), Arrow and Scitovsky (1969) and Lichfield et al. (1969).

But not every politician will realize that rather severe criticisms were raised recently on cost-benefit analysis, specifically in the field of transport policy. See, for example: Hoos (1972), Self (1975) and Taylor and Hawkins (1972, the contribution of R.A. Long).

One of the critics substitutes his own alternative: a "goals achievement matrix." This "GAM" is applied both to evaluate alternative transport plans theoretically and to a case study of transport plans for Cambridge, England. See Hill (1973).

[10] "Today the railway role has become that of environmental conservator, mainly because it now seeks to exploit through automation the potential capacity of its guided system, within its existing infrastructure. Road and air, on the other hand, now devour and pollute land and air space with increasing social impact." Taylor and Hawkins (1972, pp. 243–244).

bit. Does not the argumentation of this proposal [nrs. 1–5] prove again the truly humanistic character of a more communal way of life?"

(Interruption: "What about cabs?")

"Oh yes, I include cabs. They too are in line with the old principle: "According to one's needs."

(Interruption: "Workers need a cab to go to their weekend camping??"). Therefore, my party . . ."

And so on and so on. Then, after long debates, the ax fell again. The Prime Minister appeared. He informed the House that this policy was one of the four proposals for reforming society on which this Cabinet would stand or fall. So, a majority voted for it. Other political processes had interfered with this one. What does this story add up to? Politics, is it black? Let us put it mildly: politics look black . . . most of the time.

5. WHY POLICYMAKING IS GREY

One thing seems clear: every planning is imbedded in some kind of politics. Every process of conceiving or developing a policy is intertwined with a broader and deeper process of policy making which is essentially a political process. Do we know much about it? It may sound strange, but there are many outstanding authors whose answer is: "No."

"We have the accumulated experience of human history . . . but we are merely beginning to systematize our comprehension of what the process of policy formation is about" (Bauer and Gergen, 1971). "As yet no clear theory or methodology for the study of policy has evolved" (Hofferbert, 1974, p. 24). "The whole issue of rational planning policy in a political context has barely begun to be explored" (Ranney, 1969, p. 165). "Contemporary scientific approaches are inadequate for meeting the requirements of relevance and the needs of humanity" (Dror, 1971, p. ix). "The idea of making 'the policy making process' itself a major focus for specialized inquiry is still so new that no one seems to want to answer the question of what is supposed to be included in the process and what excluded from it" (Lindblom, 1968, p. 3). And all that was said notwithstanding the presence of an overwhelming planning literature.

If and when these things are true, then every new effort in this field should be welcome and none should be called preposterous. It is against this background, that the Political Science Department of the Amsterdam Free University — with some record in the field of "policy analysis" — some time ago started a research project with the name "Methods of Policy Development." We like to explain the objectives of this program in terms of Pendleton Herring's "The Four I's": if politics is made of interacting

Ideas, Institutions, Interests and Individuals, then let us try to disentangle them (Bailey, 1968, p. *x*).

In this connection a strict but cautious analytical distinction—as used above — between "policy development" (a planning process) and "policy making" (a political process), proves itself to be increasingly useful and worth while (e.g. Baker et al., 1975, p. *viii*). This distinction as such, apart from terminology, is certainly an old one. What should be tried, however, is to apply it more consciously, more consistently, more fruitfully.

Although embedded socially, a planning process is essentially an intellectual process. The participants in it are few. That's why it seems to be so "white." The political process however, in which that planning is embedded, is essentially a power process. The participants in it are whimsically numerous. That's why it seems to be so "black."

There are special rules governing a planning process. We call them "methods." They prescribe how a planner could or should design a policy. Methods of policy development vary from rules of the thumb (e.g. "Do it incrementally")[11] to intricate codes (e.g. "Do it on the basis of a cost-effectiveness analysis, which consists of . . . ", etc.).

Essentially different are the rules governing a power process as such. We call them "procedures." They prescribe how a policy or elements thereof could or should be decided upon. They vary from solemn legal norms (such as: "The Congress shall have the power to levy and collect taxes") to unwritten binding conventions (such as: "Before taking a measure, all categories of people who will be affected by it are to be consulted").

Now, "methods" and "procedures" (in this sense), just because of their profoundly differing nature, usually badly interconnected, often clash and put us on the horns of many a dilemma. They confuse us again and again. Nevertheless, we feel intuitively that "a good policy" depends on: (1) "good methods"; (2) "good procedures" and (3) "good mutual adjustment of methods and procedures."

There are catch words characterizing a policy formation process. Some of them refer typically to the involved intellectual processes rather than to the social processes, whereas others refer typically to these social processes rather than to the intellectual processes. Examples:

Policy development specifically: (planning: intellectual)	*Policy making in general:* (politics: social)
— to design	— to decide
— working out something	— fighting for something
— discussion	— debate
— research	— negotiation

[11] Famous term coined by Lindblom (1968, pp. 24–27).

— to convince	— to persuade
— optimum solution	— settlement
— practicability	— acceptability
— team	— coalition
— refinement	— compromise
— viewpoint	— standpoint

Terms like these may help us to analyze what is happening at a given moment. But the discernment of what is an "intellectual act" within a political context is no easy job. When a planner after some research rejects a measure, is it because he doubts its effectiveness or is it because he knows that the measure will be opposed by some important political actor?

Notwithstanding all that, the distinction holds. It works. It is inevitable. It helps us to see why the work of a planner, although his products seldom survive undamaged, is seldom in vain: decision making would be impossible without it. It also throws some light on how and where methods of planning could be improved: not by changing unsatisfactory political procedures (of course, a planner can be instructed to conceive such a change), but by changing unsatisfactory planning methods or by developing planning methods where they are embarassingly non-existent and by changing, resp. developing them in harmony with such improved policy-making procedures as the system in question might have introduced or might be considering. One word in this connection about the popular idea of "communicative planning."[12] We subscribe to it in so far as it combines a modern idea of democracy with a modern necessity of planning. We do not expect much good from it, however, because it confuses what we have called "methods" and "procedures."

Anyway, we can better explain now why "planning" is not as "white" as it seems to be. It is because politics is interfering with it from the beginning. The voices of power are being heard all the time. They speak through the instructions. They speak through the agencies that are represented in a team of planners. They are anticipated by the planner (he has to). They are felt by the planner whenever his work is interrupted by new events ... which are always translated politically.

The reverse is that "politics" is not so "black" as it seems to be. It is because politics thrives on plans. In politics, power is a central and indispensable phenomenon. But too many people have supposed too long that politics is nothing but a "struggle for power." The fact is that much, if not most, politics is described better as a "struggle about policies." And policies incorporate ideas. Granted, ideas are being used to achieve or to expand power, but in the end power is applied — by individuals, in the name of interests, through institutions — to realize specific ideas. So,

[12] Propounded in the Netherlands by, amongst others, Van Gunsteren (1976).

sticking to the terminology according to which "a policy-making process" is nothing but "the politics of a specific policy," we should conclude: the policy-making process is grey.

6. FINAL REMARKS

Returning to our subject of "Transport Policy and Politics": the economic sciences have a lot to say here.

You have to do, first of all, with scarce goods. There is more than one market here. There is "demand and supply" here. It is about investments and returns. And about individual preferences. You can calculate "trade-offs." And so on.

But you also have to do with, first of all, the decision-making processes of a collectivity. And here there is always more than one collectivity. There is a "political system," where, according to Easton, the inputs are "demands and support"; where individual preferences in some mysterious way are converted into social "preferences"; where institutions and individuals associate each idea or interest with a host of others. And so on. If political scientists have something to say, it is about things like these.

I think, therefore, that Tissot was right. Economists and political scientists could and should work together more closely in the future. Especially in the grey fields of policy making.

REFERENCES

Arrow, K.J. and Scitovsky, F., eds. (1969). *Readings in Welfare Economics.* London: Allen and Unwin.

Baily, S.K. (1950; 1968). *Congress Makes a Law: the Story Behind the Employment Act of 1946.* New York – London: Columbia University Press.

Baker, R.F., Michaels, R.M. and Preston, E.S. (1975). *Public Policy Development: Linking the Technical and Political Processes.* New York: John Wiley.

Bentley, A.F. (1949). *The Process of Government.* Evanston: The Principia Press.

Dahl, R.A. and Lindblom, Ch.E. (1963). *Politics, Economics and Welfare.* New York: Harper Torchbooks.

Dror, Y. (1971). *Design for Policy Sciences.* New York: American Elsevier.

Easton, D. (1965). *A Systems Analysis of Political Life.* New York: John Wiley.

Foster, C. (1968). "Future Research Needs of Transport Planners," in Young, M., ed., *Forecasting and the Social Sciences.* London: Heinemann.

Van Gunsteren, H.R. (1976). *The Quest for Control.* London: John Wiley.

Hill, M. (1973). *Planning for Multiple Objectives.* Philadelphia: Regional Science Research Institute.

Hofferbert, R.I. (1974). *The Study of Public Policy.* Indianapolis–New York: Bobbs-Merrill.

Hoos, I.R. (1972). *Systems Analysis in Public Policy.* Berkeley–Los Angeles–London: University of California Press.

Kuypers, G. (1973). *Grondbegrippen van politiek.* Utrecht: Het Spectrum.

Lasswell, H.D. (1947). *The Analysis of Political Behaviour.* London: Kegan Paul, Trench, Trubner and Co.

Lichfield, N. and Associates (1969). *Stevenage Public Transport: Cost-Benefit Analysis.* Stevenage Development Corporation.

Lindblom, Ch.E. (1968). *The Policy-Making Process.* Englewood Cliffs: Prentice-Hall.

Morde, P.M. and Bacon, L.W., eds. (1967). *Operation Research for Public Systems.* Cambridge, Mass.–London: Cambridge Press.

Ranney, D.C. (1969). *Planning and Politics in the Metropolis.* Columbia: Merrill.

Schneider, L.M. (1971). "Urban Mass Transportation: A Survey of the Desicion-Making Process," in Bauer, R.A. and Gergen, K.J., eds. *The Study of Policy Formation.* New York: The Free Press.

Self, P. (1975). *Econocrats and the Policy Process: The Politics and Philosophy of Cost-Benefit Analysis.* London: MacMillan.

Taylor, B. and Hawkins, K., eds. (1972). *A Handbook of Strategic Planning.* London: Longman Group.

Wade, L.L. and Curry, R.L. (1970). *A Logic of Public Policy: Aspects of Political Economy* Belmont, Cal.: Wadsworth.

PSYCHOLOGY — AID OR GUIDE FOR TRAVEL-DEMAND ANALYSIS?

J.A. MICHON

1. THE CRISIS IN TRAVEL-DEMAND ANALYSIS

In recent years travel-demand analysis has become a rather unrewarding affair. Although the mathematical sophistication of demand modeling has increased considerably, and although computers can now handle virtually unlimited amounts of data, the results have nevertheless lost a good deal of their credibility. Only studies at the micro-level seem to have a reasonable validity.

If we look at the assumptions that are characteristically made in traditional modeling the reason for this relatively unsuccessful performance becomes clear. Consider, for example, the Netherlands "Integral Traffic and Transportation Study", a national long-term transport forecast study carried out in the late sixties that took several years and several million guilders to complete. Among the various limiting conditions imposed on the model developed for this study we find, among others, the following restrictions (Netherlands Economic Institute, 1972, p. 14, my free translation):

In the study it is assumed that the government will not change its policy with regard to — among other things — private car ownership and usage, and that there will be no appreciable change in the vehicle tax system or the taxes on gasoline, etc.

In the study it is assumed that in the future traffic participants will continue to react in the same way as they do now, when the circumstances are the same.

Although we must take into consideration that these restrictions were in fact imposed by the Dutch government which sponsored the study rather than by the investigators, it should be clear that such assumptions help to make any attempts at travel-demand forecasting practically useless in the fast-changing society in which we live. Yet, all over the world millions of dollars are still being spent on such studies every year.

Some reasons for this state of affairs have been indicated by Gilbert and Jessop (1977):

— naiveté of the users who believe that the modeling results are suitable for design.
— forgetfulness about the changes over time that are likely to affect the structural parameters of society.
— the size of the investments in time and money to set up a complex model.

The authors continue: "It would perhaps be embarrassing to admit that the resulting forecasts are not valid for a length of time sufficient to cover the construction of large schemes in whose planning they are supposed to be assisting" (p. 128).

Even the road users' naiveté has its limits, however: in several countries the authorities and the public have expressed their worries in a more or less explicit form. And this, in turn, has made the forecasting experts worry too. Thus, Stopher and Meyburg (1974, p. 45) reached the conclusion that "unless models can be developed that can be demonstrated to assist decision making to a noticeable extent, the opportunity to regain respect for travel-demand modeling may be lost for all time."

In short: there is a credibility gap. How did this sad state of affairs arise, and what can be done about it?

2. THE IMPORTANCE OF INDIVIDUAL LIFE-STYLE VARIABLES

Classical travel-demand studies commonly take two main types of inputs. The first consist of geographical or zonal data. The area for which a forecast is made is divided into square sub-areas, or into more naturally delineated sectors. Then the travel between these areas is determined on the basis of extensive observations. Changes in travel over time are predicted on the basis of certain, usually unduly simplistic assumptions about structural changes in each particular area; it may be assumed, for example, that the number of shops will grow linearly over time. The second input consists of socio-economic data, such as income bracket or the number of cars in the household, that are derived from census polls or home interviews.

My contention is that both types of input are gradually becoming ineffective as forecasting variables. The reason is simply that they are becoming socially less and less meaningful. For an increasing number of people the personal and social values that they consider important are not related to the status of their residential area or to their income. Also the demographic pattern of household composition has exploded into unprecedented pluriformity. It appears that *life-style* variables are beginning to dominate the zonal and socio-economic variables that have been used hitherto. In other words, psychological variables are rapidly becoming the important determinants of travel demand.

The increasing importance of individual life-style variables coincides with some recent changes in transportation policy that have emerged in many developed countries.

(1) Until the late sixties government policy by and large followed actual

or expected travel demand. Today the policy is to control or regulate demand. Demand control, however, implies direct interference with individual mobility needs, and the ability to interfere in a democratically-acceptable way depends on a detailed knowledge of the decision-making processes that underlie individual travel patterns.

(2) In recent years travel patterns in the developed countries have become much more uniform due to the general availability of private cars and the massification of, for instance, recreational travel. A clear egalitarian attitude towards the availability of transport has developed and government transportation policy is frequently directed explicitly at further decreasing the still-existing inequality in travel potential (De Boer 1976).

(3) The introduction of citizen participation as a recognized way of communication between the government and the public at large requires considerable sophistication on the part of the authorities in putting to use the information obtained in this way. At the same time citizen participation has considerably increased the need for explicit knowledge of the psychological principles of communication and persuasion.

These trends support the conclusion reached earlier in this section: psychological variables are becoming the principal determinants of travel demand. The consequences for travel-demand analysis will be clear.

3. DISAGGREGATE MODELING

Of course travel-demand analysts have not remained inactive while this general change in perspective took place. In an attempt to deal with individual factors in travel demand in a more appropriate way disaggregate models were introduced. Unlike the classical aggregate models that take grouped average data as inputs, the disaggregate models take individual data. The probability that a particular individual will make a particular trip by a particular transportation mode is determined relative to the set of alternatives available to that individual for making that trip. Disaggregate models require the determination of (subjective) utility functions which are weighed according to the extent to which the individual believes that a particular trip alternative does indeed possess the attributes to which utilities are assigned. On this basis direct and cross-elasticities can be determined (Richards and Ben Akiva, 1975).

While disaggregate models tend to do justice to individual travel patterns and thus conform to the developments outlined in the previous sections, they have one major drawback for which no completely satisfactory solution has been found thus far. This problem is known as the aggregation problem: it is extremely difficult to find a procedure for expanding the individual trip choices into a reliable and unbiased forecast of group behavior. If no simplifying assumptions are made it is even impossible to derive predictions from a disaggregate model.

In the context of the present discussion it is not necessary to take a stand in the issue of aggregate versus disaggregate modeling, an issue that we may qualify as a choice between the Scylla of the unbelievable and the Charybdis of computational intractability. It may be taken for granted that each type of model will produce useful predictions about future travel as long as they are supplied with the appropriate data. In line with the arguments in the earlier sections of this chapter it is assumed that the appropriate data will ultimately have to be psychologically-relevant variables.

4. PSYCHOLOGICAL APPROACHES: AID OR GUIDE

There are two options for the psychologist who is prepared to accept the challenge of providing applicable psychological inputs for travel-demand analysis. One option seems too modest in its pure form, the other may turn out to be too optimistic. The first implies that the psychologist will more or less unconditionally accept that the traffic scientist is indeed capable of providing the most suitable conceptual framework for discussing transportation and traffic problems. Choosing this option the psychologist will act as a behavioral technician and as such may contribute a number of methodological and experimental techniques to aid the collection and analysis of data. The alternative option is to assume that behavioral science, when it is applied to the phenomenon of human travel, could raise a number of relevant problems that may, but need not, coincide with the classical problems. This approach, in other words, could offer a genuine change in perspective, that might well be more in line with the observed changes in travel determinants. Both approaches may yield pragmatic solutions for specific categories of problems, although in the long run the application of psychological methods and techniques will not be terribly fruitful unless fertilized by more substantial ideas derived from psychological theory. The following sections will illustrate this in some detail, as specified in Table 1.

5. REINFORCEMENT SCHEDULES

One of the basic problems of the recent attempts to change the balance between the private automobile and public transport in favor of the latter

Table 1. Summary of illustrative examples of psychology as aid or guide at the aggregate and disaggregate levels.

Level of travel-demand analysis	*Level of psychological contribution*	
	Aid	*Guide*
Aggregate	Optimal reinforcement of desired travel behavior (technique: operant conditioning)	Search for stable control variables that affect actual travel behavior (theory: adaptive information processing)
Disaggregate	Attitude surveys about travel and transportation (technique: attitude measurement)	Behavioral decision analysis of travel behavior (theory: behavioral decision theory)

is the surprising inelasticity of modal choice. Very large changes in trip duration, the cost of fuel, or public transit fares are required before an appreciable change in modal split can be observed. Even free rider-ship and cheap season tickets have frequently turned out to be failures. In a recent experiment, the Netherlands Railways offered some 6,300 season tickets at the very low price of 600 guilders. A ticket entitled all members of a household to unlimited travel by train for one whole year. The experiment was a failure; only 800 households obtained a ticket, predominantly households whose train travel was already well above average. Car-owning households had a much lower acceptance level (24 percent vs. 9 percent).

Similar effects have been observed with car pooling. Car pooling was widely advised and advertised in the Netherlands during the energy crisis in 1973–74, but practically nobody followed the suggestion.

Yet, in some cases successes have been reported in other countries under seemingly similar circumstances. Thus, in Los Angeles a car pooling campaign during the energy crisis was highly successful. In this case however, cars with three or more occupants were granted certain privileges: they were, for instance, allowed to use the special rapid bus lanes on the expressways (Cone and Hayes, 1978). The margin between success and failure of such measures aiming at mobility control may be quite narrow and may depend on the subjective pay-offs involved.

The psychological theory of the systematic manipulation of pay-offs, that is, of reward and punishment to reinforce behavior, known as operant conditioning, is quite advanced. It has even produced a "social technology," especially due to the sustained efforts of B.F. Skinner. Operant conditioning is based on a basic assumption in learning theory that a positive (desirable) outcome of an activity will increase the tendency to perform that activity again, whereas a negative (undesirable) outcome will reduce this tendency. Systematic manipulation of these outcomes therefore provides the possibility to influence the (operant) activities that produce these outcomes.

The methodological strength of this approach is its systematic search for the reinforcing factors that are maximally capable of producing the desired behavior. Surprisingly, there are only very few systematic studies applying these principles to travel behavior (Foxx and Hake, 1977; Everett et al., 1977; see also Cone and Hayes, 1978). In the studies by Everett and his associates, transit riders were offered small token rewards (coupons) that they could use in shops, or for further bus trips. The values and the probabilities of receiving a coupon were systematically varied.

Although, unfortunately, this study as well as the other based on this experimental paradigm have been performed on too small a scale to permit very general conclusions, it suggests three practical points:

(1) Reward, or positive reinforcement, should be given contingent upon the use of public transport *as an alternative* to the use of the private car, rather than upon the use of public transport as such. The latter is likely to attract new travelers rather than to influence modal choice. Also, success should not be measured in bus passengers as is usual, but in the number of moving cars per 100 m in the service area of the public transport authority during the period in which reinforcement is given.

(2) Of course token incentives have frequently been used in various places on an experimental basis. Invariably such experiments were discontinued after some time because of imminent bankruptcy of the transport authority concerned. The available empirical evidence shows, however, that it is possible to design intermittent reinforcement schedules that will keep bus rider-ship at a high level, while being cost-effective or very nearly so.

(3) Rather than offering a small token reward with certain value, it may be feasible to tie the token incentives to a lottery that offers a small chance of a high reward (e.g. the national lottery that most countries have). There is some evidence that many users would favor such a scheme. (The scheme should, of course, be personalized to avoid selling and buying of the tokens.)

Applying this systematic methodology to such a long-standing problem may have the flavor of doing something very trivial. Offering bus riders token rewards in order to increase the use of public transport does not seem a terribly original development, and it isn't. The answer one obtains from an analysis of reinforcement schedules, however, is not *what* one should do, but how one should do it and when. In short, it suggests a systematic and methodical search for the optimal application of something that frequently "even a child might have thought of." Its inherent limitation is that it depends very heavily on *a priori* knowledge about the ways in which people arrive at their decisions to make one trip rather than another or none at all. It offers no help at all in establishing what moves people.

In summary, this approach offers a suitable aid to the optimalization of the control of travel behavior that has already been identified by the transport scientist. It does not really add a new perspective for the discovery of determinants underlying such behavior.

6. STABLE BEHAVIORAL VARIABLES

Psychology offers various theoretical frameworks that each specify a different kind of approach to the determinants of mobility (Michon, 1976). Here I shall restrict myself to only one of these possibilities: one that is based on the assumption that the human organism is to a large extent a system that adapts to its environment and that, in the face of disturbing influences, will try to regain its equilibrium. Acceptance of this point of departure in social affairs, such as travel, requires a major shift in the way control should be exercised. Scitovsky (1976) has recently proposed this adaptive approach as a behavioral foundation for economic theory. In his view the maintenance of an optimal level of arousal or activation rather than drive satisfaction is taken to be man's primary motivational principle. "Comfort derives from being at that optimal arousal level, but pleasure derives from changes in arousal level; and behavior is often governed by habits reinforced by past experience of pleasure, rather than by rational weighting of all the available options" (Lea, 1978, p. 442).

Accordingly traveling people should be considered as problem solvers trying to stabilize certain bio-psychological variables. And if authorities wish to influence travel behavior, they must know which variables impose basic psychological constraints on travel demand. Such variables would qualify as "control variables" in policy making.

The use of time may illustrate this point. Time qualifies eminently as a control variable of the kind we are looking for. People try to stabilize their daily travel at an average of 1.1 hours per day (Hupkes, 1977; Zahavi, 1977), although they will, of course, not always be successful in staying within these limits. The 1.1 hour interval appears to be a stable behavioural measure, related to a basic bio-psychological need for exploring the environment and achieving sufficiently variable environmental inputs. Man shares this need with most higher animals.

The 1.1 hour value holds over a remarkably wide range of geographical and cultural conditions. If people do not succeed in keeping average travel time constant at 1.1 hours per day, stress will result and they will in various ways try to reinstate equilibrium. Thus, in big cities where the distances between home and office may require many hours of travel, special "residential" or "recreational" behaviors may develop: people will, for instance, transform their cars into little living rooms, and when traveling long distances by public transit typical non-travel behavior may be observed. If there are no possibilities for substitute behavior, tensions will build up that may lead to taking a different job, moving, or to political action.

One of the implications of this "law of constant travel time" is that if a community is in a state of equilibrium an increase in the speed or efficiency of the available transportation system will not make them save travel time. Instead they will travel longer distances, thus obtaining a greater freedom for performing a number of activities farther away from home.

Money enters as a complicating factor. People spend not only a constant time budget on their daily travel, but also a certain money budget. This travel-money budget too is remarkably constant. As the distribution of money is not very egalitarian, it is necessary to take people's socio-economic positions into account, but with this proviso the money budget tends to be a stable factor.

Zahavi has proposed that people try to control a combination of travel-time budget (T), and travel-money budget (M). He has expressed this relation formally as:

$$\frac{M}{T} = \bar{v} \cdot \bar{c}$$

in which $\bar{v}$ represents the mean daily speed and $\bar{c}$ the average cost per unit distance traveled at the average speed. The left-hand side of this equation represents what the subject is willing to spend, both in money (M) and time (T), while the right-hand side represents "the product that they would like to purchase from the system supply, in terms of system's performance and the price of using it" (Zahavi, 1977).

In this formulation Zahavi's "fundamental equation of travel demand" offers a framework for describing a large number of mobility-related behavioral tendencies. For instance, it explains the very marked tendency towards fast travel. If people have to rely on slow travel systems, they will exhaust their travel-time budgets long before they have exhausted their travel-money budget. This creates a disequilibrium that can only be restored by buying faster travel. For the individual this means in most cases a faster private car; for households it means *more* cars. For the policy maker, on the other hand, it suggests various possibilities for influencing actual travel behavior. Supposedly people are willing to trade a considerable part of their surplus travel-money budget for a system of public transport that would be considerably faster, one of the major disutilities of public transport being the long relative house-to-house travel time. In Dutch cities, for example, bus trips take on the average between two and five times as long as the same trip made by private transport (Michon et al., 1976).

Time is, of course, not the only stable behavioural control variable. Another candidate is, for instance, the perceptual complexity of the environment, which is presumably kept at an individually- and socially-acceptable level (Michon, 1978). Further analysis of life-style variables that influence travel pattern would presumably uncover other stable adaptive variables.

7. ATTITUDE SURVEYS

Among the few psychological "gimmicks" that have found application in transport and traffic research, attitude surveys are foremost. They are widely applied in almost every large-scale travel-demand study, but until recently they stood apart from the other kinds of data that enter in such studies because there was no way of quantitatively incorporating the results into the models. The attitude survey was mostly used as an aid, a mirror that supposedly reflected the satisfaction of a community with the available transportation facilities. But as happens with mirrors: the reflections will show different images, depending on who is looking into it.

Although the concept of attitude has had various interpretations the generally-accepted definition now is that of Fishbein and Ajzen (1975): an attitude is a learned predisposition to respond in a consistently favourable or unfavourable manner with respect to a given issue (object or activity). This implies that an attitude may be considered as an affective evaluative "loading" towards whatever a person knows or believes about the issue in question.

The rationale behind attitude measurement is the assumption that a fundamental relation exists between the motivations and attitudes that people display towards certain issues and the way in which they behave with respect to these issues. The empirical fact is, however, that there is frequently a considerable distance between what people feel, what they say, and what they do. While fundamental attitude research in the forties and fifties was rather favourably oriented toward the existence of a connection between attitude and behavior, the late sixties brought a period of serious doubt. The results from many well-controlled experiments turned out to be either inconclusive or irreplicable. Sometimes this was attributed to the research method used, sometimes to the theoretical status of the attitude concept. Thus Tarter (1970) concluded that "attitudes as presently conceptualized play no real role in behavior," and O'Riordan (1976) observed that "most polls only monitor weakly-held cognitions, mostly of a socially-acceptable kind, regarding matters that most respondents have thought little about (especially the various implications of their statements) but to which they are to give spontaneous answers, often a very limited array of rather simplistic choices." The upshot is clear: although someone may easily underscore or oppose certain statements of opinion, most of these opinions refer to aspects of the issue that have no particular significance for the person. This should result in variability and inconsistency in the attitudes and the behavioral intentions toward an actual issue.

A further reason why the relation between attitude and behavior is frequently found to be so weak is that behaviors and more particularly behavioral intentions, are also influenced by the normative system held by the subject and by his environment. The influence of social norms is presumably considerable and they are likely to dilute whatever influence of attitudes on behaviour there may be.

Five years ago these insights had almost brought attitude research into a state of theoretical disrepute — although the practical use of attitude surveys did apparently not suffer from this. Due to some important theoretical studies (see in particular those by Fishbein and Ajzen, 1975, 1977) the attitude towards attitudes has recently become somewhat more positive. Fishbein and Ajzen have stressed the point that if an attitude towards some issue is measured and the relation with the behaviour displayed with respect to this issue is to be established, the investigator should take great care in making certain that he is indeed measuring attitude and behaviour at the same level of generality. It is no use asking what one's attitude toward "public transport" is and then measure behavior only by looking to see if one will actually take the special bus to the football stadium on Sunday afternoons. If that particular activity is indeed to be studied one should relate it to attitudes about driving versus public transit riding to football stadiums for recreational purposes. Fishbein and Ajzen have reviewed 109 methodologically "clear" studies and they have produced convincing evidence that there is indeed a high correlation between attitude and behavior in cases where the levels of generality of the behavioral criteria and of the attitude scales are compatible.

This is an important result, because attitude data are now increasingly incorporated as regular variables in disaggregate travel-demand modeling. In particular studies of Golob and Recker (1977), and Recker and Stevens (1976) are highly interesting in this respect. In the field of transportation planning, as in other applied areas, the earlier distrust toward attitude measurement never made itself felt. Hartgen and Tanner (1971) and Sommers (1970), among others, explicitly claimed that attitudes might profitably be used as explanatory variables in models of travel behavior. And even more optimistically Recker and Golob (1975) claimed that "recent investigations of the journey to work indicate that attitudes may be better predictors of modal choice than are traditionally-used objective measures such as time and costs." In this light the recent rehabilitation of attitude measurement seems to be of great importance as it provides the necessary theoretical support for the optimistic opinions ventilated by Recker, Golob, and others, as well as for the recent attempts to use attitude data in disaggregate modeling.

Attitudes seem particularly suitable as inputs to disaggregate models, as they supposedly are among the principal determinants of individual travel decision making. Several authors have indeed undertaken to develop procedures for the disaggregate use of attitude scales (among others Hartgen 1974; Hensher et al., 1975; Westin and Watson 1975). A study by Recker and Stevens (1976) most easily serves as an example, since it provides the most complete and clear-cut description of the problems involved.

The procedure followed in their study consists of several steps. First a factor-analytic condensation of the number of attitudinal scales is obtained. The authors stress that it is necessary that the ultimate factors to be used in the disaggregate model reflect concepts that are meaningful to planners. "Planners necessarily think in terms of attributes such as travel time, waiting time, or even personal security", and in order to be effective as a planning tool the factors should be specified in such a way that they "reflect the policy options available to the planner" (Recker and Stevens, 1976, p. 362). This point of view reflects the position of psychology as an aid in a much too extreme fashion, and it should not be adopted. In contrast one could easily envisage an approach that would provide the planner with new concepts or tools that could prove equally or more effective than the conventional travel time or waiting time.

Once the appropriate attribute scales have been derived from a factor analysis of the attitude survey data, the subsequent steps in the procedure proposed by Recker and Stevens are conventional. Utility functions are derived from the attribute scores and trip probabilities determined by means of the multinomial logit model (Richards and Ben Akiva, 1975). Finally direct and cross-elasticities are calculated. Since they are based on normalized attribute scores, the elasticities are independent of the actual numerical scores assigned by the subject to the attributes.

In their study Recker and Stevens show that attitude data processed in this way can indeed provide policy-sensitive outcomes. Thus, for example, the private car when used for grocery trips in Buffalo, N.Y. showed the elasticities listed in Table 2.

This table shows, among other things that the decision to use the private

Table 2. Elasticities of several attitude factors for grocery trips by private car, according to Recker and Stevens (1976).

Factor	Elasticity
Car flexibility	.549
Car cost	.154
Walking time	.533
Bus status	.780
Taxi cost	.558
Day-time safety when walking	.217

car for a grocery trip depends strongly on the extent to which the person is convinced of the flexibility that private transport provides, and much less on his or her knowledge that it costs more than public transport. The extra personal safety provided by private as opposed to public transport (because of the walking involved) does apparently not (yet) play a considerable role.

For other types of trip making different factors were found to be elastic, but Recker and Stevens indicate that usually one will find only a few subjective perceptions (attitudes) that are sufficiently elastic and at the same time are related to policy sensitive variables. Thus, if (and only if) for a particular type of trip the perception of the private car as offering a high degree of privacy is found to be important, such trips will be sensitive to countermeasures that regulate car pooling. If (and only if) car cost is perceived as important, parking tariffs will be effective.

8. BEHAVIORAL DECISION ANALYSIS

Application of the attitude survey as a psychological aid for the recognized problems of the travel-demand analyst does not exhaust the contribution of psychology in the area of disaggregate travel-demand analysis. In fact, this area can be considered very effectively from the perspective of the psychology of choice and decision making, an area of psychological research that has undergone a rapid development in recent years, both theoretically and empirically. The predominantly normative approach of the past was successfully challenged and psychological processes that underlie observed choice behavior are now investigated in detail (for a comprehensive, recent review see Slovic, Fischhoff and Lichtenstein, 1977). In particular the standard paradigm of comparing actual behavior with the prediction from axiomatic utility theory has, by and large, been replaced by research based on the recognition that people have only limited information-processing capacities that force them to use simplifying assumptions and heuristic strategies to keep their decision trees pruned to a manageable size (see Vlek and Wagenaar, 1979).

Travel behavior seems particularly suited for the possibilities that are offered by these developments. It requires individual decision making on a day-to-day basis. Accordingly travel-demand analysis at the disaggregate level should be based on a thorough behavioral decision analysis of travel patterns (rather than on the customary normative analysis). Recently the Traffic Research Centre of the University of Groningen has embarked on a research project that is aimed at just such an analysis: specifying the processes that underlie the individual's travel decision making and relating them to his actual travel behavior.

Prior to the actual decision analysis subjects are questioned very thoroughly about their travel habits. Also the range of their knowledge about the alternative options and the consequences of choosing them is probed systematically by direct questioning, and by comparing the answers with an "objective" analysis of the real options that are available to each subject. This provides the basis for explicating the subjective representation of travel alternatives, the "travel space" within which the subject solves his trip-making problems; actual trip-making behavior is presumably consistent with the properties of this subjective representation of alternatives.

The actual experiment will begin when we offer the subject a monetary compensation on the condition that he or she agrees to reduce the annual mileage driven in the private (perhaps household) car by some 40 percent, over a period of one whole year. Needless to say, acceptance of this proposal must indeed have a major effect on the mobility of the subject and his or her household.

The size of the compensation is determined by negotiation but must remain within a realistic bracket. The subject is offered a legal contract and if he agrees he is left with the problem of coping with an entirely new situation. From that moment on the subject (and his or her household) will have a difficult time: there will be situations that do not fit the new "travel space", requiring a fundamental change in the old "decision habits" as well as in the mobility pattern that derives from these habits. Such changes will be followed at close range during the experimental period. They reflect the restructuring of the processes that guide travel decision making. The subjects can be observed as they are adapting realistically to entirely new circumstances. By looking at the subjective "travel space" through such a powerful magnifying glass one may hope to find out the necessary details for better understanding of what moves people, thus providing a psychologically relevant underpinning of disaggregate travel-demand analysis that is presently lacking.

9. SUMMARY AND CONCLUSION

When social values change travel-demand forecasting should adapt to those changes. In this paper I have argued that indeed there is such a change, and that it involves a shift from socio-economic factors toward psychological and life-style factors as trip determinants.

Psychology can aid travel-demand analysis both at the aggregate and the disaggregate level, but only to a limited extent. Unless the theoretical underpinnings of such techniques as instrumental conditioning or attitude measurement are brought into play, only a simple technical contribution is to be expected. In Section 5, I already pointed out the intrinsic limitations of the operant conditioning approach. Similar arguments have been raised in the case of the attitude survey. Fishbein and Ajzen (1977, p. 914) suggested that "attitude measurements, even by means of sophisticated instruments, may add little to our understanding of social phenomena," because the necessary correspondence between the attitude measured and the level of behavior to be predicted requires a considerable knowledge about social processes and behavioral determinants.

Psychology can be an aid to travel-demand analysis, but it apparently can only fulfil that role if it is also accepted as a guide at the same time. Consequently, the rhetorical question that served as the title of this contribution must be restated before it can be answered in the affirmative: psychology should be both aid *and* guide for travel demand analysis.

10. ACKNOWLEDGEMENT

The present paper is partly the result of a discussion initiated by the Dutch Transportation and Traffic Research Committee, TNO. It has greatly profited from discussions with C. Wildervanck, G. Kok, E. van Essen, H. van der Colk and C. Vlek, all of the University of Groningen.

REFERENCES

Cone, J.D. and Hayes, S.D. (1977). "Applied behavior analysis and the solution of environmental problems," in I. Altman and J.F. Wohlwill, eds., *Human Behavior and environment*, vol. II. New York: Plenum Press.

De Boer, E. (1976). "Mobiel en niet-mobiel. Een verkenning van de sociale betekenis van ons vervoer," in J. Overeem, ed., *Stedelijk verkeer en vervoer langs nieuwe banen?* Toekomstbeeld der Techniek nr. 21. The Hague: Stichting Toekomstbeeld der Techniek.

Everett, P.B., Hayward, S.C. and Meyers, A.W. (1974). "The effect of a token reinforcement procedure on bus ridership," *Journal of Applied Behavior Analysis* 7:1–9.

Fishbein, M. and Ajzen, I. (1975). *Belief, attitude, intention and behavior: An introduction to theory and research.* Reading, Mass.: Addison-Wesley.

Fishbein, M. and Ajzen, I. (1977). "Attitude-behavior relations: A theoretical analysis and review of empirical research," *Psychological Bulletin* 84:888–918.

Foxx, R.M. and Hake, D.F. (1977). "Gasoline conservation: A procedure for measuring and reducing the driving of college students," *Journal of Applied Behavior Analysis* 10:61–74.

Gilbert, D., Jessop, A. (1977). "Error and uncertainty in transport models." Paper presented to the PTRC Summer Annual Meeting 1977. University of Warwick.

Golob, T.F. and Recker, W.W. (1977). "Mode choice prediction using attitudinal data: A procedure and some results," *Transportation* 6:226–286.

Hartgen, D.T. and Tanner, G.H. (1971). "Investigations of the effect of traveler attitudes in a model of mode-choice behavior." *Highway Research Record* 369. Washington D.C.: Highway Research Board.

Hartgen, D.T. (1974). "Attitudinal and situational variables influencing urban mode choice: some empirical findings," *Transportation* 3:377–392.

Hensher, D.A., McLeod, P.B. and Stanley, J.K. (1975). "Usefulness of attitudinal measures investigating the choice of travel mode," *International Journal of Transportation Economics* 2:51–75.

Hupkes, G. (1977). *Gasgeven of afremmen: Toekomstscenario's voor ons vervoerssysteem* (2 vols.). Deventer: Kluwer.

Lea, S.E.G. (1978). "The psychology and economics of demand," *Psychological Bulletin* 85:441–466.

Michon, J.A., ed. (1974). *Kwaliteitsaspecten van het openbaar vervoer.* Report nr. VK 74–03 (C). Groningen: Traffic Research Centre, University of Groningen.

Michon, J.A. (1976). "Menselijke factoren in stedelijke vervoersprocessen," in J. Overeem, ed., *Stedelijk vervoer langs nieuwe banen*? Toekomstbeeld der Techniek nr. 21. The Hague: Stichting Toekomstbeeld der Techniek.

Michon, J.A. (1978). "Searching stable parameters for the control of human mobility." Paper presented to the *International Association of Traffic and Safety Sciences Symposium on "Mobility for Man and Society"*. Tokyo 19–22 September, 1978.

Netherlands Economic Institute (1972). *Integrale verkeers- en vervoersstudie* (Hoofdrapport). The Hague: Staatsuitgeverij.

O'Riordan, T. (1976). "Attitudes, behavior, and environmental policy issues," in I. Altman and J.F. Wohlwill, eds., *Human Behavior and Environment*, Vol. I. New York: Plenum Press.

Recker, W.W. and Golob, T.F. (1975). "A behavioral demand model incorporating choice constraints," *Advances in Consumer Research* 3:416–424.

Recker, W.W. and Stevens, R.F. (1976): "Attitudinal models of mode choice: The multinomial case for selected non-work trips," *Transportation* 5:355–376.

Richards, M.G. and Ben Akiva, M.E. (1975). *A disaggregate travel demand model.* London: Saxon House Studies/Heath.

Scitovsky, T. (1976). *The joyless economy.* Oxford: The Oxford University Press.

Slovic, P., Fischhoff, B. and Lichtenstein, S. (1977). "Behavioral decision theory," *Annual Review of Psychology* 28:1–39.

Sommers, A.N. (1970). "Toward a theory of traveler mode choice," *High Speed Ground Transportation Journal* 4:1–8.

Stopher, P.R. and Meyburg, A.H. (1974). "Introduction and summary of research recommendations," *Transportation Research Board Special Report nr. 149.* Washington D.C.

Tarter, D.E. (1970). "Looking forward: The case for hard-nosed methodology," *American Journal of Sociology* 5:276–278.

Vlek, C.A.J. and Wagenaar, W.A. (1979). "Judgement and decision under uncertainty," in J.A. Michon, E.G. Eykman and L.F.W. de Klerk, eds., *Handbook of Psychonomics*, Vol. II. Amsterdam: North-Holland.

Westin, R.B. and Watson, P.L. (1975). "Reported and revealed preferences as determinants of mode choice behavior", *Journal of Marketing Research* 12:282–289.

Zahavi, Y. (1977). "Equilibrium between travel demand system supply and urban structure," in *Transport decisions in an age of uncertainty*, Proceedings of the third World Conference on Transport Research. Rotterdam, 26–28 April, 1977. The Hague-Boston: Martinus Nijhoff.

PLANNING OF RAILWAY TRANSPORT AND OF LAND USE: EXPERIENCES AND PERSPECTIVES IN ITALY

F. SANTORO

1. LAND USE PLANNING AND TRANSPORT

It is possible to examine problems of transport and of land-use planning in relation to the progress of theoretical studies and methodologies utilized in this field of research. It is also possible to examine such problems in relation to the actual questions existing for policy and to the solutions adopted in having to carry out transport planning connected with the planning of land use.

For the former, we cannot say that in Italy this kind of study has led to particularly new points of view or to techniques of a substantially innovative character. However, we can say that problems of rational land use, as premises for transport planning, have gained more and more importance in the course of the sixties. Their significance has increased considerably because of the concentration of production in limited areas of some regions of Italy and, above all, because of the expansion of urban centres and regional areas. In Italy, as elsewhere, many economic problems have arisen and their induced effects have become clearly evident in the problems of transport. Many problems derived from the connection of land use with transport planning have become clearly visible as a result of the difficulties met in transport (Collida et al., 1968; Colombo, 1974).

It is evident that transport has been unable to solve all the problems caused by economic growth. Such problems could be solved only by general economic planning, which would also include the perspectives of housing settlement and population growth. In this kind of planning, transport could be treated as only one element among many others.

Real transport planning has had a difficult start. General regulations and procedures to carry out a planning process both for economic activity as a whole and for transport have been lacking in Italy. Initially, it was necessary to set up, in 1970, autonomous regional governments and administrations and then, in 1972, to acknowledge their competency in economic planning and land use in order to establish a broad direct connection between land use and transport planning programs (Ministero del Bilancio, 1969). At the same time, this has led to an advancement in related research and technologies.

Methods followed in this field of research are obviously very complex and their results depend mostly on the capability and experience of the staffs that are to be appointed by private or public organizations to carry out the studies.

Research on land use, so important for transport planning, is producing an improvement in this field that will leave a mark on scientific methods relative to this kind of economic research (Del Viscovo, 1976; Brambilla, 1973). Furthermore, the connection between the variables that characterize economic growth and those that more directly concern the field of transport are thoroughly examined in this way. Of course, also in Italy, deep doubts accompany the effort to quantify the effects of the growth variables on transport needs and hence on the programs for the development of the transport system. The consciousness that the complexity of economic life does not allow us to simplify relations in the real world is actually widespread. Defects are deeply rooted in every methodology. Besides we can observe that even where sophisticated techniques have been used to draft complex transport programmes, it has been impossible to complete such programmes because of the limited resources that can be allocated to them.

Looking at the past, we can say that, for many of the questions solved through the use of advanced methodologies, common-sense foresight could have been sufficient. We can say that normally it is enough to note previous deficiencies and gaps in order to know what to do.

2. ITALIAN PLANNING EXPERIENCE

Looking at previous experiences of Italian transport planning and at the criticism they have been subjected to, we can certainly formulate some conclusions.

First, planning has gone on only for separate transport sectors; secondly, planning has not caused rational land use (Caglozzi, 1975; Cecchini, 1973).

We cannot reject totally this kind of criticism, especially that pertaining to the harmonization of separate sectorial plans (Fiorentini, 1977). We must recall a few facts in order to bring at least the criticism within proper limits, especially for what pertains to development necessities of regional areas.

First, the Italian transport system, in all these years, has satisfied transport demand trends and their specific propensities. In such a way one of the more criticized aspects of Italian transport policy can be justified: the development of road and private transport have been excessively favoured. On the other hand, nothing too different from what has happened in other countries has happened in Italy. By preferring private road transport, possibilities of investment in other sectors, especially railways, have been limited. Good results have really been achieved by specific railway planning, and large amounts of funds have been spent, but it cannot be stated that all the necessary improvements proposed at the beginning have been obtained. As the funds that were assigned appeared to be insufficient because of increasing costs, many projects had to be postponed.

A second observation is that general economic plans, especially those related to the southern part of the country, have been disappointing failures. Mistakes have been made in national planning and uncertainty has marked the dimensions, time, and areas for economic development, causing serious doubts with regard to the formation of transport plans.

Once again a well-known difficulty to those who have to deal with problems of transport planning has appeared: transport facilities have to precede economic growth, but the direction and dimension of this growth cannot always be clearly outlined in advance. Particularly such uncertainty in transport planning has had a large influence in the destiny of the South, as it was unthinkable to build new railway lines in order to face the transport problem raised by industrial growth as it has been promoted in those regions (Santoro, 1977). Hence the necessity of modernizing the existing railway network, increasing its traffic capacity to meet the increase of transport demand and providing a better quality of the services, attainable by an improved standard of the railway installations. But also on this point, although the railway plans have always foreseen the necessity to reserve a great share of funds for improvements in the South, financial resources, however, have never been sufficient and the problem of the railways in the southern areas is always on the agenda of Italian transport policy. In conclusion, even if more funds had been available than those foreseen in the sixties, when the country became aware of the necessity to make a big effort to increase the southern railway network, there would have been serious delays in the realization of the programmes. The same can be said concerning other targets of increasing the potential of the railway network, such as regional area services and rapid and sufficient connections with both ports and foreign railways. As a consequence, the possibility of a more penetrating railway policy with respect to land-use planning and its economic organization has been sensibly reduced. These efforts to carry out economic development and transport plans are and continue to be, in their interrelationship, a subject of the most lively debate.

3. THE ROLE OF THE REGIONS IN THE FIELD OF TRANSPORT

Before examining the Italian experiences in transport planning, either drafted or in the process of formulation, some indications are useful with regard to the effect on transport of the regional administrative system which came into being in Italy in 1970.

The creation of regions was provided for in the Italian constitution but it had always met obstacles which had delayed their establishment. Only at a certain point did the conviction that this important reform in the Italian constitutional system should take place prevail. Certainly political considerations have influenced the decision, but certain demands derived from economic planning in general and transport planning more in particular have also acted in this sense.

General economic planning started in Italy with the quinquennial plan 1966–70. It has provided the opportunity to start regional planning policies as a means to reach an integrated national planning, which looks not only at national economic developments but also at problems of the single regions.

The insufficiencies of the Italian transport system were more visible in regional than in national matters of transport. In the regions, the picture showed numerous defects in transport and raised the belief that the direct power of regional authorities could achieve evident advantages.

Maybe it was too optimistic to believe that a reinforcement of regional powers was sufficient to assure a good regional communication system. Certainly nobody could foresee that in transport alone regions had to deal with so many difficulties, as they do now. Neither is it exaggerated to say that among the many reasons for the creation of regions was the intention of a direct intervention in the planning of land use and in the organization of transport.

For a long period before the creation of regions, a pre-eminent attention had been given to the transport system in the programmes of the political parties, of the trade unions, in many conferences, and in the national press. This was a proof of the general dissatisfaction widespread among the users of urban and metropolitan transport services and a clear sign of the deep crisis in this sector (Cirenei, 1972).

In urban transport the most striking difficulties were caused by the increase of transport demand and the insufficient equipment to meet it. The evident problems were, first of all, those caused by congestion, involving extra costs and inconveniences to car drivers. Solutions and plans had been suggested to correct the disequilibrium between the demand for transport services and their supply through reducing mobility. Therefore, it was necessary to develop an adequate development plan for regional areas.

First of all, regions were compelled to face up to this double set of problems, both connected to the expansion of regional areas. Therefore, Italian legislation regulating the competencies of the regions in the field of transport has to be judged on these premises. The extent of the jurisdiction laid in the hands of the regions is certainly larger than would have been required by the sole needs of this particular sector, and this because of the links of regional transport both with regional economic development and with national traffic.

4. RAILWAY TRANSPORT IN NATIONAL TRAFFIC

A considerable part of the regional legislation concerning the metropolitan areas is devoted to transport activity, especially railways. It may be noted that the idea of setting up a General Transport Plan had arisen from railway planning. In the railway sector planners meet the most complicated problems.

We can approach these problems according to three different aspects: (1) the contribution of regional governments to the formation of transport plans and especially to railway plans; (2) action by the regions in the field of railway services; (3) the direct intervention of the regions, i.e. in substitution of the State administration (Bordusio, 1974; Talice, 1976).

The regional administrations have no legal jurisdiction in the programming of railway development, but since their beginning they have participated in the formation of plans for the improvement of the railways. The results of this participation have been very positive. Some people were suspicious about this participation, fearing that the regional governments would favour commuter lines in metropolitan areas at the expense of railway planning that would have to be concerned with national and international traffic and with economic development viewed on a national basis. This fear has been dispelled and we can be certain that in the future the participation of regional authorities in the formation of the General Transport Plan will not cause a serious inconvenience.

5. THE REGIONS AND THE MANAGEMENT OF RAILWAYS

The initial idea which was to provide the regions with a large power in reorganizing transport in metropolitan areas has led to the inclusion, in the sphere of regional legislative activities, of regional bus lines (ANAC, 1972). Such a competency is exercised through concessions granted to private transport firms or by setting up new public managing agencies, such as public consortiums, regional corporations, etc. Also new possibilities for the regions to intervene in railway transport have been created. The regions can intervene directly in matters of railway lines at present granted to private companies and even of secondary lines of the state railways which are not of much interest for transport seen from a national point of view. Moreover the regions can intervene in services of a regional character that take place on lines that, because of their national character, can never be separated from the state railway network.

Complex and delicate problems have arisen from this tangle of both state and regional competency in dealing with this group of lines whose budgets often show large deficits and continually require the support of public funds. As yet the regions have avoided assuming the management of regional railway lines and it is doubtful that despite their power to intervene to improve this branch of transport they may be interested in managing lines that are in great financial difficulties.

At present it is urgent to analyze accurately the problems of these local railway lines that were built in the nineteenth century when other technical alternatives to railway transport were non-existent and the railway represented the only means of modern transport. In any case, the imminent drafting of the General Transport Plan should solve this preliminary problem which concerns, after all, the role of railways in the metropolitan areas. It is reasonable to foresee that some of these lines will be confirmed in their regional role, and will also assume a new importance in urban transport. Consequently, these lines will be modernized and their capacity increased. Other lines, however, should be eliminated and the railway services should be taken over by bus lines which can prove to be more suitable and less expensive.

6. NEW RAILWAY LINES FOR REGIONAL TRANSPORT

The expansion of the metropolitan areas and the increase of commuting movements of regional masses — workers and students especially — have made the building of new railway lines on the regional level, either independent or linked with urban transport lines, an urgent need (Clerici, 1968).

At present we cannot say what lines will be considered necessary and will be really built in the future. In the early seventies the push in this direction has become more impelling. The accelerated growth of many large areas of the country has given rise to important problems in regional communications, at least in the ten largest urban areas. Scenes of congested road traffic in these big centres and their surrounding areas seem to leave no other alternative but to provide services of modern railway lines particularly equipped for this kind of circulation. Some regional plans for economic development have underlined this need. The most recent developments in the Italian economy, stricken by both temporary and structural crises, and the subsequent decline in road traffic, have lessened for some time the pressure for these initiatives. If the process of economic growth will start again, the problem of regional communications, the construction of new lines, and a new policy must be decided upon. According to some experts, it would be more convenient if initiatives for new lines which could be used for other users of transport besides workers and students, should be taken within the whole of the network of the State Railways. But if metropolitan lines with specialized passenger facilities are decided upon, the best solution would be that of initiatives from outside the State Railways, to be undertaken by the regional authorities, who are in charge of short-distance communications.

7. ACTION TAKEN BY THE REGIONS WITH RESPECT TO RAILWAY TRANSPORT

The existing network of the State Railways still plays an important role in regional traffic. In this field there are numerous problems, of which the technical ones are predominant. It is the general opinion that these railway services are now working in an unsatisfactory way, but their improvement involves a number of interrelated problems. So there are serious difficulties determined by the insufficient capacity of fixed installations and still more of the railway lines themselves, account also being taken of the peak-hour needs of local services. Clearly long-distance traffic and freight traffic interfere with this kind of services.

A specific programme has been prepared by the State Railways to ameliorate this situation, and part of it is being carried out. The program will be carried out completely when the long-term plan prepared in 1976 will come into effect. This plan now awaits inclusion in the General Transport Plan.

On the whole the initiatives taken by the railways are able to improve regional communications, through upgrading goods and passenger stations and above all through doubling and quadrupling lines. These are now the most important works to increase the capacity of the Italian railway network.

More in general we cannot say that the railways are setting about solving by themselves all the problems of land-use reorganization in the regional areas. Nor can we say that in such a way the railways are setting about solving the problems of economic development in the regional areas. This would not be the specific role of the State Railways, for they could not entirely deal with such a task even if it were to be decided to use the railways as an instrument for reaching those purposes. In any case, how the transport problems in regional areas must be faced and can be solved more economically is still an open question. And if new lines are needed, it is not at all clear that it is the State Railways that should provide for them.

Of course regional planning involves a wide range of problems and the contribution of the railways to their solution is very important. In any case, it is necessary to stress that railway projects included in the plans for regional economic development have a limited importance with respect to the regional transport requirements. The contribution of the railways to the development of regional traffic will depend for the largest part on the fulfilment of the specific programmes contained in their multi-annual plan.

8. THE ROLE OF THE REGIONS IN THE MANAGEMENT OF RAILWAY SERVICES

The regions will also have to intervene in organizing railway services on lines which, by their nature and connection with the national railway network, can never be transferred to regional jurisdiction.

If we consider commuter movements, only part of this traffic takes place on lines having a regional function, and could therefore, after fulfilment of certain conditions, be transferred to regional jurisdiction. The largest part of railway services of a regional character is carried out on lines of the national rail network. The regions have been unwilling to take over the management of the typically regional lines. The real problem concerns the extent of the power that could be given to the regions as regards the running of these railway services and the question of what can be done to make these services more useful to the needs of regional movements. It is just here that a greater understanding of the complex needs of the management of an entire railway system is more desirable. On the other hand, it is equally desirable that railways should satisfy as much as possible the needs of regional economic organization, because of the new responsibilities of the regions in the transport sector and their role in regional, economic, and land-use planning.

To facilitate a better understanding, in some regions specific committees have been formed; in other ones, the relations between railways and regions have been improved by direct contacts. Unfortunately, the laws that regulate the powers of the regions in the field of transport have not established specific regional agencies for co-ordination and in many cases the effects of their absence have been felt.

9. THE FUTURE OF PLANNING IN THE FIELD OF TRANSPORT

For the planning of transport and economic development the most pressing problems at present are those concerning the formation of the General Transport Plan and the long-term railway plan, which will have to be integrated into the General Transport Plan. The new long-term railway plan has been preceded by a set of limited plans in which the more urgent problems caused by insufficiencies in the Italian network as a modern transport system have been faced as they turned up. In the government acts dealing with the provision of funds, the aims to be pursued in increasing the capacity of the network have been indicated; namely, the improvement of traffic with foreign railways and with the major ports of traffic in the South and of that within the regional areas.

Specific criticism of some part of these programs can be advanced, but on the main point here in discussion — the close connection of railway plans with the development of regional economies — the general outlines of railway planning are beyond discussion. The main purpose of the railway plan was in fact the upgrading of the existing network (infrastructure and rolling stock). The criticism has been that by this policy no propulsive effects on production and trade would be obtained. However, it would already be much if in this way obstacles deriving from railway insufficiencies could be overcome. More positive results could not have been expected from plans sustained by limited funds.

An important turning-point in Italian transport planning that opened the way to the planning of a new conception and of a larger dimension occurred in 1974. For both intentional and accidental reasons, Italy has entered a new phase, in which transport planning came to manifest itself in a broader perspective.

According to an Act adopted by Parliament in 1974, the railways had to present a new comprehensive plan, ultimately in 1976, that would have to take account of all requirements in this sector. Criticism in Parliament stressed that once again the government was following a policy of sectorial instead of overall planning. Therefore, the Act provided that the railway plan would have to be inserted in the General Transport Plan.

The long-term railway plan was drafted and presented in 1976 as a corollary of the plan of 1962–72. But the most noteworthy point is that now the General Transport Plan is considered as the primary instrument of general transport planning and as a point of confluence of economic planning in both national and regional spheres. At the same time, the policy of land-use reorganization, especially by the regions, will enable the attainment of concrete results. At present we already have the long-term railway plan, but not yet the General Transport Plan. For the moment, we must wait for the results of new studies and reflections on transport planning in Italy.

10. THE RAILWAY PLAN: OUTLINES AND CRITICISM

The State Railway Plan is meant to increase the network capacity of the major lines and to standardize this capacity in order to provide for a bigger volume of traffic and to improve the quality of services. The programme's primary design is to operate in the fundamental sector of the railway network (the great dorsal and cross lines), i.e. where the greater share of Italian railway traffic is concentrated today. The concentration of Italian railway traffic is indeed very high: 80% of railway movements take place on one third of the network.

Improvements of lines which play a complementary role are included in the programme. Secondary lines, which really sustain a limited traffic and whose survival has been frequently discussed in the past, are not included, on the condition, however, that these lines are not relevant to specific programmes of economic development. This is not the only point that has recently caused criticisms, but undoubtedly it touches upon a preliminary question. It has been observed that the railway plan is not connected with the general transport programme. This is true; but as we mentioned before, the railways had to present their own programme within a certain time and preceding the General Transport Plan. Of course, the railway plan will in any case have to be compared and checked with all the projects in transport planning. Another observation regards the premises of the railway plan. The plan has been based on some hypotheses of traffic growth in order to foresee what may be necessary to meet such growth. However, it has been objected that this is the wrong method of planning, because there is no clear proof that the enlargement of the capacity of the railway system will produce a stimulating effect on the economy. According to such criticism the State Railways have been presenting a plan viewed from the interests of the railways, but not a plan integrated with land-use planning and related to economic development. This criticism has also been made for that part of the plan that more in particular concerns southern Italy.

The criticisms that have been mentioned are mostly based on a clear misunderstanding. To widen the traffic canals by making them adequate both to the quantitative and the qualitative needs of the future transport demand means also to face the needs of future economic development. Nonetheless the railways are still conscious of the natural limits of the effects of railway initiatives which derive from the economic features of the railway system, especially concerning its cost. Aside from other considerations, it must also be noticed that railway programmes are expected to satisfy needs which cannot be neglected at the level of national interest and which deserve, on the contrary, priority in their satisfaction. Here we have to recall again the needs of communications with foreign countries, ports, metropolitan areas and so on. Furthermore, other initiatives in communications, in order to promote economic development in areas that do not possess good links with the national railway network, could not be included in the plan because they require so much funding that it is doubtful whether they could be completely carried out within a reasonably short period. On the other hand, serious doubts exist that railway construction can really foster regional economic development in an age in which railway transport becomes convenient only for high-volume traffic—this kind of growth being completely unlikely for the backward areas in Italy.

For these reasons we cannot criticize the plan of concentrating only on the main lines of the railway network also in the southern regions. It is correct to avoid the risks of expensive programmes in areas which will not be able to support mass traffic in a foreseeable future. The railway plan could not ignore and does not ignore the need of increasing the capacity of the southern railways, but it considers them with reference to the major lines in southern Italy where the traffic meets more difficulties than in any other part of the network. This problem is particularly serious, because in the South transport is more dependent on the railways than in the other parts of the country.

11. TRAFFIC CONCENTRATION

Some people assert that by the new railway plan a policy of traffic concentration is pursued in a stronger way than in the past.

In many ways, such a criticism is well-founded. A first remark concerns the plan's exclusion of lines run at present on the basis of private concessions or of governmental management. It may be remembered in this regard that the diversity in management does not prevent connections with main lines and with services which are being produced by means of old and well-known forms of co-operation.

We must leave aside political motives that may lead to nationalization determined only by the fact that for these minor railways both public and private initiative can exist.

If certain tendencies regarding alternatives for the programmes included in the State Railway Plan will prevail, some of these local lines might be transferred to the State network. The problem concerning lines granted to private companies, however, is not to transfer all of them to the State Railway network, but to decide which lines have to be kept and brought up to an adequate working standard, especially if they have to play a distinct regional role, and which have instead to be taken over by road services. It is the General Transport Plan that will take care of this matter. There is also the possibility of assigning their management to the regions. Therefore, a sufficiently wide range of solutions still exists.

A parallel problem — and a parallel criticism — exists for the smallest State lines that not only are left out of consideration in the State Railway Plan for what concerns the improvement programmes, but even are considered to be eventually closed and replaced by road services. This subject also will be treated in the General Transport Plan, in order to establish which of these lines will still have a role to play, especially in regional communications.

12. ALTERNATIVES FOR RAILWAY CAPACITY INCREASES IN THE MAJOR LINES

In facing the problem of increasing the capacity of the great Milan–Naples dorsal, which sustains the biggest share of Italian railway traffic and which is the basic line of North-South communications, the railways have been following a rational policy. At present the traffic over this line is already considerable. An annual increase of a certain measure will cause difficulties in absorbing the traffic, and therefore quadrupling of sections where capacity is insufficient will become necessary.

Following this line of thinking, the capacity of the Rome–Naples line has been increased and traffic from and to southern Italy now requires only the construction of a direct line avoiding Naples. The new direct line from Rome to Florence is already in an advanced stage of construction. The State Railways then only will have to quadruple the Florence–Milan line Works for reaching that purpose have already started. It is not true that in this way a mere company interest is being pursued. On the contrary, because of this programme the principal Milan–Naples line will be brought in a better condition for dealing with the future traffic increase. It is also clear that the interest of the regions and of economic activities using this major railway line will be served by making traffic easier and cheaper.

The development of other lines, however, could offer valid alternatives to those put forward by the railways. In such cases, other areas of Italy would benefit from improved communications, and the capacity increase of the railway network would be more widespread.

It is logical that, at present, the far-sweeping dimensions of capacity increasing programmes proposed in the long-term railway plan do revive some old proposals and stimulate new ones. Such a gigantic plan as the long-term one conditions many other initiatives; therefore, it is necessary to consider each of them carefully, independently of the scheduled time of their realization. Strong pressures towards alternative solutions, and the prospect that the completion of the new Rome–Florence line could absorb funds originally assigned to other works, have led to the decision of giving up the last section from Arezzo to Florence.

The idea of variant lines, as opposed to the improvement of existing major lines, is certainly a fascinating one, both because it would allow the improvement of communications in other zones of the national territory and because of the broader possibilities for railway transport itself. Moreover these proposals are in harmony with a tendency which appeared in Italy some years ago, when the doubling of congested sections of the "Autostrada del Sole" was proposed. The advantages derived from new railway itineraries would still be greater, because the natural risks connected with concentration of operations in only a few railway junctions would be reduced. Above all, however, the needs of a more efficient land use would be better satisfied by providing more rapid communications in large regional areas which at present are being served by inadequate railway communications.

The comparative costs and the feasibility of these solutions are still unknown. We can only hope that these questions will be examined in detail by railway and regional planners in preparing the General Transport Plan. In particular, studies and investigations are necessary in order to consider and evaluate single projects before their inclusion in the more general planning of communications in Italy.

13. THE PLANNING OF TRANSPORT TODAY

Many times we have mentioned the long-term State Railway Plan in which the future railway network is extensively surveyed. Under the most favourable circumstances, the plan could be carried out in about ten years, but considering the difficulties of providing it with public funds, we can foresee a longer period. We have also mentioned that the General Transport Plan which, on account of its comprehensive character, should integrate the railway plan and the highway plans, should also include ports, alpine tunnels and airports, and that it should provide for new arrangements of urban infrastructures, at least those connected with the more relevant kinds of transport, especially of a regional character.

Such a plan involves complex problems of various sorts. Among these are the institutional problems, because it has still to be decided which central administration will have the authority to harmonize single-region plans and to make the choices which have to be made. Furthermore, the way of eliminating contrasts that can arise between regions and the development of criteria necessary for ranking the priorities of initiatives included in the General Transport Plan, in view of the impossibility of financing all projects, still have to be determined.

Greatest attention must be paid not only to the last mentioned topics, but also to other ones of a more general nature — those touching the essence of the planning which is being undertaken with the General Transport Plan.

First of all this is an operation based on more than one framework of planning. One is certainly on the national level. In this context are to be mentioned policies concerning the development of the national economy, with themes such as the growth of traffic with foreign countries and the connections with seaways. Then problems of development of the southern regions must be solved and the needs of modern transport in a country with the particular length and geographical shape of Italy must be satisfied. It would already be much if, because of prompt financing, the most difficult projects could effectively be started. Above all, the difficulty presents itself to determine the correct point in which a transport development programme can function as a stimulating factor in economic growth. This point can be discovered and mastered. Doubts rise, however, in relation to the functioning of the General Transport Plan concerning regional planning and more in particular the regional planning of land use.

The planning that the regions are about to undertake in the field of transport has to start from a preliminary land-use planning. The alternative possibilities in this respect are logically of a considerable breadth. We cannot exclude that in such operations there is a tendency to exaggerate, because of possibilities and hypotheses that may never be realized or may be carried out only in a distant future. The regional budgets are not directly concerned in this matter and therefore there is no limitation in projecting such programmes.

Certainly the present moment in which an extensive planning is undertaken by drafting a General Transport Plan is the least favourable one for urging large projects. No indication can be provided at the moment about the real needs; only for what concerns the railways we can point out that their long-term plan requires investments amounting to 20,000 billion lire (price level 1976). And probably this will not be the largest requirement, as compared with what can be expected in all sectors and at various levels, including the regional plans.

It is easy to foresee that in the future a limited supply of funds could cause quite a few disillusions to those people who, in 1974, when the railway plan of 2,000 billion lire was passed, saw a favourable moment and the best opportunity for promoting a general planning of transport.

REFERENCES

ANAC (1972). *Le autolinee in concessione per il trasporto di persone.* Rome.
Bordusio, A. (1974). "Rassegna di legislazione regionale in materia di trasporti," *Le regioni.*
Brambilla, F. (1973). *Teoria matematica dei trasporti.* Rome: Centro Studi sui Sistemi di Trasporti.
Cagliozzi, R. (1975). *L'ammodernamento delle ferrovie e il ruolo del trasporto ferroviaro nel Mezzogiorno.* Milan: Giuffrè.
Cecchini, D. (1973). *Trasporto stradale e struttura insediativa nel Mezzogiorno.* Milano: Giuffrè.

Cirinei, M. (1972). "Trasporti di massa," *L'Impresa Pubblica.*

Clerici, A. (1968). *Le ferrovie al servizio delle aree metropolitane.* Milan: Ciriec.

Collidà, A., Fano, P. L. and D'Ambrosio, M. (1968). *Sviluppo economico e crescita urbana in Italia.* Milan: F. Angoli.

Colombo, V. (1974). *La ricerca urbanistica;* Indagini primarie. Milan: Giuffrè.

Fiorentini, F. (1977). *Trasporto e territorio.* Milan: F. Angeli.

Ministerio del Bilancio (1969). *Progetto '80: Rapporto preliminare al programma economico nazionale 1971–1975.* Rome.

Piano Poliennale di sviluppo della rete FS (1976). Rome: Documento del Ministero Trasporti, Direzione Generale delle Ferrovie dello Stato.

Santoro, F. (1977). *Politica dei trasporti.* Milan: Giuffrè.

Talice, C. (1976). "Il trasferimento delle funzione amministrative nella materia dei trasporti terrestri", *Stato e Regioni,* UTET.

Viscovo, M. Del, and Naddeo, A. (1976). *Modelli econometrici per la domanda di trasporto.* Rome: Centro Studi sui Sistemi di Trasporti.

DEVELOPMENTS IN THE RESEARCH ACTIVITIES OF THE EUROPEAN CONFERENCE OF MINISTERS OF TRANSPORT

A. DE WAELE

1. INTRODUCTION

The editors of this Festschrift have asked me to contribute this short article for two reasons. First, in their view the European Conference of Ministers of Transport (ECMT) has developed into an important platform for research and study of the various aspects of transport economics and transport policy; a survey of the work performed in this respect would, it seemed to them, be interesting in itself. Second, they wanted to know if particular trends were discernible in ECMT research work at the international level, or if any would be desirable particularly with reference to the relationship between research and the formulation of political opinions and the taking of political decisions within the framework of the ECMT.

2. THE ECMT AND ITS RESEARCH ACTIVITIES

The ECMT was established as a forum for the Ministers of Transport of 19 European countries by a Protocol signed in Brussels in October 1953.

The Ministers meet as a Council twice a year, the agenda being prepared by a Committee of Deputies, assisted by a Secretariat which has its headquarters in Paris.

The aims of the Conference are:

(a) To take whatever measures may be necessary to bring about at general or regional level the maximum use and most rational development of European inland transport, this being a matter of international importance.

(b) To co-operate and promote the activities of international organizations concerned with European inland transport, taking into account the work of supernational authorities in this field.

The regular research activities of the ECMT started in 1964 when the first symposium was held. In response to a suggestion made in 1963 by the late Mr. Louis Armand of the Académie Française on the occasion of the commemoration of the 10th anniversary of the foundation of the Conference, the Council decided to organize a symposium to be attended by representatives from various walks of life (universities, business, transport) on the general theme: "Theory and Practice in Transport Economics" (ECMT, 1965). The theme was subdivided into three series of specific topics: the progress made in the theory of transport economics, the relationship between theory and practice and the role of quantitative knowledge and econometrics.

These subjects which were discussed at the first symposium are still topical 15 years later during which time 7 symposiums and 44 round table conferences have taken place and a wealth of research information has been assembled. Similarly, ECMT Council meetings have discussed a large number of subjects which have been noted with interest by research workers and those concerned with practical applications. In addition to the original matters discussed since 1964 research subjects have been introduced over the past 15 years and these have tended to supplant some of the older ones. It would be interesting to study these changes of emphasis and to seek an explanation for them in the changing requirements of policy makers but this is beyond the scope of the present article which seeks to establish whether the abundance of study and research results has made any real contribution to the quality of political decision making and the factors which are at issue in this process. A summary of the research and study topics handled in the symposiums and the round table conferences is annexed to this article. This summary is sub-divided according to the nature of the topics treated and in a chronological order. So it becomes possible to have an opinion about the interest these different topics had and at what time.

3. DEVELOPMENT TRENDS

An analysis of the themes of the symposiums and round table conferences reveals several clear development trends. This is less so where other developments are concerned since they are not so obvious in themselves, although they have influenced ECMT procedures. We shall return to this point in both of the following sections.

In the beginning, programmes contained topics concerned with methodology and issues of a very general nature, but these gradually gave way to more specific themes and topics with a more direct bearing on actual problems. The four main reasons for this can be set out as follows:

(a) after several years general and methodological topics proved to be incapable of providing any new insights. In any case it was found desir-

able to leave such topics temporarily in abeyance before tackling them
again in the light of new data or insights;

(b) topics of the type mentioned, in view of their nature, failed to arouse
a great deal of interest among the political organizations of the ECMT,
which tended to see them — not always justifiably — as academic
exercises on the part of theorists and therefore not entirely appropriate
to an institution endeavouring to adopt practical measures for the
improvement of international transport (see the aims mentioned in
Section 2);

(c) it was found desirable to link the research and political activities of the
ECMT more closely together. The political side urged that the research
aspects of a particular issue should be dealt with before political discussions took place, with a view to making available in the political
committees the results of preliminary studies as well as the outcome of,
for instance, the round table conferences;

(d) the energy crisis and the subsequent economic changes increased the
need for better information. In other areas, too, more acute transport
problems have presented themselves in recent years, some examples
being: the evolution of the division of duties between the various
branches of transport; the more efficient use of available space; the
time factor in transport; protection of the environment and developments in the sphere of employment conditions.

A parallel development, to a certain extent influenced by the above
factors, was the introduction of a two-tier documentation system within
the ECMT consisting of an electronic system for obtaining and passing
on information on important publications and a system for keeping a
record of current research activities. By means of this system requirements and gaps in research could be more easily pinpointed, and
current activities brought into line with needs.

4. PROCEDURES

The co-ordination of the scientific and political approaches to the issues
being dealt with is without doubt of prime importance and it is indeed
constantly being striven for, although in practice co-ordination is no easy
matter. Once a theme has been agreed upon, one or more experts or institutions must be found with sufficient scientific knowledge to enable them
to deal with the subject. The new system of documentation has proved
particularly valuable for this purpose but recent research work is not
always available on themes which suddenly become the object of political
interest. Even given the most favourable circumstances, the preparation

and compilation of preliminary documents takes a considerable time. An adequate international discussion panel has also to be formed, representing as many countries as possible and covering the various avenues of approach (government, business, universities). On the other hand, the urgency with which a topic needs to be discussed does not make any allowance for the time which needs to be spent on research and preparation. For this reason it is not always possible to base a political debate on thorough and detailed research, as could be seen in the recent rapid development of transport links with the Near East: when this issue reached the political agenda there had been little research carried out on it.

Precisely because there is a time lag between setting up research and conducting political debate on the basis of its findings, the attempt should be made to set the research in motion at the earliest possible moment and those carrying out research should recognize the importance, including the political importance, of a particular problem as soon as possible. In fact, however, it is usually only the public authorities who can authorize research work of this nature and it is therefore their responsibility to see to it that delays are avoided at the outset.

5. INTERACTION BETWEEN THEORY AND PRACTICE

As we have already indicated, the problem of effectively integrating theory and practice has not yet been solved but the ECMT is working on solutions on several fronts. If the issue is viewed realistically, it must be admitted that progress to date has been disappointing; at the same time it must also be recognized that the conditions of true interaction are not easily fulfilled.

First and foremost, political decision making within international organizations is exceedingly complex. It is scarcely realistic to require, or even expect, of research that it should contribute to the solution of problems as such and at the same time take into account political realities which usually produce factors extraneous to the topic itself and which in many cases differ from country to country. This does not mean, of course, that research should not be fully alive to the complexities of international political decision making.

The study — known as "Action 33" — on future long-distance travel requirements in Europe is, in our view, an example of research being very much on the ball. According to the terms of reference the study, undertaken by twelve countries from 1973 to 1976, was: "to assist the participating Member Countries in the task of devising long-range strategies to meet the growing demand for passenger transport between major metropolitan regions of Western Europe." By developing four different strategies Action

33 was able to demonstrate the possibilities of a realistic and integrated policy which formulates the often vague aims more explicitly and shows more clearly ways in which these aims can be realized by means of specific combinations of government measures. International activity is at present restricted to the co-ordination of analyses of the study's findings at national level. However, it is not inconceivable that individual countries will have a preference for a particular strategy ("scenario") and that political diversity will again prove to be a barrier to integrated international transport policy as far as both infrastructure and operation are concerned. It therefore seems reasonable to see Action 33 as simply a preliminary activity to be followed by further advisory studies; after all it is necessary to study requirements in this respect regularly and perhaps even to go further and study other aspects which are much more difficult to quantify, such as the motives of travellers. This would facilitate analysis of specific requirements as well as decision making with respect to infrastructure based on this analysis.

On the general issue of insufficient integration of theory and practice, it may be postulated that many misunderstandings and obstacles to progress could probably have been avoided in the past if both concepts had been more clearly defined since, on closer acquaintance, they have very little to do with highly-developed ability to abstract or a thorough grasp of reality. Seen in these terms, something which is not particularly interesting is often dismissed as irrelevant theory and "practice" becomes synonymous with a lack of vision whereas it is in fact a question of a different approach: the difference lies in the fact that research tends to place an issue in a broader framework with respect to related aspects and to the time factor.

The first attempt at integration confirmed this diagnosis. When the political authorities requested that conclusions be drawn from research work which were capable of application to the practical situation, "seminars" were introduced, i.e. working groups of civil servants were formed to discuss the findings of the round table conferences with a view to deciding whether they were practicable.

It soon became clear that this procedure was too concerned with "quick successes" and that important areas of the sociology of meetings were ignored. In fact, the recommendations of the round table conferences did not become any more applicable after being "filtered" through the seminars; indeed, in some cases the procedure was counterproductive in that knotty problems were simply eliminated.

In reality a political body cannot be expected to turn a scientific report into something that can immediately be translated into action.

What is required is a collective will to absorb the contents of such reports in order to promote a type of collective awareness. In addition to this and more often than not following upon it there must be a political will to look for solutions, engendered by the collective awareness.

The development of an awareness of this type is, however, obstructed by the fact that not many policy-making officials subject themselves to a type of "*éducation permanente*" in their own disciplines. To exaggerate a little, it could be said that in a society where more is written than read; many a responsible public official relies on expertise dating from his student days, roughly twenty-five years ago. When this happens, outdated ideas tend to colour both thought and action and more up-to-date knowledge is not exploited.

6. FUTURE DEVELOPMENTS

The division between concept and action, research and practice is obviously not conducive to good decision making and should, at least as far as officials assigned to the preliminary work on decisions are concerned (who are not therefore tied to a political mandate), be eliminated.

The question is how? Any institutional distinction between "thinkers" and "doers" only creates more barriers. The most efficacious solution would appear to be the fusion of the two tasks. A step in the right direction would be to ensure that the official concerned had a sound up-to-date academic background, thereby eliminating the time lag between a study and the action based on it as well as the psychological barrier which so often prevents the assimilation of someone else's know-how. Of course, such an integration at the personal level cannot be achieved completely and certainly not overnight. Once it has been accepted as desirable, however, it can be gradually given more definite form: by suitably modifying procedures and by taking a critical look at the criteria used to assess the operation of the official hierarchy.

In the next few years, the aspects touched upon here — which are of prime importance in the development of research activities and their interrelation with policy making — will need to be treated as a separate overall issue — and this applies not only to work carried out within the ECMT.

ANNEX

*Main themes of ECMT economic research activities**

1. *Transport policy and organization of transport*
   (a) *Transport policy and economic policy*
       — Possibilities of applying the principles of the market economy in the transport sector (S 1).
       — Utility of transport from the social point of view. Social costs in transport economics (S 1).

— Effects of specific government intervention on the organization and efficiency of transport concerns (S 3; RT 22).
— Role of transport in an anti-cyclical policy (RT 41).
— Transfers through the transport sector; evaluation of re-distribution effects (RT 48).

(b) *Transport plans and organization*
— Methodological studies for the establishment at the national and regional level of overall transport plans (RT 15).
— Changes in the planning, organization and finance of transport required for the 1980's (S 5).
— General transport plans: methods, gaps and prospects (RT 27).
— Organization of regional passenger transport (RT 35).
— Decentralization and regional environment (passengers and freight) (S 8).

(c) *Organization of international transport*
— Re-distribution of economic activity and trade; transit and infrastructure (S 8).
— Infrastructural capacity problems raised by international transit (RT 45).

(d) *Transport statistics*
— Transport and national accounts (S 1).
— Indicators for evaluating transport output (RT 43).

2. *Investments, regional development, land-use planning*
(a) *Choice of investments*
— Criteria governing the choice of investments (S 1).
— Analysis of the factors governing the choice of investments to determine the basic criteria. Optimum scale and programming (S 2).
— Application of modern methods (with special reference to planning, programming, budgeting techniques) to the choice of investment projects (RT 10).
— Cost-benefit analysis (RT 36).
— Choice of investment priorities (S 7).

(b) *Investments and land use planning*
— Transport and regional problems; mutual influences (S 1).
— Transport in conurbations, considered as an integral part of regional development policy (S 3).
— The impact of infrastructure investment on economic development (RT 4).
— Impact of infrastructure investment on industrial development (RT 25).

— Land-use resources and transport (S 6).
— Transport systems and regional development (S 8).

3. *Transport and Energy*
   — Raw material resources and transport (S 6).
   — Costs and benefits of general speed limits (RT 37).

4. *Transport and Environment*
   — Social costs of urban road transport (noise and pollution) (RT 18).
   — The impact of transport on the quality of life (S 5).
   — Costs and benefits of general speed limits (RT 37).
   — Mobility and life style (S 8).

5. *Demand and behaviour of the transport user*
   (a) *Passenger transport*
      i. *Determination of demand*
         — Characteristics of supply and demand (S 1).
         — Components of demand and need in the transport market (S 2).
         — Elaboration of models for forecasting demand and need in the transport sector (RT 5).
         — The impact of high-speed ground transport on demand (RT 8).
         — The impact of changes in society on the demand for passenger and freight transport (S 5).
         — Passenger transport demand in urban areas. Methodology for analysing and forecasting (RT 32).
         — Evaluation of demand (S 7).
         — Forecasting demand (Action 33).
         — Mobility and life style (S 8).

      ii. *Modal split*
         — Choice of mode of transport (RT 3).
         — Choice between individual transport and public transport: psychological factors; influence of the organization of transport and of prices (S 4).
         — Determination of elasticities of demand for the various means of urban transport (RT 13).
         — Influence of cost, quality and organization of terminal transport and interchanges on the choice of passenger transport mode (RT 19).
         — Psychological motivation (RT 34).

    iii. *Demand and the factor time*
- Theoretical and practical research on an estimation of time-saving (RT 6).
- Economic problems of traffic peaks (RT 29).
- Value of time (RT 30).
- The influence of a high-speed network (Action 33).
- Holiday traffic (RT 44).
- The impact of high-speed ground transport on demand (S8).

  (b) *Transport of freight*
- Economic implications of the development of productivity in the transport field for an economically-efficient distribution of goods traffic between the various modes of transport (S3).
- Studies (notably from the econometric approach) of factors determining the demand for freight transport (RT 16).
- Demand for freight transport — practical results of studies on market operation (RT 20).
- The impact of changes in society on the demand (S 5).
- Evaluation of demand of freight transport (S 7).
- Redistribution of economic activities and trade; transit and infrastructure (S 8).
- Evaluation of the behaviour of shippers and forwarding agents (S 8).

6. *Urban transport (see also 4)*
  (a) *Supply of transport*
- Influence of the existing transport infrastructure on the choice of techniques to provide modern urban and suburban transport lines (RT 17).
- The impact of innovation on the supply of passenger transport (S 5).
- Freight collection and delivery in urban areas (RT 31).
- Scope for the use of certain old-established urban transport techniques (trams and trolley-buses) (RT 38).
- Semi-collective transports (RT 40).
- Scope for railway transport in urban areas (RT 47).
- "Social service" transport: school and works buses; transport for elderly and handicapped persons (RT 51).

  (b) *Public and private transport policy*
- Price policies in public transport and subsidy problems; technical possibility of special taxation according to the congestion caused by private users (S 2).
- Basic economic problems of urban transport (RT 2).
- Economic criteria for the maintenance, modification or crea-

tion of public transport services which may not necessarily be profitable (S 4 and RT 24).
— Economic problems of traffic peaks (RT 29).
— Optimal use of transport networks (S 7).
— Influence of measures designed to restrict the use of certain transport modes (RT 42).
— Tariff policies other than road pricing for urban transport (RT 46).

(c) *Transport and urbanism*
— Transport in conurbations, considered as an integral part of regional development policy (S 3).
— Impact of the structure and extent of urban development on the choice of modes of transport (RT 28 and 33).
— Mobility and life style (S 8).

7. *Combined transport*
— Impact of innovation on the supply of freight transport (S 5).
— The economic influence of containerization of transport systems (RT 21).
— Changing patterns of economic activity and trade; combined transport: technical, economic and commercial aspects (S 8).
— Scope for the various kinds of combined transport; importance of trans-shipment technology (RT 53).

8. *Railway transport (see also 5)*
(a) *Role of the railways and the future*
— The efficient participation of the railways in the market economy (RT 14).
— Impact of innovation on the supply of transport (S 5).
— Economic problems of traffic peaks (RT 29).
— Optimal use of transport networks (S 7).
— Prospects for a European high-speed network (Action 33).
— Infrastructural capacity problems raised by international transit (RT 45).
— Scope for railway transport in urban areas (RT 47).
— Economic prospects for railways (RT 39).

(b) *Tarification*
— The benefits and costs of government intervention in the normal process of setting freight transport prices (RT 22).

(c) *Social problems*
— Effect of productivity and technological progress on transport workers (RT 26).
— Human factors and transport (S 6).

9. *Inland-waterways transport (see also 5)*
   — Economic criteria for determining the capacity of the fleet of inland waterways with a view to obtaining an optimum balance between supply and demand (RT 12).
   — Effects of productivity and technological progress on transport workers (RT 26).
   — Human factors and transport (S 6).
   — Competitive position and future of inland-waterway transport (RT 49).

10. *Road transport (see also 5)*
    (a) *Supply of transport and road infrastructure*
       — Economic criteria for determining the capacity of goods transported by road with a view to obtaining an optimum balance between supply and demand (RT 11).
       — Impact of innovation on the supply of transport (S 5).
       — Economic problems of traffic peaks (RT 29).
       — Optimal use of transport networks (S 7).
       — Holiday traffic (RT 44).
       — Infrastructural capacity problems raised by international transit (RT 45).
    (b) *Tarification*
       — Allocation of infrastructure charges (S 1 and S 2).
       — Pricing the use of infrastructure (RT 7).
       — The benefits and costs of government intervention in the normal process of setting freight transport prices (RT 22).
    (c) *Structure of enterprises*
       — Effects of specific government intervention on the organization and efficiency of transport concerns (S 3).
       — Optimum structure and size of freight transport firms; positive and negative effects of specialization (RT 23).
11. (d) *Social aspects.*
       — Effects of productivity and technological progress on transport workers (RT 26).
       — Human factors and transport (S 6).
       — The working conditions of professional drivers; effects on productivity and road safety (RT 52).

---

*S 1–S 8: Symposia held in the period 1964/79.
RT 1–RT 44: Round tables held in the period 1968/78.
RT 45–RT 52: Provisional round tables planning for 1979 and 1980.

(e) *Safety in road transport*
   — Costs and benefits of road safety measures (RT 9).
   — Costs and benefits of general speed limits (RT 37).
   — The working conditions of professional drivers; effects on productivity and road safety (RT 52).

REFERENCES

European Conference of Ministers of Transport (1965). *International Symposium on theory and practice in transport economics*, Strasbourg 5–9 October 1964. Paris: OECD.
Organization for Economic Cooperation and Development (1977). *The Future of European Passenger Transport* (Study undertaken in liaison with the ECMT and EEC) Paris: OECD.

TRANSPORT AND LOCATION: AN INQUIRY INTO PRINCIPAL EVOLUTIONS

W. WINKELMANS

The principal concern of this paper is to show that "transport" as a locational element merits our full attention. First of all it seems to be one of the most important location factors in the context of the locational decision making of large firms, and moreover in the framework of a regional economy and for development policies it often becomes a driving force, a kind of stimulus for the creation of a growth pole.

Therefore, in this paper transport (facilities) will be discussed not only from the point of view of an individual enterprise, but also in connection with agglomeration economies and the creation of industrial complexes.

1. INTRODUCTION TO THE RELATIONSHIP BETWEEN LOCATION FACTORS AND LOCATION RESEARCH

Location theories aim to elucidate and at its best to operationalize the process of locational decision making, i.e. by analyzing and weighting locational influences and interdependences of various factors, motivations and conditions, which determine the final choice of location.

The prime *theoretical bases* on the location of economic activities are to be found in the work of Von Thünen (1826) and Weber (1909). Basically the main problem to be solved was the minimization of production costs; in our context this means determining the site(s) with the lowest costs.

After Weber many authors — e.g. Predöhl (1925), Engländer (1926), Ritschl (1927), Palander (1935) and Hoover (1948) — concentrated more and more on a total cost concept, whereas others, such as Hotelling (1929), Smithies (1941) and Lösch (1954) finally became aware of the interdependence of the location factors (the so-called locational interdependences).

Note that the principal difference between "site with the lowest cost" and "total cost concept" is primarily a question of mentality, i.e. of "knowing" that the optimal location need not always or necessarily coincide with the location where all "known" production costs are minimal. In other words, the latest location conceptions are much more dynamic in character, although the words of Lösch (1954, p. 16) remain true: "Dynamically there is no best location, because we cannot know the future."

Furthermore practically all these considerations remained highly theoretical even in spite of the rationality behind them.[1] It is indeed self-evident that in reality any location factor is to be considered in relationship with almost all other relevant location factors, because several are strongly intercorrelated (Winkelmans, 1973, pp. 288/90).[2]

Empirically, however, the study of location aims at practical conclusions with respect to the factors, motivations, conditions and situations which determine the choice of a certain site.

By means of comparisons between industries, sectors and regions, theoretical knowledge about the location issue may be extended. In this context it is advisable to distinguish between general and specific location factors. The former are forces operating on a national or regional level. By definition they apply to all industries or sectors (think of social and fiscal regulations). The latter are particular to a sector or even subsector (think of energy and transport demands) and therefore often will direct an activity to a particular region (see also Greenhut, 1956, p. 103). "A locational force of no great significance to one kind of plant (indeed) can be of critical significance in a different type of operation" (Chinitz and Vernon, 1960, p. 136). Consequently it might be interesting to know as much as possible about changes in both the absolute and relative rating values of the various location factors.

Our classification of location factors as a function of time (see Table 1) gives some theoretical information in this respect.

(1) For the general factors there are $5 \times 10 = 50$ possibilities of quotation. The actual number of quotations, 21, therefore gives a quotation ratio of approximately 40%.
    For the specific factors the number of possible quotations is $24 \times 10 = 240$. The quotation ratio therefore is approximately 60%. The conclusion is that general factors are less quoted than specific factors. In recent years apparently there has been a change in this respect, which in fact relates to the growing influence of government.
(2) Most specific factors are still quoted many times; some receive more attention, like the psycho-social factors, and others are little or less quoted, such as those relating to additional financial advantages.

Anyhow, statements like the above remain too vague and, more important, are not always even in correspondence with the practice of location decisions.

Therefore it is necessary to make *inquiries* per kind of industry or business. Not all industries however are equally location-dependent. The question of *location-dependence* is a rather tricky one. For a long time many

---

[1] As a typical example the general location equations of Lösch (1954, pp. 95–7) may be quoted; in theory full account was taken of the reality of interdependences, but in practice it was not possible to solve the system.

[2] The importance of locational interdependences and/or interactions was also brought forth by our factor analysis of various location patterns (Winkelmans, 1977, p. 151).

Table 1.   Classification of location factors as a function of time.

G *General Factors*	L*	18	47	56	61	61	63	68	68	69	70	Σ r
		1	2	3	4	5	6	7	8	9	10	
G1 Fiscal policy		—	1	1	—	—	—	—	—	1	1	4
G2 Parafiscal policy (government loans + subsidies)		—	—	—	1	1	—	1	—	1	1	5
G3 Governmental regime and regulations		1	1	—	—	1	—	1	1	1	1	7
G4 Communicational facilities		—	—	—	—	1	—	—	—	1	1	3
G5 Climate		—	1	—	—	—	—	1	—	—	—	2
Quotation ratio G-factors: 42%		1	3	1	1	3	0	3	1	4	4	21

S *Specific factors*												
S1 Transport conditions	S1	1	1	1	—	1	1	1	1	—	—	7
S2 Transport (costs) — transport ways	S2.1	1	—	1	—	1	1	1	1	1	1	8
— raw materials	S2.2	1	1	1	1	1	1	—	—	1	1	8
— product markets	S2.3	1	1	1	1	1	1	—	—	1	1	8
S3 Labour conditions — quantitative	S3.1	—	1	1	1	1	1	—	1	1	1	8
— qualitative	S3.2	—	1	—	1	1	1	—	1	1	1	7
S4 Labour costs	S4	1	1	1	1	1	1	—	—	—	1	7
S5 Production conditions — sites	S5.1	—	1	—	—	1	1	1	1	1	1	7
— energy	S5.2	1	1	1	—	1	—	—	1	1	1	7
— water	S5.3	—	1	1	—	1	1	—	1	1	1	7
— pollution control	S5.4	—	—	—	—	1	1	—	1	—	—	3
S6 Production costs — cost prices of S5	S6	—	1	1	—	1	1	1	1	—	1	7
S7 Agglomerations — industrial	S7.1	1	—	—	1	1	1	—	1	1	1	7
— industries annexes'	S7.2	1	—	1	—	—	1	—	1	1	1	6
— commercial	S7.3	—	—	—	—	1	—	—	—	1	1	3
— research	S7.4	—	—	—	—	—	—	1	1	1	1	4
S8 Additional financial — subsidies	S8.1	—	—	1	—	—	1	—	—	—	—	2
advantages — fiscal	S8.2	—	—	1	—	—	—	—	—	—	—	1
— capital needs	S8.3	1	—	1	—	—	—	—	—	—	—	2
S9 Psycho-social factors — social climate	S9.1	—	—	1	—	—	1	—	1	1	1	5
— economic climate	S9.2	—	—	1	1	—	—	—	1	1	1	5
— life climate	S9.3	—	1	1	—	—	1	1	1	1	1	7
— personal reasons	S9.4	1	1	1	1	—	1	1	1	1	1	9
— contacts	S9.5	1	—	—	1	—	1	1	1	1	1	7
Quotation ratio S-factors: 59%	Σ c	11	12	17	9	14	18	8	16	17	19	141

L:

1. Groothoff (1931, p. 50).
2. U.S. Department of Commerce (1947, pp. 1–3, 8).
3. Greenhut (1956, p. 317).
4. Nourse (1968, p. 10).
5. Schilling (1968, p. 8).
6. Vanneste (1967, pp. 302–5).
7. Schröder (1968, p. 179).
8. Stedenband Twente (1968)
9. Davin (1969, pp. 896–904).
10. Falise and Lepas (1970, p. 107).

people believed, e.g., in such a thing as the "seaport-linked" industry. After analysing thoroughly the phenomenon of seaport industrialization in Antwerp and Rotterdam (Winkelmans, 1973) it became clear that at most one could speak about "port-directed" industries and then only for very few industries. In other words other location factors than merely (sea) transport factors are equally involved in the location decision process. Schröder (1968, pp. 137–142) arrived at 14 location-dependent industries against 15 location-independent ones on the criterion that the location-relevant costs, viz. the transport-, energy-, fuel- and water-supply costs, represent at least 5 percent of the total output.

In the same year Nourse (1968, p. 18) put forward that cost information is insufficient to determine the most profitable site. Many location factors are often of decisive importance, but do not always appear as such in the production cost structure of the enterprise.

Security considerations with respect to energy supply, special facilities with respect to transport, etc., may be quoted in this connection.[3] Enlargement of the sales market is another example. In other words: besides pure cost factors of location, cost-reducing factors as well as revenue-increasing factors are to be taken into consideration. In view of the increasing importance of the "agglomeration economies" such secondary location factors, which are indeed closely tied to the phenomenon of the economies of scale — which is the very basis of the agglomeration economies (Nourse, 1968, p. 85) — can not be neglected any longer in the framework of location theory.

The emphasis placed upon the traditional location factors has indeed been shifting since the post-war years, most of all in connection with alterations in the supply of raw materials, energy and water. These three elements have also been influenced by radical *changes in transport technology.*

Dynamically seen few industries or firms are optimally located (cf. also Lösch, 1954, p. 16), because the chance always exists that due to unforeseen or unexpected circumstances the location finally chosen will become less attractive or sometimes even become a serious drawback.

Indeed: "What we really want to know for different locations is the relative level of production costs, freight rates and other costs *for a quarter of a century ahead,* as well as the long-run distribution of markets and supply sources" (Chinitz and Vernon, 1960, p. 126). In other words, this is something impossible!

But, precisely for that reason, i.e. with a view to adaptation possibilities, the question arises of what the factor "transport" means in the framework of location theory and research.

[3] In the feasibility study of the North Sea Island Project, the factors "availability of energy sources" and "sufficient area" got high mean ratings, and fairly low standard deviations (Winkelmans et al., 1974, Table A2–10.3–T2).

2. THE LOCATION FACTOR "TRANSPORT" IN RELATIONSHIP WITH THE LOCATION DECISION PROCESS

For Weber the main question in his general location theory consisted in finding the minimum *transport cost sites* ("die Transportaufwandsoptimal-orte"). He believed that transport was a kind of vital force in the framework of location, or as Holmes (1930, p. 31) said: "the all-time leader in plant locations." Meanwhile much has changed. Greenhut stated (1956, p. 279) that "most reflections on plant location over-emphasized the locational importance of the transport and processing cost factors".

The declining role of transport as a factor in plant location (Barloon, 1965, p. 170) was in a certain sense a logical consequence of the idea that many of the location factors are not at all cost-related. In other words the optimum location will not be realized by optimizing only transport costs. At least one should take into consideration the substitution possibility between transport costs and the prices of other production inputs.

For that reason Isard (1956) introduced into location theory the concept of "*transport input*," which was according to Schärlig (1969, p. 22) a more than valuable contribution to location theory ("une idée très profonde, et certainement une des principales contributions de Walter Isard à la théorie de la localisation optimale"). Interesting to know is that initially Isard called this notion "distance input" (Isard, 1949, p. 489). Isard's change in opinion was in fact the result of becoming conscious that not only "distance" but also additional factors, such as terminal facilities, are important in view of site selection. Before this Ohlin (1973, pp. 191–199) had indeed already shown that in fact it is transport relations, not distance relations, that have economic importance. In other words the transportability of goods and products is often more important than the geographical distance. Many transport-related expenses are not proportional to transport distances, like all terminal and infrastructural investments, whereas distance itself is a very relative notion; apart from the geographical distances, one has to consider the psychological distances, the trade resistances, the kind of commodities to be traded, the number of transhipment operations, etc. (cf. also Linnemann, 1966, pp. 25–29).

Nonetheless it remains worthwhile to set apart explicitly transport inputs, "because the study of their variations is basic to an understanding of the operations of the space-economy" (cf. Isard's spatial transformation function; Isard, 1956, p. 222).[4]

---

[4] In the spatial transformation function the various *transport inputs* are evidently included as explanatory variables:

$$\varphi(y_1, y_2, \ldots y_k; m_A s_A, m_B s_B, \ldots, m_L s_L; x_{k+1}, x_{k+2}, \ldots, x_n) = 0$$

$y_1 \ldots y_k$ are inputs other than transport; $x_{k+1} \ldots x_n$ are the outputs.

Another important factor of the change in transport-location relation-ships consisted in the rise of low-cost technologies for moving bulk and other commodities in large units, which indeed meant also a serious decline of the *relative importance of transport cost* per unit-cif. Furthermore, because transport rates are generally less than proportional to distance, this point is of major significance for industrial location (Isard, 1975, p. 90). "With tapering transportation costs ... an intermediate location becomes dis-tinctly less likely" (Lloyd and Dicken, 1972, p. 178).

In other words, the locational pull of the raw material source or of the market location is easily strengthened. However, it may be misleading to take transport costs in a narrow sense: many other costs such as those in connection with storage, stocks, rentals, etc., are directly related to the availability of specific transport facilities. The type of service guaranteed sometimes plays the most decisive role. There is, therefore, a clear tendency of a diminution of the locational importance of transport cost, because the availability of certain facilities on the site of location or in the direct neighbourhood of it, may very well reduce — at least indirectly — trans-port cost. In the relevant cases business will look for sites with extensive and varied transport facilities, whether they are intermediate points or not! This reasoning is the more realistic because "the same circumstances which make it advantageous to locate industries in given districts tend also to draw labour and capital to them" (Ohlin, 1933, p. 225).

In consequence our conclusion is that although the transport-related factors no longer seem to play an important role in theoretical respect, in practice they continue to play — and sometimes more than ever — a very "active" role in almost every location decision process.[5]

Often they are one of the few cost factors left which may still be in-fluenced by the enterprise itself, all other factors being imposed by local and/or governmental regulations and international situations (think of raw materials, energy, labour, etc.). In this case transport aspects may become predominant with respect to the search for the optimum location.

3. THE LOCATION FACTOR "TRANSPORT" IN RELATION TO REGIONAL DEVELOPMENT

A special feature of some location factors consists in the implications they may have as regards regional development and growth-pole creation. This is especially true with respect to "labour" and "transport."

Investments in transport infrastructure are often seen as stimuli for the establishment of enterprises. However, not much is known yet about such

[5] "Active" does not always mean "leading" (see Section 3).

a type of interaction (Schröder, 1968, p. 197). It is a fact that those places, which are well-provided with transport facilities also enjoy an important degree of agglomeration economies, because a sufficient number of people and a sufficient amount of capital are concentrated in a clearly limited region. Precisely therefore "transport" is very often considered a predominant location factor in economic literature. It acquired, so to say, an extra dimension in the framework of the analysis of regional development and the follow-up of industrial interrelationships.

The problem is always "where, when and how" such an interrelated growth process will start. Even the successful seaport industrialization of the sixties did not prove the existence of a direct and prevalent influence of transport factors. Rather than now haphazardly exploring the economic literature of the early seventies on the changing role of transport in connection with industrial location and expansion, we prefer to discuss this recent and not yet so well understood phenomenon by means of one of the most typical, and maybe symptomatic, examples of location shifts.

An analysis of a number of characteristics of 40 industrial enterprises, established either in the port of Antwerp or in that of Rotterdam, finally could not explain the variation in the ratings given by those industries to two specific location factors, viz. the "availability of various transport facilities" and the "level of sea-transport cost."[6]

In terms of the original location decisions only 50 percent of the ratings of the location factor "sea-transport cost" and barely 35 percent of those of the "availability of transport facilities in a seaport" could — up to a 1 percent confidence level — be explained by the dependence of firms on import or export over sea. Whereas, when firms had to answer the same question in the real context of the beginnings of 1970, the "explanatory variables" mentioned did not any longer explain the new answers, not even at a much lower confidence level.

Apparently individual attitudes of companies with respect to the location issue had changed substantially, because neither the averages of the different variables (dependent and independent ones) nor the respective standard deviations showed any significant variation as between the first and second estimation.

What, therefore, are the basic determinants of the so-called seaport industrialization? Are transport factors really so predominant in the establishment of certain industries near deep-water facilities as is usually thought? Directly the answer is yes, because there would indeed not exist such a phenomenon as seaport industrialization if there was no deep-water infrastructure and related transport technology at hand. However, the question is not to be put that way! The question is whether the location

---

[6] See for further statistical details: Winkelmans (1973, pp. 91–2 and Appendix 1).

of all industries settled in the port is to be explained by the presence of the port as such. And here the answer is no. Other location factors, such as the available and reserve area, the benefits of industrial interrelationships have definitely played a more decisive role in many location decisions.

An investigation into determinants of a possible location shift to a man-made island in deep sea[7] also did not reveal overwhelming influence of the "transport cost" and "transport service" factors.

The same as for the seaport industrialization, the basis of the island industrialization process is to be found mainly in the field of production.

By means of a factor analysis performed on qualitative locational data of some 80 potential island and/or mainland industries, it was possible to come to a fairly well-defined bifactorial structure, in the sense of a specific island-location-minded group versus a specific mainland-seaport-location-minded group (Winkelmans, 1977, p. 147–149). The resulting factor measurements showed that a lot of normally very important location factors such as "transport service," "deepdraught facilities" and "real estate cost" are disrated in the case of concrete alternatives of location.

In other words location patterns for one and the same activity may be fundamentally different according to the "spatial" situation (Winkelmans, 1977, p. 151). In view of the increasing problem of priorities with respect to the attraction of industries as well as other activities in the framework of a regional economic policy, it is of highest importance to have a good insight into the interaction between the various location factors. This might help the government in deciding which location aspects for a given region are to be promoted, or to which most attention is to be paid, in order to ameliorate the weak feature(s) of the selected sites in a regional, national or international context.

The foregoing may show that one cannot always be sure whether transport location factors will predominate in the final location of an industry.

4. CONCLUSIONS

All this of course will not mean that "transport," in the sense of infra- and superstructural facilities, is not still playing its crucial role in the economy. This is so, even when transport investments do not have any longer a multiplier effect in connection with anti-cyclical policies.

As regards the location of business, especially for industries, "transport" is still a very important factor, though not always in an absolute sense.

From a micro-economic point of view its importance depends princi-

[7]Cf. the "North Sea Island Project", commissioned to Hydronamic B. V. by the North Sea Island Group during the years 1973 to 1976 (Winkelmans, 1977, p. 139).

pally upon some relevant production ratios such as the transport cost ratios for inputs and outputs, which in fact are measures of the transport sensitivity of the firm. Also the specific commercial situation in which the managing of an enterprise takes place determines the transport-location relationship. Therefore the relative importance of transport as a locational element may vary from minor to major influence. Indeed it should not be forgotten that the transport bill may be important in an industry because transport, though cheap in comparison with other inputs, is still not cheap in relation to the low value of the industry's product (Edwards, 1970, p. 272).

From a macro-economic viewpoint and in accordance with the economic evolution of the last decennia, transport facilities will continue to play a clear role — from indicative to directive — as regards the establishment of economic activities.

One has to take note, however, that in the present time:

(1) the qualitative aspects of transport are often valued higher than trans-
    port costs;
(2) first of all a number of technical-economic features in connection with
    the choice of location will be taken into consideration; only then might
    the transportation features of the selected site(s) become decisive.

In the framework of a (regional) economic policy the question still is: what are the right priorities vis-a-vis the attraction of industries? Governments, nowadays, may indeed prevent the settlement of an industry on any site, but, on the other hand, they cannot oblige the same industry to settle on a particular site: they can only try to facilitate such settlement. But on what basis and by which means? Here we still have a rather open field of investigation in which modern research techniques such as multi-criteria analysis, factor analysis and location models (cf. The Industrial Location Project of Rijnmond Public Authority, 1973) ultimately might yield the necessary tools to analyse the extremely interrelated and interactive data both of a quantitative and a qualitative nature concerning the issue of locational choice.

REFERENCES

Barloon, M.J. (1965). "The interrelationship of the Changing Structure of American Transportation and Changes in Industrial Location," *Land Economics* 49:169–179.
Chinitz, B. and Vernon, R. (1960). "Changing Forces in Industrial Location," *Harvard Business Review* 38:126–136.
Davin, L. (1969). "Les facteurs de localisation des industries nouvelles," *Revue Economique* 5:894–904.
Edwards, S.L. (1970). "Transport Cost in British Industry," *Journal of Transport Economics and Policy* 4:265–275.

Falise, M. and Lepas, A. (1970). "Les motivations de localisation des investissements internationaux dans l'Europe du nord-ouest," *Revue Economique* 21:103–109.

Greenhut, M.L. (1956). *Plant Location in Theory and Practice.* Chapel Hill: University of North Carolina Press.

Groothoff, A. (1931). "Het vraagstuk van industrieterreinen in verband met de vestiging van nieuwe industrieën in Nederland," *De Ingenieur* 46, nr. 18:49–56.

Holmes, W.G. (1950). *Plant Location.* New York: McGraw Hill.

Hoover, E.M. (1948). *The Location of Economic Activity.* New York: McGraw Hill.

Isard, W. (1956). *Location and Space-Economy.* Cambridge, Mass.: The M.I.T. Press.

Isard, W. (1975) *Introduction to Regional Science.* London: Prentice-Hall.

Linnemann, H. (1966). *An econometric Study of International Trade Flows.* Amsterdam: North Holland.

Lloyd, P. and Dicken, P. (1972). *Location in Space.* London: Harper and Row.

Lösch, A. (1954). *The Economics of Location.* New Haven: Yale University Press.

Nourse, H. O. (1968). *Regional Economics.* New York: McGraw-Hill.

Ohlin, B. (1933). *Interregional and international trade.* Cambridge: Harvard University Press.

Schärlich, A. (1969). *Localisation optimale et théorie des graphes. Contribution à la théorie de la localisation optimale de la firme dans une structure de concurrence.* Cahiers Vilfredo Pareto. Genève: Librairie Droz.

Schilling, H. (1968). *Standortfaktoren für die Industrieansiedlung. Ein Katalog für die regionale und kommunale Entwicklungspolitik sowie die Standortwahl von Unternehmungen.* Stuttgart: Kohlhammer.

Schröder, D. (1968). *Strukturwandel, Standortwahl und regionales Wachstum.* Stuttgart: Kohlhammer.

Stedenband Twente. (1968). Vestigingsfactoren. Twente: A5 (55).

Vanneste, O. (1967). *Het groeipoolconcept en de regionale economische politiek. Toepassing op de Westvlaamse economie.* Antwerp: Standaard.

Winkelmans, W. (1973). *De Moderne Havenindustrialisatie.* Rijswijk: Nederlands Vervoerswetenschappelijk Instituut.

Winkelmans, W., Delwel, A., Stuiver, M. and Swart, W. (1974). *Economic Considerations,* vol. 2 of Report Phase A of the North Sea Island Project. Sliedrecht: Hydronamic.

Winkelmans, W. (1977). "Towards a Research into Island and Mainland Seaport Location Patterns by Means of Factor Analysis," *Empirical Economics* 3:137–173.

U.S. Department of Commerce (1947). *Basic industrial location factors. Guide for Evaluating an Area's Resources for Industrial Development.* Industrial Series nr. 74. Washington D.C.

THE AUTHORS

G.J. BLAUWENS, born in 1944, has a degree in Business Administration and holds a Ph.D. in Applied Economics (thesis on the price elasticity of the demand for freight transport, 1973).

Since 1974 he has been an Associate Professor at the University of Antwerp, UFSIA, where he teaches a course on the economics of the transportation firm.

He is Director of Research at the Study Centre for Economic and Social Research, SESO. He has worked mainly on transport economics and on investment decisions. Some of his publications since 1975: *Een vijfjarenplan voor het Belgisch Wegennet* ("A five-year plan for the Belgian motorway network," with Kirschen, E.S. *et al.*, 1975); *Een overzicht van prognosemodellen voor het goederenvervoer* ("A survey of forecasting models for freight transport," Bedrijfskunde, 1975); *Statische en dynamische selectieregels voor onafhankelijke en interdependente overheidsinvesteringen* ("Static and dynamic rules for selecting independent and interdependent public investments," Cahiers Economiques de Bruxelles, 1976); *Het wegvervoer in België* ("Road transport in Belgium," Tijdschrift voor Vervoerswetenschap, 1977).

H.A. VAN GENT, born in 1941, obtained his degree in Economics at the Free University in Amsterdam in 1969. He is a staff member in the Transport Economics Section at that university and has worked very closely with Professor Tissot van Patot for a number of years.

The studies he wrote were mainly for internal purposes, but he has also published some on various transport matters.

R.A. KUYVENHOVEN was born in 1953. He obtained his degree in Economics in 1977 at the Free University of Amsterdam. In the course of his studies he has been an Undergraduate Assistant in Transport Economics. After having finished his university studies he was for some time a staff member in the transport economics section at the Free University.

K.M. GWILLIAM was born in 1937. He studied in Oxford where he obtained his B.A. (Politics, Philosophy and Economics) in 1960.

He has been Professor in Transport Economics at the University of Leeds since 1967 and has been Director of the Institute for Transport Studies of the same University from 1969 to 1977. He is an editor of the *Journal of Transport Economics and Policy*; a member of the Planning and Transport Research Advisory Council to the Departments of Transport and Environment; and Member of the Board of the English National Bus Company.

His main publications are: *Criteria for investment in transport infrastructure* (1973, EEC Transport Studies), with J. Zighera, F. Voigt and S. Petricione), *Economics and Transport Policy* (1975, with P.J. Mackie). Some of his most recent articles are: *Urban Road and Rail Policy* (Institute of Transport Journal, 1977), *Transport Policy in the U.K.* (with M.E. Beesley in Journal of Transport Economics and Policy, 1977) *Institutions and Objectives in Transport Policy* (Journal of Transport Economics and Policy, 1979).

R. HAMERSLAG, born in 1931, studied Civil Engineering at the Technical University Delft, where he obtained a Ph.D. in 1972. He has worked at the Netherlands Institute of Transport and with Netherlands Railways. Since 1972 he has been Head of a transportation modelling unit of DHV Consulting Engineers. Amersfoort.

In 1978 he was appointed Professor in Transportation Models at the Technical University Delft.

His main publications are: *Prognosemodel voor het personenvervoer in Nederland* ("Forecasting model for passenger transport in the Netherlands," Ph.D. thesis, 1972); *The interrelation of transport, land use and employment* (paper for the XVe Congrès Mondial de la Route, Mexico, 1975); *The interdependence between environment and transportation planning* (paper for the International conference on mathematical models for environmental problems, University of Southampton, 1975). *The multiproportional estimation method for the simultaneous determination of the value of the deterrence function by mode; theory and experience* (PTRC, Summer annual meeting, London, 1976) and *Binaire calibratie; de schatting van coëfficiënten in een verkeersmodel met gebruik van verschillende soorten waarnemingen* ("Binary calibration; the estimation of coefficients in a traffic model, using different kinds of observations," Verkeerskunde, 1978).

ARNOLD HEERTJE, born in 1934, studied Economics at the University of Amsterdam, where he gained a Masters degree with honours in 1956. He obtained his Ph.D. with honours in 1960 on a thesis "Some aspects of price formation of consumer goods in monopolistic and oligopolistic markets."

From 1955 he was a Research Assistant to Professor P. de Wolff, in the field of Mathematical Economics at the University of Amsterdam. He became Professor of Economics at this university in 1964.

Dr. Heertje has given guest lectures at the Universities of Bochum, Münster, Tübingen, Saarbrücken, London, Antwerp, Brussels, Naples and other cities. He published articles in various economic journals over the last fifteen years. Among the more recent of these are: *A Dynamic Interpretation of Edgeworth's Duopoly Model* (Kyklos, 1971); *An Essay on Marxian Economics* (Schweizerische Zeitschrift für Volkswirtschaft und Statistik, 1972); *Welfare Economics and the Cambridge Controversy*, with D. Furth (Revue d'Economie Politique, 1977); *On Marx's theory of Unemployment*, with D. Furth and R.J. van der Veen (Oxford Economic Papers, 1978).

In 1973 his *Economie en Technische Ontwikkeling* appeared. It was published in an English edition in 1977, entitled *Economics and Technical Change*.

A.A.I. HOLTGREFE, born in 1942, in 1978 was appointed Professor of Transport Economics at the Free University, Amsterdam, where he succeeded Professor J.P.B. Tissot van Patot.

He is also Chief of the Management Information Department of Netherlands Railways. Prior to this last function the author worked with Netherlands Railways in such areas as operational research, economic research and long term planning. Holtgrefe holds a degree in Economics from the Erasmus University in Rotterdam. He became a Ph.D. on a thesis entitled *An optimizing medium-term planning model for the Netherlands Railways* (Rotterdam, 1975).

LEO H. KLAASSEN, born in 1920, has been a Professor in Regional and Socio-economic Research at the Erasmus University, Rotterdam, since 1959.

He is President of the Board of the Netherlands Economic Institute, Rotterdam, and holds a number of other positions in the Netherlands and abroad. In the last 15 years he participated — mostly in advisory functions — in more than 30 special development studies and projects in African, South and Central America, Asian and European countries.

Many of his numerous writings are published in books in combination with one or more co-authors, e.g.: *Integration of Socio-Economic and Physical Planning* (with J.H.P. Paelinck, 1974); *The Quality of Life in European cities* (with several co-authors, 1974); *Social Issues in Regional Policy and Regional Planning* (with several co-authors, 1977).

Some of his recent publications in the Series "Foundations of Empirical Economic Research," published by the Netherlands Economic Institute, are: *Integral planning, some considerations* (1974); *Some elements of a theory of governmental behaviour* (with J.H.P. Paelinck, 1975); *Optimum governmental welfare policy for regions and cities* (with L. van den Berg and C.H.T. Vijverberg 1975); *Towards better integration of transportation behaviour in spatial models* (with J.H.P. Paelinck and A.C.P. Verster, 1976); *Elements of a theory of urban development* (with C.H.T. Vijverberg and L. van den Berg, 1977); *Spatial systems* (with J.H.P. Paelinck and S. Wagennar, 1979).

VOJISLAV KOLARIĆ, born in 1920 in a village of Komirić, Serbia, studied as a part-time student at the Economic Faculty in Beograd and obtained his Ph.D. in 1955.

During that period he worked at a railway workshop and later on at the General Directorate of the Yugoslav Railways, which he left in 1962 as Deputy General Manager. In that year he was appointed Professor at the Economic Faculty in Beograd, in the Economics and Organization of Transport Enterprises.

Besides his teaching work he directed scientific research at the Transport Institute and was a consultant to the General Manager of the Railways. He has taken an active part in the work of international railways organizations and in all the symposia of the ECMT.

His principal publications are: *Characteristics of the transport market* (1960); *Transport organization and problems of self-management in transport enterprises* (1964); *Railway Transport Economics* (3 vols., 1968); *Economics and organization of transport enterprises* (1972); *Theory of Cost Dynamics* (1973); *Transport Organization and Economics* (1978).

H.C. KUILER, born in 1914, studied at the Erasmus University (formerly the Netherlands School of Economics) in Rotterdam, where he obtained his Ph.D. in 1946. He began lecturing there in 1947 and in 1951 was appointed Assistant Professor and in 1962 Professor of Transport Economics at this university.

In addition to his academic post he worked at the Netherlands Central Bureau of Statistics from 1940 to 1978, for a long time as Head of the Department of Transport Statistics and in recent years as an adviser in charge of a special study treated by him in this book.

His main publications are *Enige aspecten van europees verkeer* ("Some aspects of European traffic," 1955); *De ontwikkeling van de vervoerseconomie en die van de Europese vervoersintegratie* ("The development of transport economics and of the European integration of transport," 1963); *Achtergronden van de tweede vervoersrevolutie* ("Backgrounds of the second transport revolution," 1971); *Inleiding tot de vervoer-en haveneconomie* ("Introduction to transport and to port economics," 1973) and *Changing patterns of economic activity, trade and freight transport. Redistribution of economic activity and trade; transit and infrastructure* (ECMT, 1979).

GIJSBERT KUYPERS, born in 1921, is Professor of Political Science at the Free University in Amsterdam. He is the author of *De Russische problematiek in het Sowjet-staatsbeeld* ("Russian elements in Soviet political theory," 1953); *Het politieke spel in Nederland* ("The political game in the Netherlands," 1967); *Grondbegrippen van politiek* ("Basic concepts in politics," 1973) and *Beginselen van beleidsontwikkeling* ("Principles of Policy Development," forthcoming).

JOHN A. MICHON, born in Utrecht in 1935, studied Psychology at the University of Utrecht. He obtained his Ph.D. in Leiden, in 1967, on a thesis "Timing in Temporal Tracking."

From 1960 till 1973 he worked at the Dutch Institute for Perception-TNO, from 1969 onwards as head of the then newly-created Department of Road-User Behaviour.

Following a part-time appointment in 1971, he was appointed in 1973 : rofessor of Experimental Psychology at the State University of Groningen. From 1971 till 1977 he combined this work with the special Chair for Traffic Studies, also in Groningen.

His connection with the fields of transport and traffic continues in his present Chairmanship of the Traffic Research Center of the University of Groningen. He also is Chairman of the Netherlands Foundation for Psychonomy.

The main fields of his research have been the processing of information by the human organism, in particular its temporal structure, the processing of information by traffic participants — especially with respect to traffic safety — and applications of the social sciences to the problem of mobility.

From his hand numerous publications have appeared, the most recent of which are:

The mutual impacts of transportation and human behavior (1976) and *Le traitement de l'information temporelle* (1978). He has further been a co-editor of the *Handboek der Psychonomie*, 1976 (English edition: "Handbook of Psychonomics," 1979) and of *Sociale Verkeerskunde* ("Social Traffic Studies," 1977).

FRANCESCO SANTORO was born in 1910. After finishing his studies in Economics and Commerce in 1930, in 1934 he entered the Italian Railways (FS) which he served in various functions. He now is a member of the Board of Administration of FS. In the years 1965–71 he was Head of the Cabinet of the Minister of Transport and a Director-General in the Ministry.

Many-fold have been his activities in international organizations in the field of transport, especially in the International Railway Union, the ECMT and the EEC.

Since 1971 he has been Professor in Economics and Commerce at the University of Trieste. Santoro has published articles in a variety of periodicals. He also wrote several books, of which may be mentioned: *Struttura economica e tecnica delle tariffe ferroviarie* (1947); *Economia dei Trasporti* (1966); *La politica dei trasporti della Comunità Economica Europea* (1975) and *Politica dei trasporti* (1977).

ARTHUR DE WAELE, born in 1931, studied at the Universities in Ghent, Louvain and Cologne. For seven years he assisted in different studies in the field of Regional Economics and Physical Planning in Belgium. After that period he was in charge of the Centre of Studies on Transport Economics of the Flemish Economic League. In 1968 he started working at the Secretariat of the European Conference of Ministers of Transport in Paris, where he is Head of the Division for Research and Documentation, charged with preparing the Symposia and the Round Table Conferences of the ECMT.

Some of his publications: *Die Koordinierung der Binnenverkehrsmittel in Belgien* (1962); "Die praktische Berücksichtiging der Wegekosten bei der Gestaltung des Margentarifs, (co-author W. Hamm, *Zeitschrift für Verkehrswissenschaft*, 1967); Les problèmes de prévisions en matière de transport de marchandises," (*Echos des Communications*, 1970); *Eisenbahn der Zukunft, Zukunft der Eisenbahn?* (co-author G. Strosberg, 1972); *Impact des possibilités de transports terrestres à grande vitesse sur la demande de transport* (ECMT, 1970); *The efficient participation of the railways in the market economy* (co-author J.H. Rees, ECMT, 1971); *Economic problems of traffic peaks* (ECMT, 1975).

W. WINKELMANS was born in Antwerp in 1941. He obtained a Ph.D. in Commercial Sciences in 1972.

Since 1972 he has been Senior Assistant at the Department of Applied Economics of the State University Centre of Antwerp. In 1977 he became Professor in Port Management.

From 1973–75 he participated as an economic advisor in a feasibility study for an artificial island in the North Sea. For the period 1977/80 he is serving as promotor and director of the research program on the "Feasibility of cost-based port tariff-making in ten EEC seaports."

His publications are mostly in the fields of the economics of seaports and of shipping. Some of his articles: *Changements de structure dans la navigation maritime et leur rapport avec le traffic portuaire* (Echos des Communications, 1971); *Towards a research into island and mainland seaport location patterns by means of factor analysis* (Empirical Economics, 1977) and *The importance of smaller seaports in the Benelux* (Rivista Internazionale di Economia dei Trasporti, 1977).

Besides his Ph.D.-thesis *De moderne havenindustrialisatie* ("The modern port industrialization", 1973) he is the author of the study *National Economic Consequences for the Dutch Economy of the Establishment of Industries on an artificial North Sea Island* (1975).

THE EDITORS

JACOB B. POLAK was born in Amsterdam in 1933. He holds a degree in Economics from the University of Amsterdam.

After a number of years in the General Policy Department of Netherlands Railways he became Senior Assistant at the Institute of Transport Economics of the University of

Amsterdam. Since 1975 he has also been Professor of Transport Economics at the University of Groningen, where he had been appointed as a Reader in 1967.

His research and publications have been mainly in the fields of the theoretical aspects of transport policy, the evaluation of transport projects and urban transport economics. Lately he was the editor of a special number of the Netherlands Magazine for Transport Science on *Analysis and Decision-making for Transport* (1977) and headed a study of parking problems in one of the Dutch provincial capitals (1978). He also holds a number of advisory positions.

JAN B. VAN DER KAMP, born in 1921, got a degree in economics from the Netherlands School of Economics, Rotterdam, in 1946. At the end of an eight-year period in Indonesia he gained his Ph.D. in 1955 under the guidance of Professor Dr. P.L. van der Velden at the University of Indonesia (Djakarta). In 1956 he entered the Netherlands Railways in the General Policy Department, then headed by Dr. Tissot van Patot. At present he is in charge of policy development activities both in the freight and the passenger sector.

He has published a number of articles in the Netherlands Magazine for Transport Science and in other Dutch periodicals on topics related to transport policy.